ISLAM AND THE WORLD

THE RISE AND DECLINE OF MUSLIMS AND ITS EFFECT ON MANKIND

SAYYED ABUL ḤASAN ʿALĪ NADWĪ

UK ISLAMIC ACADEMY

ISBN 1 872531 31 8 (HB)
ISBN 1 872531 32 6 (PB)

Translation: Dr. Muhammad Asif Kidwai
General Editor: Iqbal Ahmad Azami

Published by
UK ISLAMIC ACADEMY
PO BOX 6645
LEICESTER LE5 5WT
UNITED KINGDOM

Website: www.ukiabooks.com
E-mail: info@ukiabooks.com

British Library Cataloguing in Publication Data
A catalogue record for this book is available from the British Library

Design and Typesetting: Sohail Nakhooda

CONTENTS

بسم الله الرحمن الرحيم

In the name of Allah, Most Gracious, Most Merciful

FOREWORD

The most important need today is to help the Muslim acquire confidence in himself and in his past so that he is able to face the future with hope, courage and determination. His faith in the religion he professes, but whose genius he does not always understand, has to be revived and vitalized. His bonds with Islam are sadly mainly those of heritage. He is a Muslim because he is born to Islam. He has rarely made any serious attempt to acquire a real understanding of his religion.

Of all the books, both ancient and modern, I have read on an understanding of Islam, this book, by Sayyed Abul Ḥasan ʿAlī Nadwī, deserves particular attention. The teaching of Islam is essentially a teaching of leadership and world welfare. One of its most important characteristics is that it teaches its follower how to acquire self-confidence without conceit or egotism; it breathes into him the fervour of faith and conviction, free of self-deception and, by weaning him from all dependence on others, instils in him complete trust in God with a faith that never falters nor weakens.

This faith requires the Muslim to shoulder the responsibility of humanity at large and enjoins on him the trusteeship of the entire human race. It is the duty of Muslims to guide to the right path those who have gone astray, and lead men, with the help of the light and guidance given by God, from darkness into light. The Holy Qur'ān says: *You are the best of people evolved for mankind. You enjoin what is right and forbid what is wrong and you believe in God* (Āl ʿImrān 3:110). Also: *Thus We have made you a people justly balanced (of the Middle Path) so that you could be a witness (an example) to people and (just as) the Prophet is to you* (al-Baqarah 2:143).

This book succeeds in stimulating an awareness of this responsibility in its readers and in bringing home to them its validity. In its style and treatment, however, it does not pander to mere sentiment or excite passions of dogmatism. The claims that the book makes are sustained by solid scholarship and objective research in a manner that appeals to both the mind and the heart. The enlightened and unprejudiced approach of the author is clearly revealed by the scrupulous care and deep concern for truth with which historical events and their sequences are recorded and environmental effects and ramifications analyzed. Decisions are left to the discernment of enlightened minds and to consciences that are sensitive to truth. Topics have been discussed, arranged and interfused in such a manner that no conclusion is ever forced on the reader.

What was the condition of the world before the advent of Islam and the state of affairs in the East and the West, the North and the South? What was the intellectual temper of man from China to India, from Persia to Rome? What was the colour and texture of contemporary society? In what state were those religions of the world that are based on Heavenly sanction, such as Judaism and Christianity, and those that preach idol and fire-worship, such as Hinduism and Magianism? These questions with which the book begins are dealt with in a concise but comprehensive manner. The picture presented of that age is clear-cut and delineates its features with accuracy and insight. In preparing the picture, the author never gives the impression that he is self-opinionated or bigoted. He quotes non-Muslim authors, particularly those who have been notorious for their enmity towards Islam and for their persistent efforts to belittle Islam and the achievements of the age associated with Muslim glory. The age before Islam was steeped in ignorance in which the mind and the spirit of man had become benighted and high standards and values of life debased. It was an age of tyranny and slavery in which the very roots of humanity were corroded by a criminally luxurious and wasteful life on the one hand, and hopelessness and frustration and despair on the other. In addition, clouds of scepticism, agnosticism and infidelity hovered overhead and the religions of the world were helpless to dispel them. Religions that called themselves Heavenly had already fallen victim to interpolations and disintegration. They, and particularly the Christianity of the day, had lost their prestige and had become a body devoid of all spirit. There was no life, no vitality left in them. They had become, in short, a depository of certain rituals and symbols, the meaning and pertinence of which had lost all its validity.

After describing the salient features of the age of ignorance, the author outlines the part played by Islam in the reconstruction of humanity. He shows how, when it had the opportunity, Islam liberated the soul of man from superstitions and banalities, emancipated him from the evils of slavery and degradation, and lifted him out of the slough of filth and disease. The author makes it clear how Islam saved human society from degradation, and civilization from disintegration and ruin, and liberated man from the tyranny of kings and the dominance of priests. Islam constructed life on new foundations, purified belief and morality and gave them new sanctions. It imparted a high resolve to life, endowed it with noble values and stimulated love for freedom and creativeness. It blessed life by giving it faith and knowledge, fraternity, justice and self-confidence. It prepared and trained men to bring out, through constant effort and endless toil, the hidden potentialities of life so that it could develop and flower into a just, healthy and balanced system. By a correct appraisal of men and their aptitudes, Islam put the right people in the right place for the reconstruction and development of life and took from each according to his worth.

All this was achieved when Islam had a controlling hand in the affairs of the world and had the opportunity to fashion life according to its own special genius. Since Islam is pre-eminently a faith that inspires leadership, its real mettle is tested and proven only when it assumes responsibility. It can lead the caravan of life. It cannot be a camp follower. Then came a period whereby Islam lost its leadership. This was mainly due to the failure of the Muslims to efficiently sustain and discharge the great responsibility of the trusteeship of mankind which Islam had enjoined upon them.

The author succinctly describes the reasons for the material and spiritual decay of the Muslims and identifies the harm the Muslims sustained by deviating from the principles of their faith and turning away from the responsibilities it entailed. In describing what happened to the world when it was deprived of this noble leadership and when it reverted to its previous state of ignorance, the author points out, in no uncertain terms, the horrible depravity towards which the world is heading today. Unfortunately this depravity belongs to a time when knowledge has opened out new paths and vistas and man has made considerable material progress. In identifying this depravity, the author does not indulge in fiery rhetoric or sensational writing, but instead employs a critical and objective approach to events. He presents facts in a manner free from all exaggeration or attempts at "fine" writing.

The historical analysis Sayyed Abul Ḥasan ʿAlī Nadwī gives compels one to believe strongly that the time has come when the present leadership should be changed and humanity brought back from darkness to light and from ignorance to knowledge and wisdom. The reader soon realizes how important such guidance is to the world today and, in losing it, what a terrible loss humanity has suffered. This loss is sustained not only by the Muslims, but is shared by the world at large. It is a loss that encompasses the past, the present and the future, both immediate and distant. If upon reading this book the Muslim is filled with shame and contrition for his criminal neglect and carelessness, he also becomes acutely aware of the tremendous potentialities that have been given to him and begins to feel an overpowering desire to regain the world leadership he has lost through his own neglect and lack of appreciation of its qualities.

One particularly praiseworthy feature of the book is that the author, whenever he speaks of the general depravity of mankind (the depravity that has come about because the Muslim failed in his leadership), he calls it Ignorance. This approach clearly shows what, according to the author and his way of thinking, the difference is between the spirit of Islam and the spirit of materialism which prevailed before the advent of Islam and which has again prevailed in the world ever since Islam lost its world leadership. Ignorance and lack of wisdom remain the same in its temper in whatever period of history it is found. It is not confined to any particular interval between two periods of time. It is a typical attitude of mind and comes to the forefront when those standards and norms of behaviour sanctioned by God give way to those inspired merely by sophisticated and debased appetites. The world is enduring this ignorance today as it did in earlier periods of history.

Another outstanding feature of the book is that the author displays a deep and correct understanding of the spirit of Islam and of its principles and essentials in their wider aspects and implications.

For these reasons this work is not only a refreshing example of religious and social research but also of how history can be recorded and interpreted from the wider Islamic viewpoint. Scholars of the West have written the history of the world from their own Western point of view. They could not, naturally, escape from being conditioned by their upbringing, their philosophy and their national and religious prejudices. Purely and simply because they forgot or underrated, consciously or unconsciously, certain important values of life, the histories written by them contain many aberrations and travesties. Unless these values are understood and appreciated properly, no history of man can be recorded in its completeness, nor can facts be interpreted and conclusions correctly deduced from them.

Furthermore, owing to national and religious prejudices, European scholars are inclined to consider Europe as the centre of the world and so pay but scant notice to important historical movements and their repercussions, simply because they do not emanate from Europe. If they mention them at all, they try to belittle them, minimizing their influence and importance.

For quite some time, we in the East have, unfortunately, become accustomed to borrowing from the West not only its products but also the techniques of recording history used by its scholars with all their imperfections and shortcomings. This in spite of the fact that it has now been proved that their methods of approach and treatment are usually inadequate and not in keeping with historical veracity. The fact that they apprehend life from a specific and narrow point of view often leads them to draw the wrong conclusions. When premises are wrongly stated, conclusions cannot but be wrong. The current work, however, has kept all these considerations carefully in mind and has given special attention to movements and values that have conditioned and influenced man and his life. In short, nothing has been left out which has had any effect on life.

The reader, for instance, would hardly expect from an author who is concerned with the fortunes of Islam, who is a believer and believes implicitly in the spiritual strength and vigour of Islam and whose heart nurtures a strong desire to entrust Islam once again with the leadership of the world, that he would, while describing the genesis of this leadership, also dwell on its industrial and martial potentialities and qualities and discuss at some length a modern system of education and economic and industrial self-sufficiency. All this, the author does with rare insight and it is a great pleasure to say that he does not leave these aspects inconclusive.

This book presents a systemic and well-knit analysis of all the factors that have influenced and conditioned life. It has reviewed history with this purpose in mind and has offered suggestions to the Islamic world that are balanced and free from extravagance or polemics. It is a remarkable example of how history should be recorded. It shows how a Muslim can take up his pen to record historical events and discuss their sequence without borrowing from European historians and copying their style which often lacks balance, historical veracity and adequate scholarship and research. I consider it a great privilege that I have had the opportunity to record my impressions of *Islam and the World: The Rise and Decline of Muslims and its Affect on Mankind* and further that I was fortunate enough to have read it in Arabic.

> *In it is advice for those who have (an understanding) heart and who lend their ears to it and bear witness to its truth.*
>
> Qāf 50:37

Hulwan, Egypt SAYYID QUṬB

بسم الله الرحمن الرحيم

In the name of Allah, the Most Benevolent, the Most Merciful

TRANSLATOR'S NOTE

This valuable book was originally written in Arabic and published in Cairo in 1950 for the Academy of Research, Translation and Publication in Egypt. It was an instant success with critics and the general public alike in Arabic-speaking countries. The book has also been translated into Persian and Turkish. Its Urdu version, from which this translation has been made, was produced in India in 1954 in response to persistent demand.

This book does not claim to be a history of the rise and fall of the Muslims – it deals only with the effects thereof. The author's main ambition, however, has been to stir Muslims to an appreciation of Islam's glorious role in the story of human progress and to promote in them a desire to look at themselves with a view to finding out how far they have been true to their mission and duty towards the world. The author feels that his labours would be amply rewarded if he succeeds, in however small a measure, in moving the Muslims to think of the great harm they have done, not only to themselves but to the whole of mankind, by shutting their minds to the creative impulse that underlies the teachings of Islam.

For, indeed, as Muhammad Asad has so beautifully and so correctly said: "It was not the Muslims that made Islam great; it was Islam that made the Muslims great." It is impossible to over-emphasize the fact that Islam is not a religion in the popular sense of the term. It is a religion as well as a way of life that embraces most decisively all the manifold aspects of human existence – spiritual and material, moral and physical, emotional and intellectual, personal and social. It is the conflux of this world and the Next, the meeting point of the body, the mind and the spirit, where all three unite to form a single reality, the basis of which is a real, living consciousness of God. Islam does not, however, stop there. It also shows us the way – the practical way – of reproducing this reality, this unity of Idea and Action, within the limits of our earthly sojourn, in our lives and our consciousnesses. It refrains from demanding of man, as a necessary condition to salvation, a belief in dogmas that may either be difficult to comprehend or are opposed to scientific truths. In fact, no dogma of any kind is found in the structure of Islamic beliefs and practices. No Original Sin, no misdeeds of a past life stand between man and his destiny. No mortification of the flesh, no renunciation of the world is required to open the secret door to spiritual prosperity. Such things are utterly foreign to Islam. For Islam is neither a mystical doctrine nor a philosophy, but rather a programme of personal and social behaviour that not only leaves no inherent conflict between the physical and the moral existence of man, but insists on their co-existence as the natural basis of life.

Precisely because of this ability to strike a harmonious balance between the world of faith and the world of action, Islam has never presented a barrier to progress and science. History cannot cite an instance of any other religion that has given such encouragement to scientific progress as has Islam. Who, indeed, can know this better than the Europeans themselves, who are now so eager to distort its Message, for is it not to Islam and to the Muslims that Europe owes its intellectual and cultural rebirth after it had sunk deeper and deeper into barbarism from the fifth to the tenth centuries? In the words of Robert Briffault: "It is highly probable that but for the Arabs modern European civilization would not have arisen at all; it is absolutely certain that but for them, it would not have assumed the character that has enabled it to transcend all previous phases of evolution."

With the dismal spectacle of cultural and social decay staring one in the face everywhere in the Muslim world, a strong tendency is created in the minds of Europeans to attribute the faults and weaknesses of the Muslims of today to the teachings and influence of Islam and to use it as an argument for advancing the theory that the sooner the Muslims are freed from the shackles of their faith and induced to adopt Western ways of life, the better it will be for them and for the rest of the world. In this book, Sayyed Abul Ḥasan ᶜAlī Nadwī tries to expose the falsity of this view. No unbiased person who cares to study the teachings of Islam will contend that there is anything contrary to reason or progress in them, or anything that can be bracketed with sensuality or crude materialism. The decline of the Muslims is due not to any shortcomings in Islam, but to their failure to live up to it. The Muslims, themselves have reduced Islam to a body without a soul. They have deprived it of its social content, its sense of purpose and dynamism, and made it a mere dry husk of belief and practice. But, fortunately, the idea underlying the precepts of the Qur'ān and their interpretation through the *Sunnah* of the Prophet ﷺ has remained intact and there is no reason why it cannot be put into practice once again.

Belief in Islam as a Law decreed by God to be followed by humanity at all times and everywhere is an article of faith for Muslims. It is an eternal plan of life that was brought into the world by one who was not a mere Law-giver among many other Law-givers, but rather the Supreme Messenger of God who always acted under Divine inspiration. Such being the case, those among the Muslims who, in imitation of Western critics of Islam, want to change it in order to bring it, as they say, into harmony with the spirit of the times, betray their own inner insolvency. A law which is the result of Divine Revelation cannot be bound by the rules of organic life. It can never become obsolete. What appears to be the decay of Islam is, in fact, nothing but the decay and the bankruptcy of the hearts of the Muslims themselves: basically they have become too small and too lazy to respond to the Divine Call.

Muslims who talk of reforming Islam have neither an honest solicitude for their religion, nor a genuine feeling for their community. Their real aim is to recast the teachings of the Qur'ān in such a way as to find in them a justification for the degenerate ways of living and thinking they have borrowed from the materialistic civilization of the

West. The blind admiration for everything Western that has come to be regarded as the hallmark of progress in most Islamic countries has produced a dangerous urge among the so-called modernized sections of Muslims for the modification of the practical teachings of Islam consistent with the social and economic concepts and attitudes of the Western world. That the very roots of Islam as a moral, practical, personal and social code would be destroyed in such a process does not appear to worry them in the least, for what rules over their hearts and minds is not Islam but the West.

The reader will find enough food for thought in the following pages as far as the social destinies of Western civilization are concerned. With its mask removed, he will be able to judge for himself how cruel and catastrophic the consequences of the transfer of world leadership from Muslims to Western peoples have been. For Western appetites are purely material and are built on a structure of life that is utterly inimical to the needs of the human mind and spirit.

Chapters V and VI, which may be described as the core of the current book, constitute something of a challenge to the West. That is to search its heart as to whether it has made any real contribution to the happiness of mankind by separating the quantitative from the qualitative and subordinating transcendental ethics to practical utility. Despite its tremendous advances in the field of science and technology, the West has led mankind into a wilderness of fear, greed, loneliness and spiritual despair. The author boldly asserts that all scientific achievements will be of no use until a corresponding improvement is attained in human behaviour. This by rebuilding humanity and its surroundings on the foundations of the Islamic faith and way of life. Will the West listen to this voice? The future progress of humanity, to a large extent, will depend on an answer to this question.

What Muslims need to do to bring about a regeneration of the Islamic world is not to reform Islam but to reform themselves by creating that inner awakening, that permanent consciousness and that sense of responsibility in all their thoughts and actions which distinguished the lives of the Companions of the Prophet of Islam ﷺ.

I have undertaken the translation of this book into English in the earnest hope that it will help kindle in the hearts of English-speaking Muslims that flame of faith which once enabled the followers of Islam to contribute such a glorious chapter to the book of man's social and cultural advancement.

Another notable feature of this admirable book is the wealth of material it contains regarding the religious, social, moral and political state of the pre-Islamic world, particularly on the eve of the prophethood of Muḥammad ﷺ. There is, perhaps, no other book in any language which provides such an elaborate account of that moribund period in human history. Here, as everywhere else, the author has supported his statements by reference to reliable authorities. In so doing, he has also greatly facilitated the work of future biographers of the Prophet ﷺ.

I have endeavoured to capture the mood of the original in the translation. How far I have succeeded is not for me to say. I need hardly add that the responsibility for the facts stated and views expressed rests entirely with the author.

Lucknow M. ĀSIF KIDWĀI

بسم الله الرحمن الرحيم

In the name of Allah, the Most Benevolent, the Most Merciful

PREFACE

What the World has Lost with the Decline of the Muslims

The initial decline of the Muslims, their failure and retirement from the leadership of other nations thereafter, and finally their withdrawal from life and action was not an event that had hitherto happened or one which was repeated in history, like the decadence of other peoples and nations, or the disappearance of other governments and states. It was instead unlike any other event in history.

What happened did not concern the Arabs alone, nor was it the private concern of those peoples and nations which accepted Islam, let alone the families and relations which lost their states and countries. It was rather a general human tragedy, more wretched and widespread than history had ever seen before. Had the world realized the reality of this disaster and the extent of its loss, and had it thrown aside the veil of racism, it would have adopted this day as a day of commiseration, condolence, weeping and wailing; and it would have worn the clothes of mourning. Alas, this did not take place in a day, but rather happened gradually over the course of decades. Moreover, up till now, the world has not considered this event in the right way nor has it given it its due weight, nor has it perceived the right scale for its wretchedness and loss.

The world does not lose anything by the disappearance of a state which rules for a moment in time, conquers a number of countries and regions, enslaves groups of people and lives in luxury, enjoying itself to the detriment of the weak and of those governed. Nor does humanity suffer from the transfer of power and governance from one man to another, or from a group to another similar to it in its transgression, injustice and abuse. Nor does the universe grieve or become saddened solely for the decadence of a nation struck by old age and one which is weakened, or, for that matter, for the fall of a state whose roots have decayed and whose components have become disjointed.

Quite the contrary, universal law requires this to happen. Moreover, human tears are too dear to be shed every single day on a deceased king or on an evanescent power. One can well dispense with such tears, just as one is too busy to mourn someone who has never worked towards one's happiness or exerted effort towards one's benefit. The heavens and earth are too harsh on such events, and these have occurred a thousand times before and, indeed, continue to occur every day.

> *How many were the gardens and springs they left behind, and corn – fields and noble buildings,*
> *And pleaseant things werein they had taken such delight!*
> *Thus (was their end)! And We made other people inherit (those things)!*
> *And neither heaven nor earth shed a tear over them: nor were they given a respite (again).*
>
> Holy Qur'ān, Al-Dukhān 44:25–9

In fact, many of those kings and nations were but a burden on the face of the earth, a woe to human kind and a chastisement for small and weak nations. They were also the source of corruption and disease in the body of human society. From this source, poison spread to its veins and nerves until it reached even those parts which were sound. Hence, the need for surgery, for cutting off this sick part and removing it from that which was sound. In this, then, was a great manifestation of the lordship and mercy of the Lord of the worlds. Such manifestation obliges praise and appreciation from all members of the human family, indeed, from all the elements of the universe.

> *Of the wrong-doers the last remnant was cut off Praise be to Allah, The Cherisher of the Worlds*
>
> Al-Anʿām 6:45

The decline of the Muslims, the disappearance of their state and the stagnation of their might (being the carriers of the Message of the Prophets, and being to the human world like good health is to the body) was not, however, the decadence of a people or of a human element or of a nationality. Had this been the case the blow would have been light and with little impact. The truth though is more harsh for it represented the decadence of a message which is to human society like the spirit is to the body. It was also the collapse of a foundation upon which was established the orders of the *dīn* and the world. Hence, one may ask: has the decadence and withdrawal of the Muslims, in reality, been regretted by man both in the East and West centuries after this event occurred? Has the world, which is rich with nations and peoples, really lost anything with the decadence of the Muslims? If so, what did it really lose? What has become of this world after this collapse? What happened to these different nations when European powers assumed the leadership of the world and established a vast territory on the ruins of the Islamic state? What impact did this great transformation have on the leadership of nations and the world at large in the domains of religion, ethics, politics, general life and the destiny of humanity?

It is these questions that we will try to answer in the pages which follow.

ABUL ḤASAN ʿALĪ AL-HASANI

I

BEFORE THE ADVENT OF PROPHET MUḤAMMAD ﷺ

Sixth Century CE

The sixth century of the Christian era, it is generally agreed, represented the darkest phase in the history of our race. Humanity had reached the edge of the precipice, towards which it had been tragically proceeding for centuries, and there appeared to be no agency or power in the whole world which could come to its rescue and save it from crashing into the abyss of destruction.

In his melancholy progress from God-forgetfulness to self-forgetting, man had lost his direction. He had grown indifferent to his destiny. The teachings of the prophets had been forgotten; the fire that they had kindled had either been put out by the storms of moral anarchy or the light they shed had become so feeble that it could illumine only the hearts of a few men, most of whom had sought refuge in passivity and resignation. Having been vanquished in the battle between spiritualism and materialism, they had shut themselves up in monasteries or gone into the wilderness. Those who were left in the whirlpool of life had aligned themselves with the ruling classes of their lands. They helped them in the satisfaction of their sensual desires and in the maintenance of unjust political and economic systems, and co-operated in reaping unlawful benefits out of the wealth of the people.

The Romans and the Persians, who enjoyed the monopoly of leadership in the West and the East respectively, had sunk into a state of utter moral depravity. They wallowed in the deep-rooted vices of their corrupt and decaying civilizations. Their empires had become store-houses of confusion and mischief. The governing classes, drunk with power, indulged in reckless debauchery and sensuality. The middle classes, as is their wont, took great pride in aping the modes and manners of the rich. As for the common people, they lived in grinding poverty. They filled their bellies like lower creatures and toiled and sweated like cattle so that others might live in voluptuous luxury. They would solace themselves with narcotics and cheap entertainment, or fall blindly into carnal pleasures whenever their miserable lives afforded them a breathing space.

Spiritual Inactivity

Great religions became playthings in the hands of debased clergymen who corrupted and twisted them beyond recognition, so much so that, if it were possible for their founders to return to the physical life, they would not have recognized them.

As a result of the moral debasement of the great centres of civilization and general disorder and unrest, people everywhere became entangled in their internal problems. They had no message to offer to the world. The world had become hollow from within; its life-springs had dried up. It possessed neither the light of religious guidance for personal conduct, nor any abiding and rational principles for running a State.

Christianity

Christianity had never possessed a comprehensive or elaborate code which could provide the framework of a civilization or the basis of a government. Consisting mainly of the barest outlines of the teachings of Christ, it did little more than dimly reflect the simple creed of monotheism. But even this distinction was removed by the baneful influence of St Paul. After that the flickering flame of the Divine Truth was utterly extinguished. St Paul did not let go of the old pagan rites and customs and introduced them into Christianity. Later, during the reign of Constantine, the very roots of the Christian faith were destroyed.

Thus, by the fourth century, Christianity had become a curious mixture of Greek mythology, Roman idolatry, Egyptian Neo-Platonism and Monasticism, in which the pure and simple teachings of Christ had been lost like a drop of sweet water in the ocean. The religion had been reduced to a hopeless mess of meaningless doctrines and empty rituals which could neither elevate the spirit, illuminate the intellect, nor move the emotions. Instead of opening fresh avenues for the display of cultural energies, this great religion had become a stumbling block in the path of human progress. Centuries of morbid disintegration had ushered the faith of Jesus into the lap of Paganism. Sale, who translated the Holy Qur'ān into English, says of Christianity in the sixth century: "The worship of saints and images, in particular, was then arrived at such a scandalous pitch that it even surpassed whatever is now practised among the Romanists."[1]

Religious Strife in the Roman Empire

Doctrinal divisions had turned Christendom into a seething cauldron of warring sects. Homes, schools and churches had been transformed into war camps. The land was involved in a civil war. The main dispute was over the combination of the divine and human natures in Jesus. The Melkite Christians of Syria held that he was both divine and human, while the Monophysites of Egypt insisted on his sole divinity, the human part of his nature having lost itself in the divine as a drop of vinegar loses its identity in the ocean. The former view was, in a way, the official view of the Empire, and the Byzantine rulers did everything in their power to have it established as the united creed of the Eastern Empire. In the process they perpetrated brutal atrocities on their opponents, but the differences were not resolved. Both sides openly attacked each other as apostates and renegades, as if they belonged to two opposing religions.[2] Cruelties and persecutions of a most savage nature were witnessed during the ten years of the viceroyalty of Cyrus in Egypt (631-41 CE).[3]

Social Discontent and Economic Chaos

Social disruption had reached its peak in the Eastern Roman Empire. Taxes and other duties had multiplied manifold, though the people were already groaning under innumerable hardships. Even greater than the taxes were the hardships of confiscations and monopolies. As a result of these causes widespread uprisings and rebellions occurred. In the disturbances of 532 CE, for example, as many as 30,000 people were killed in the capital itself.[4]

The people had become so hopelessly addicted to extravagance and lavishment that it was beyond their powers of self-control to practise austerity, no matter how desperate their circumstances. There was but one reigning passion: to amass wealth by every conceivable means, and then to squander it on luxury and licentious behaviour.

The social horizon was extremely gloomy. The foundations of civilization were exposed to ruin and decay. Celibacy was preferred to matrimony, so that people could be totally free to indulge in debauchery. Justice was, according to Sale, publicly sold and corruption and breach of trust received encouragement from the nation itself.[5] Gibbon says that Rome, around the close of the sixth century, had reached, "the lowest period of her depression," and that, "the lofty tree, under whose shade the nations of the world had reposed, was deprived of its leaves and branches, and the sapless trunk was left to wither on the ground".[6]

Similarly, the *Historians' History of the World* says: "That it (Byzantine Empire) had nevertheless suffered very severely in the general decline caused by over-taxation, and by reduced commerce, neglected agriculture and diminished population, is attested by the magnificent ruins of cities which had already fallen to decay, and which never regained their ancient prosperity."[7]

North-Western Europe

The nations of North-Western Europe had not yet seen the dawn of civilization. They were steeped in the darkness of their abject state, broken down by endless bloody tumults. Muslims and Arab Spain had not yet appeared on the stage of history to show them light nor had any historical calamity of such magnitude befallen them that could have jolted them into an awakening. They were cut off from the broad stream of humanity and knew very little of the world around them. Religiously, these nations stood between the new Christianity and the old idolatry. In the words of H.G. Wells, "there was no sign of order or union" in Western Europe.[8]

To sum up: "From the fifth to the tenth century, Europe lay sunk in a night of barbarism which grew darker and darker. It was a barbarism far more awful and horrible than that of the primitive savage, for it was the decomposing body of what had once been a great civilization. The features and impress of that civilization were all but completely effaced. Where its development had been fullest, e.g. in Italy and Gaul, all was ruin, squalor, dissolution."[9]

The Jews

Of all religious communities, the Jews alone could boast of still being in possession of a large part of their spiritual inheritance. They were also the most efficient in the art of interpreting theological and scriptural terms and symbols. But they did not command a position in the fields of religion, culture or politics where they could influence others. They were destined to live in subjection to other nations and to be exposed to injustice, oppression, chastisement, extradition, troubles and hardships. Political serfdom, oppression and anguish suffered indefinitely had produced in them a typical racial character. They were notorious all over the world for their excessive pride of blood and greed. Meek and submissive in distress, they were tyrannical and mean when they had the upper hand. Hypocrisy, deceit, treachery, selfishness, cruelty and usury had become the normal traits of their nature. In the Qur'ān we find repeated references to the extent to which they had sunk into degradation in the sixth and seventh centuries.

The mutual jealousy and hatred between the Christians and the Jews, which did not permit any opportunities to settle old scores, was brought to its climax towards the close of the sixth century. In 610 CE the Jews of Antioch rebelled against the Christians, and Emperor Phocas sent his famous General Bonosus to put down the uprising, who set about his task with such enthusiasm that the entire Jewish population was wiped out. Thousands of Jews perished by the sword, while hundreds were drowned or burnt alive or thrown to wild beasts. The Jews took their revenge in 615 by instigating Khusrau Parvez to order a general massacre of Syrian Christians when he overran that country. Then, in 630, Heraclius wreaked such savage vengeance on the Jews that in the Roman Empire those alone could save themselves who were able to flee or go into hiding.[10]

Iran

Iran was Rome's equal in the governance and administration of the civilized world. Its moral foundations had never been sound. It was a hotbed of vice and folly. Conjugal arrangements considered criminal in other parts of the world were not unlawful or undesirable in the opinion of the Iranians. It is stated that Yezdegerd II, who ruled during the middle of the fifth century CE, married his own daughter and afterwards killed her,[11] and that Bahrām Chobīn, in the sixth century, had marital relations with his sister.[12] As Professor Arthur Christensen remarked, the Iranians found nothing repugnant in incestuous connections.[13] The famous Chinese traveller Hiuen Tsang stated that no relationships were excluded from conjugality in Iranian law and society.[14]

Partly as a reaction to unbounded immorality and perversion, and partly under the influence of the supposed conflict between Light and Darkness that had been the favourite theme of Iranian philosophy from the earliest times, in the third century Mānī preached his cult of celibacy as the panacea for all the ills from which humanity was suffering. Proceeding from the curious hypothesis that evil was the outcome of the conflux of Light and Darkness, he declared that, for the permanent victory of the former over the latter, it was necessary for the human race to bring itself to an end voluntarily by ceasing to procreate.

Mānī was put to death, in 276 CE, by Bahrām as: "a messenger of doom who should be liquidated before he liquidated mankind", but his teachings endured for a long time and its influence was still visible at the advent of Islam.

After two hundred years the innate licentiousness of the Iranian temperament once again revolted against the unnatural teachings of Mānī and reasserted itself in the shape of the Mazdakite movement. Mazdak advanced the view that since all human beings were descended from the same common parents, they have equal rights to the women and wealth of one another. This, he held, would put an end to all feuds and quarrels which generally arose on account of these two factors. Shahrastānī says, "Mazdak proclaimed community of women, and made wealth and women freely and equally available to all men like fire, water and fodder."[15] This movement was readily received by the young and the libertine sections of society and eventually the Iranian Emperor Qubād took it under his patronage and showed a keen interest in its progress. Under royal encouragement the tenets of Mazdak spread rapidly and the whole of Iran was thrown into sexual anarchy and erotic crisis.

"Intemperate and pleasure-loving persons," according to Ṭabarī, "jumped at the opportunity and became ardent Mazdakites. The common people were also caught in the tempest. So powerful did the movement become that everyone could walk into everyone else's house and take possession of his wife and property. The Mazdakites approached Qubād and threatened him with dethronement if he did not champion their cause. The Emperor yielded and, thenceforth, a situation quickly emerged in which neither parents could recognize their children, nor children their parents. No one had any right even over one's own property."[16]

Ṭabarī continues: "Before Qubād had joined the movement, he was counted among the good rulers of Iran but, after he had joined it, chaos and corruption swept over the land."

King Worship

The Chosroes of Iran claimed, and were accepted by their people, to have divine blood running in their veins and the Iranians also believed that there was divinity in the very nature of their rulers. The people prostrated themselves before them, sang to the glory of their godhead and swore that they could do no wrong. It was disrespectful to utter the name of the Emperor or to sit down in his presence. The Iranians believed that the Emperor had a natural right over everyone, without anyone having any right over him. Whatever he granted to his subjects was purely out of his generosity. The subjects were there to obey, and not to interfere. The Divine Right of sovereignty being vested solely in the Kayānī family, none but a Kayānī could rule in Iran. This right was automatically transmitted from one generation to another. No one dare encroach upon it. In case a male member of mature age was not available among the Kayānīs to wear the Imperial crown, the crown was placed on the head of a minor and, if no male descendant was available, a woman was crowned. The dynastic line had to be preserved in all circumstances. Thus, after Sherūya, his seven-year-old son Ardasher was accepted as the emperor and, after Khusrau Parvez, his infant son Farrukhzād was declared the emperor. Kisrā's daughter, Borān, too, occupied the throne, and so did his other daughter, Āzarmidukht.[17] It did not occur to anyone to entrust the administration of the empire to an experienced general, a great nobleman or some other able and experienced person. As the people had no choice in the installation of an Imperial dynasty, the question of their selection of a particular ruler did not even arise.

Along with the rulers the spiritual leaders, too, were regarded as superhuman and they enjoyed unlimited powers. Distinctions in class and profession were a permanent feature of Iranian life. Professor Arthur Christensen says: "There was an unbridgeable gap between the various classes of society. Common people were prohibited by law from purchasing the property of the privileged classes. It was a standing feature of the Sāsānī rule that no one should aspire for a rank higher than what he was entitled to by birth. No one could adopt a profession in which he had not been born. The Emperors of Iran did not employ the so-called low-born people into the state service. Social distinctions were rigidly enforced. Everyone had a fixed place in the society."[18]

Racial Pride

The Iranians were great believers in the purity of their blood and the superiority of their race. They considered themselves a sanctified people, holier and nobler than the rest of humanity and gifted with unique natural abilities. They looked down on the neighbouring peoples and called them insulting and ridiculous nicknames.

Fire Worship

Fire can neither educate nor inform. It can neither redeem the sinner, nor instruct its devotees in life's problems. The religion of the fire-worshippers was, therefore, but a conglomeration of certain rites and ceremonies to be performed at certain times and certain places. Outside the temples, at home and in the market places, and in other spheres of individual and collective life, fire-worshippers were free to act as they pleased. There were no spiritual ideals, no ethical Do's and Don'ts that could fit in with social or national life in Iran. The fire-worshippers had to have recourse to their own judgement or follow blindly the demands of expediency, as polytheists of all ages are known to have done.

The Zoroastrians of Iran were, as such, no better off than pagans and unbelievers in this respect. They were without the advantage of possessing a complete and self-contained religion which could be a source of moral awareness and which could furnish them with ideals that could hold good in all walks of life.

Buddhism

Due to its assimilation of the teachings of Brahmanism and its adopting of deities and gods, Buddhism had, a long time ago, lost its individuality and the simplicity of its creed. Brahmanism had swallowed it up. In any case, the two religions had melted into each other after centuries of bitterness and conflict, and Buddhism was converted into an idolatrous faith. Wherever the Buddhists went, they took the images of Buddha with them. The entire religious and cultural life of the Buddhists is overshadowed by idolatry.[19] Strangely enough, idol-worship was introduced into Buddhism when it was in the full bloom of its power in India. Professor Ishwar Topa observes that, "the kingdom that was established under the patronage of Buddhism began to present a vast scene of idolatry. The atmosphere in the monasteries was changing and heretic innovations were being introduced one after another."[20]

"Brahmanism," says Pandit Jawaharlal Nehru in his book *The Discovery of India*, "made of Buddha an 'avatar', a god. So did Buddhism. The Mahayana doctrine spread rapidly, but it lost in quality and distinctiveness what it gained in extent. The monasteries became rich centres of vested interests and their discipline became lax. Magic and superstition crept into popular forms of worship. There was a progressive degeneration of Buddhism in India after the first millennium of its existence." Mrs Rhys Davids thus describes its diseased state during that period: "Under the overpowering influence of these sickly imaginations, the moral teachings of Gautama had been almost hidden from view. The theories grew and flourished, each new step, each new hypothesis demanded another; until the whole sky was filled with forgeries of the brain, and the nobler and simpler lessons of the founder of the religion were smothered beneath the glittering mass of metaphysical subtleties."[21]

Such being the state of affairs, the Buddhists in India, China and other countries of Southeast Asia could scarcely be looked on to play a significant role in the moral and spiritual rehabilitation of man, or the promotion of peace and stability in the world. The Chinese, in particular, were leading a self-sufficient life at the eastern end of the civilized world with their spiritual and cultural patrimony securely entombed in their breasts.

Central Asia

The other nations of Eastern and Central Asia (Mughals, Tartars, Japanese, etc.) were oscillating between a perverted Buddhism and barbaric paganism. They were still in the transition stage of civilization, having only just begun to emerge from the Dark Ages. Most had yet to learn the rudiments of a civilized existence.

India

In India, the epoch opening with the sixth century was by all accounts the gloomiest in its long and chequered history. Once the cradle of great religions and mighty civilizations, it had now languished and absorbed all the features of social and moral degeneration that had overtaken the neighbouring lands, and to these it had added a few characteristics of its own, more prominent among which were: an abundance of objects of worship; sexual wantonness; and caste and social distinctions.

(i) *Ever-Increasing Gods*

In the sixth century CE, idolatry had reached its lowest ebb in India. The Vedas give the number of Hindu gods as 33. During this period as many as 330 million gods were worshipped among Hindus. Almost everything that possessed any attractiveness or utility had been vested with divine attributes. Stones and minerals, trees and plants, rivers and mountains, animals and even organs of procreation were adored as gods. Thus, this ancient religion was turned into a heap of mythical traditions, beliefs and rites. Dr Gustave le Bon says in *Les Civilisations de l'Inde*: "The Hindu, of all people, stands most unavoidably in the need of visible objects for religious worship, and although at different times religious reformers have tried to prove monotheism in the Hindu faith, it has been an unavailing effort. From the Vedic Age to the present day, the Hindu has been worshipping all sorts of things. Whatever he cannot understand or control is worthy of being adored as divine in his eyes. All attempts of Brahmans and other Hindu reformers in the direction of monotheism or in limiting the number of gods to three have been utterly unsuccessful. The Hindus listened to them, and sometimes even accepted their teachings in principle, but in practice the three gods went on multiplying until they began to see a god in every article and phenomenon of nature."[22]

Sculpture had attained its highest perfection in the seventh century CE. The idols had caught the popular imagination so powerfully that even the Buddhist and Jain religions had to bow to them in the interests of self-preservation. An idea of the popularity and the profusion of idols during this epoch may be obtained from the following account of an important event in Harsha's reign supplied by Hiuen Tsang, who stayed in India from 630 to 644 CE:

> Emperor Harsha held a religious assembly at Kanauj. First a full-size golden figure of the Buddha was installed on the top of a fifty-foot high pillar. Then a smaller statue was taken out in procession with great pomp and ceremony. Harsha himself held the canopy over its head, dressed as 'Sakr-devta', while his friend Kumara, the King of Assam, wielded the flapper to drive away the flies from it.[23]

Of the members of the family and the courtiers of the Emperor, Hiuen Tsang says that:

> Some of them were the followers of Siva; some had embraced Buddhism; some worshipped the sun; some worshipped Vishnu: everyone was free to choose any god or goddess for his devotions, or to worship all of them if he pleased.[24]

(ii) *Sexual Wantonness*

Nowhere do obscene subjects and sexual themes occupy such a conspicuous place in religion as they did in Ancient India. Extremely revolting and shameless accounts of the sexual misdeeds of gods and goddesses by way of explaining the occurrence of important mythological events and the creation of things are found in the ancient Indian religious books. It requires no great imagination to picture what indecent practices must have gone on in the name of religion. The worship of the "lingum" (the sexual organ) of Siva was prevalent throughout the land. To quote Gustave le Bon once more:

> The Hindus are deeply devoted to images and symbols...Their temples are full of these, chief among them being the '*lingum*' and the '*yoni*', as symbolising the generative power in nature. Even the pillars of Asoka are regarded by lay Hindus as images of '*lingum*'. All vertical and conical objects are held in veneration by them.[25]

Some historians say that there was a religious sect in which naked women were worshipped by men and vice versa.[26] A large number of temples had degenerated into cesspools of corruption with their priests conducting themselves as guardians of lust. The palaces of the kings and noblemen were seething with vice and immorality.

Parallel to this devotion to the flesh and sensuality, a strong movement of life-denial and self-mortification with a long routine of penances was also current in the country. Between these two extremes the moral fabric of society had been torn to shreds. While a tiny section of the population was subjecting itself to useless self-torture, the bulk indulged in vulgar self-indulgence.

(iii) *The Caste System*

Another glaring peculiarity of the religio-social structure of the India of early days was the all-powerful caste system. Its foundations had been laid by the Aryans during the later stages of the Vedic Age with a view to protecting themselves against mixing with the primitive races of the land. In the words of Gustave le Bon:

> We have seen that, towards the close of the Vedic Age, occupations had started to become more or less hereditary, and the germ of the caste system had been sown. The Vedic Aryans were alive to the need of maintaining the purity of their race by not mixing with

> the conquered peoples, and when they advanced towards the east and subjugated vast populations, this need became still more manifest and the law-givers had to pay due regard to it. The Aryans understood the problems of race well; they had come to realize that if a ruling minority did not take proper care of itself, it was rapidly assimilated with the servile population and deprived of its identity.[27]

The real credit, however, for evolving the caste system into a rigid social framework and law goes to Manu who, in the heyday of Brahmanic civilization in India, three hundred years before the birth of Christ, formulated what is commonly known as the "Manu Shastra", the sacred law of Hindu society. Manu classified the entire Hindu population into four classes with reference to their birth, namely: (i) the Brahmans or the learned and priestly class; (ii) the Kshattriyas or the fighting and ruling class; (iii) the Vaisyas or the trading and agricultural people; and (iv) the Sudras or the lowest caste people whose sole purpose in life was to serve their superiors.

The "Manu Shastra" says: "The Lord created Brahman from His mouth, Kshattriya from His arms, Vaisya from His thighs and Sudra from His feet so that the world may prosper."

He assigned separate duties to each of them for its preservation. For the Brahman he commanded: "the study of the Vedas, the presentation of offerings to gods on his own behalf and on behalf of others, and the receiving of alms."

For the Kshattriya he commanded that: "he should protect the people, give alms, offer oblations, read the Vedas and abstain from carnality."

For the Vaisya he commanded: "the service of the cattle, the giving away of alms and oblations, the reading of the Vedas and trading and agriculture."

For the Sudra he commanded: "he should serve the above three."

This law gave to the Brahmans the distinction, superiority and sanctity which raised their status equal to that of the gods. Says the "Manu Shastra":

"Anyone who is born a Brahman is the noblest creature on earth. He is the monarch of all the created things and his duty is to defend the Shastra.

"Whatever is on the earth belongs to the Brahman, for he is the highest among all creatures. All things are for him.

"A Brahman can acquire, by force, if necessary, the property of his Sudra slave. This will not at all be unlawful, because a slave can never own anything; whatever he has is his master's.

"A Brahman who remembers the Rig Veda is absolutely sinless, though he may destroy all the three worlds or partake of food belonging to anybody.

"However great be the king's need – he may even be dying of want – he must never levy any tax on the Brahmans, nor let a Brahman die of hunger in his kingdom.

"In lieu of the sentence of death, the head of the Brahman shall be shaved, while persons of other castes shall be executed."

According to this law, though higher in status than the Vaisya and the Sudra, the Kshattriya has no status in comparison with the Brahman. Says Manu:

"A ten-year-old Brahman and a hundred-year-old Kshattriya are like a father and son unto each other, the Brahman being the father."

The Unfortunate Sudras

The Sudras in Hindu society, according to this Law, were lower in status than animals and more degraded than a dog. Says "Manu Shastra":

"Nothing can be more honourable for a Sudra than to serve the Brahman; nothing besides this can earn for him any reward.

"A Sudra should never acquire property, even if he has the opportunity, for in so doing he causes pain to the Brahmans.

"A Sudra who assaults a higher caste man is liable to lose the limb with which the assault is made.

"Should a Sudra try to sit at the same place with the 'twice-born', the king should get his buttocks branded with red-hot iron and banish him from the land.

"If a Sudra touches a Brahman or abuses him, his tongue shall be pulled out from the root. If he claims that he can teach a Brahman, boiling oil shall be poured down his throat.

"The atonement for killing a dog, a cat, a frog, a lizard, a crow, an owl and a Sudra is the same."

The Position of Women in Indian Society

As compared with the Vedic Age, the position of women had deteriorated considerably during the Brahmanic Age. In the Law of Manu, according to Gustave le Bon, the woman was consistently shown as frail and referred to in disgraceful terms.[28]

On the death of their husbands, women were condemned to a state of perpetual misery. They were not allowed to remarry. They lived as slave-maids of the brothers of their husbands, or their other descendants. A widow would often commit *suttee* (self-immolation). Gustave le Bon writes: "The immolation of widows on the funeral pyres of their husbands is not mentioned in the 'Shastra', but it appears that the practice had become quite common in India, for we find references to it in the accounts of the Greek chroniclers."[29]

Arabia

The pre-Islamic Arabs possessed certain natural virtues that marked them out in their contemporary world. They were unrivalled in eloquence and in the skilful use of language. Freedom and honour they valued above their lives. They were superb horsemen. They were ardent, bold, chivalrous, plain of speech, strong of memory, fraternizing, plain, hardy, determined, truthful, loyal and trustworthy.

But centuries of isolation in the peninsula and a morbid insistence on the faith of their forefathers had severely undermined their moral and spiritual health. The sixth century CE found the Arabs steeped in depravity, perversion and dark idolatry and indulging in the characteristics of primitive life.

Pre-Islamic Idols

The belief in an over-ruling Providence had grown very feeble among them. It was confined to a select few, while the religion of the masses was gross idolatry. The idols that had originally been introduced to serve as devotional mediums had been elevated to the status of Divinity. Homage was still paid to the One Transcendent God, but only verbally; in their hearts a host of deities were enthroned, whose goodwill they sought to propitiate and displeasure avert.

Each tribe, city and locality had its own god. Al-Kalbī stated that every household in Makka had its own idol. When a Makkan set out on a journey, his last act at home would be to invoke the blessings of the family deity, and the first thing he did on his return was to pay reverence to it.[30]

People used to compete with one another in collecting idols and constructing temples. Those who could afford neither planted a slab of stone in front of the Kaᶜbah and performed the ritual of circumambulation around it. Such stones were called *anṣāb*. In the words of Abū Rajā' al-ᶜUṭāridī, as reported in the *Ṣaḥīḥ* of al-Bukhārī: "We worshipped stones. When we found a better stone than the one we had, we took it up and threw away the old one. Where no stones were available, we made a sand-mound, milked a goat over it and worshipped it."[31] When a traveller halted at a place, he used to collect four stones, worship the most beautiful of them, and used the other three to rest his pot on for cooking.[32]

Angels, stars, jinns and other objects of veneration found in polytheistic faiths were adored as divine beings by the Arabs. The angels, they believed, were the daughters of God, whom they besought to intercede with Him on their behalf. Jinns were regarded as the co-sharers of the Almighty in the practical control of the world.[33]

Al-Kalbī says that Banū Malīḥ, a branch of the tribe of Khuzāᶜah, worshipped the jinns,[34] and Sāᶜīd reports that the tribe of Ḥimyar worshipped the sun; the tribe of Kināna adored the moon; the tribe of Tamīm worshipped ad-Dabarān; the Lakhm and the Judhām, Ṭayy, Banū Qays and Banū Asad worshipped Jupiter, Canopus, the Dog-star and Mercury, respectively.[35]

Social Debasement

The Arabs' social habits were outrageous. Alcoholic drink was so common that even their literature stunk of it. The wealth of expressions contained in the Arabic language for the "daughter of the vine", and the delicate variations of meaning these expressions convey, reveal how passionately the Arabs were in love with it. Banners were flown over liquor-shops. Gambling was a matter of pride and it was considered dishonourable to decline a gambling bout. A *Tābiʿī* theologian, Qatādah,[36] stated that often a gambler would stake his entire household on a single bet, and would walk away in sorrow as he saw it pass into the hands of his rival. Such incidents would sometimes lead to bitter feuds.[37]

Usury was indulged in callously and adultery was considered a minor vice. A great interest was taken in the various attitudes and postures of sexual intercourse. Prostitution was rampant and brothels were frequently maintained.

The Position of Women

The position of women was extremely lamentable in pre-Islamic Arabia. The right of inheritance was denied. Widowed and divorced women were not permitted to remarry. It was a common practice for the eldest son to take as wives his father's widows inherited as property with the rest of his estate. They were discriminated against even in matters of food, men reserving certain dishes for themselves.

Many daughters were buried alive at birth, since pride and poverty had introduced the abominable crime of female infanticide among all Arab tribes. Haitham ibn ʿAdī tells us that one out of every ten men was guilty of it.[38] Kind-hearted tribal chiefs often bought infant girls to save their lives. Ṣaʿṣaʿah ibn Nājiyah says that before the dawn of Islam he had rescued as many as three hundred girls from this terrible fate by paying compensatory money to their fathers.[39] Sometimes a young girl who had escaped being killed at birth or during childhood (due to her father being away from home or some other reason) would be taken to a lonely spot by her father and killed. Several incidents of this nature from their past lives were narrated by the Companions after they had embraced Islam.[40]

Tribal Prejudice

Tribal prejudice was very strong. The horizon of life was painfully limited by the narrow concepts of tribal organization. A maxim among the Arabs said: "Stand by your brother, be he the oppressor or the oppressed", and they adhered to this with great passion.

Everyone thought that he came from the most noble stock. Some families considered it degrading to participate with others even in religious congregations. The Quraysh, for example, kept their distance from other pilgrims during some of the *Ḥajj* rites. They took the lead in performing the ritual of halting at ʿArafāt[41] in order to avoid coming into contact with other pilgrims.[42] There was, they thought, a class of born masters, another of born toilers and a third of the common people and the "people of the street".

The Arabs' Warlike Temperament

In keeping with their primitive, desert environment, the Arabs had a very warlike temperament. War, in some respects, was for them a necessity but, more than that, it was a pastime. Their poets portrayed war as a thing of great joy. An Arab poet says:

> If an enemy tribe we do not find,
> We go to war with a friendly tribe,
> And our lust for war is quenched.[43]

Another poet says:

> May a war break out among the tribes
> When my colt is grown up for riding,
> That I may get a chance to show
> The worth of my colt and sword.[44]

The most trivial incident could spark off a bitter inter-tribal war. The war, for instance, between the descendants of Wā'il, Bakr and Taghlib dragged on for forty years in which there were innumerable casualties. An Arab chief, Muhalhil, thus depicted its consequences: "Both the tribes have been exterminated; mothers have become childless; children have become orphans; the flow of tears does not cease; the dead are not buried."[45]

The Arabian peninsula was like a hornets' nest. One never knew when one would be robbed or assassinated. People were kidnapped while travelling with caravans, even in the presence of their companions. Powerful kingdoms of the day needed strong escorts and guarantees of safe passage from tribal chiefs for their caravans and delegations to travel from one place to another.[46]

A General Survey

R.V.C. Bodley depicted a general survey of the world at the time of the advent of the Prophet in his book *The Messenger.* He says: "The Arabs did not command any respect in the sixth-century world. As a matter of fact, no one counted very much. It was a moribund period when the great Empires of Eastern Europe and Western Asia had already been destroyed or were at the end of their imperial careers.

"It was a world still dazed by the eloquence of Greece, by the grandeur of Persia, by the majesty of Rome, with nothing yet to take their place, not even a religion.

"The Jews were wandering all over the world, with no central guidance. They were tolerated or persecuted according to circumstance. They had no country to call their own, and their future was as uncertain as it is today.

"Outside the sphere of influence of Pope Gregory the Great, the Christians were propounding all kinds of complicated interpretations of their once simple creed and were busy cutting one another's throats in the process.

"In Persia, a last flicker of empire-building remained and Khusrau II was extending the frontiers of his domain. By inflicting defeat on Rome he had already occupied Cappadocia, Egypt and Syria. In 620 AC (after Christ), when Muḥammad was about to emerge as a guide for humanity, he had sacked Jerusalem and stolen the Holy Cross and restored the might and grandeur of Darius I. It looked almost like a new lease of life for the splendour of the Middle East. Yet the Byzantine Romans still had a little of their old vitality. When Khusrau brought his army to the walls of Constantinople, they made a final effort to survive.

"Further away in the east, the march of events was leaving few landmarks. India still consisted of many unimportant petty states which struggled mutually for political and military supremacy.

"The Chinese, as usual, were fighting among themselves. The Sui dynasty came into power to be replaced by the Tang which ruled for three centuries.

"In Japan, an Empress occupied the throne for the first time. Buddhism was beginning to take root and to influence Japanese ideas and ideals.

"Europe was gradually merging into the Frankish Empire, which would eventually comprise France, Northern Italy, most of the countries east of the Rhine as far as the present Russo-Polish border. Clovis was dead and Dagobert, the last great Merovingian ruler, was soon to be crowned.

"Spain and England were unimportant petty states.

"Spain was under the control of the Visigoths, who had lately been driven out of France which they had occupied as far in the north as Loire. They were persecuting the Jews, who would, consequently, do much to facilitate the Muslim invasion which was to follow a century later.

"The British Isles were divided into independent principalities. One hundred and fifty years had passed since the departure of the Romans, who had been replaced by an influx of Nordic people. England herself was made up of seven separate kingdoms."[47]

The Political and Economic Condition of the Pre-Islamic World

Absolute Monarchy

In the pre-Islamic world, the common form of government was absolute monarchy, which was generally founded on the popular belief in the innate sacredness and inviolable superiority of certain dynasties, as in Iran where the Sāssānids believed they had a divine right to rule in succession.

On occasions, sovereignty was based on the grandeur of individual rulers. The Chinese, for instance, called their emperor the "Son of the Heaven", for they believed that the Emperor was the offspring of the marriage between the "male" sky and the "female" earth, and that the Emperor Khata I was the first issue from that alliance.[48] On this account their emperor was taken to be the sole Father of his people, and as such he had the right to rule over them as he wished. "You alone are our benefactor," they said to him by way of formal acknowledgement of their allegiance. Under the spell of this concept, when Emperor Taitsung died, the Chinese were so overwhelmed with grief that many of them pierced their faces with needles, some cut off their hair, and others bruised their ears by striking their heads against the coffin.

In some cases, sovereignty was considered to be the special prerogative of a particular group or a country. With the Romans, it was an article of faith that they were the sovereign race and all other races had been created to be subservient to them. The other races were like the veins and arteries whose sole function was to carry the blood to and from the heart, which was Rome. The Romans could override any law, violate any right and ravish any country. Community of religion or treaties of friendship with Rome were no protection against the high-handedness of the Romans.

The Roman dependencies had no legal status or administrative autonomy within the Empire. They were, so to say, like the she-camel, which gives milk and is used for transport, but receives, in return, only as much fodder as might keep its back strong and udder full. Says

Briffault: "The intrinsic cause that doomed and condemned the Roman Empire was not any growing corruption, but the corruption, the evil, the inadaptation to facts in its very origin and being. No system of human organization that is false in its very principle, in its very foundation, can save itself by any amount of cleverness and efficiency in the means by which that falsehood is carried out and maintained, by any amount of superficial adjustment and tinkering. It is doomed root and branch as long as the root remains what it was. The Roman Empire was, as we have seen, a device for the enrichment of a small class of people by the exploitation of mankind. That business enterprise was carried out with all honesty, all the fairness and justice compatible with its very nature, and with admirable judgment and ability. But all these virtues could not save the fundamental falsehood, the fundamental wrong from its consequence."[49]

Egypt and Syria under the Romans

Of the Roman rule in Egypt, Dr Alfred Butler writes:

> The whole machinery of rule in Egypt was directed to the sole purpose of wringing profit out of the ruled for the benefit of the rulers. There was no idea of governing for the advantage of the governed, of raising people in the social scale, of developing the moral or even the material resources of the country. It was an alien domination founded on force and making little pretence of sympathy with the subject race.[50]

Their rule in Syria was no better, as one Syrian historian observes:

> The Roman rule over Syria was benevolent in the beginning. But when their Empire grew old and began to disintegrate, the Romans subjected the Syrians to the worst type of tyranny. As the Romans did not annex Syria directly to their Empire, the Syrians could never acquire the rights of citizenship in the Roman Empire,

> nor did their country ever gain the status of a Roman territory. The Syrians remained a stateless people.
>
> The taxes were so exorbitant that often people had to sell their children to pay them. Slavery and forced labour were common. The splendid buildings and manufactories that were the pride of the Roman rulers were built by the toil of servile hands.[51]

The seven hundred years of Roman rule in Syria was a dismal tale of pain, suffering and bloodshed. Before the Romans the Greeks had occupied Syria for 369 years. Their regime, too, had been a dreadful curse for the Syrians. The insatiable greed of the Greeks had been laid bare by the inhuman methods they had employed in extorting money from the people.[52]

Taxes in Iran

The administrative and financial structure of Iran was neither just nor stable and was subject to the ever-changing pattern of the needs and ambitions of the rulers. The author of *Iran ba ᶜAhd-i-Sasanian* says:

> In the assessment and collection of taxes and levies those who realized them were guilty of extortion and misappropriation. It was not possible to make an estimate of income and expenditure at the beginning of the year, for the revenue varied from year to year...The result often was that while a war was on, the coffers of the Empire were empty. In such circumstances it became necessary to impose extraordinary taxes, the chief target for which almost always were the rich Western provinces, particularly Babylon.[53]

Royal Treasuries and the Private Wealth of the Iranian Emperors

A very meagre part of the Imperial revenue was spent on public welfare. The emperors of Iran believed in amassing as much wealth for themselves as possible. When the treasure of Khusrau II was shifted to a new building in Madā'in (Ctesiphon) in 607–8 CE, it included 468 million *mithqāls*[54] of gold (worth approximately 375 million gold francs). By the thirteenth year of his reign, the accumulation of gold had reached 800 million *mithqāls*. His crown was made of 120lb of solid gold.[55]

Castes and Classes

The distribution of wealth was grossly unjust. A few individuals were excessively rich, and the rest were immersed in poverty. The reign of Naushīrwān is famous in Iranian history for the justice and benevolence of his administration. The author of *Iran ba ʿAhd-i-Sasanian* says:

> In the land system of Naushirwan, greater attention had been bestowed upon the interests of the Imperial Treasury than those of the people. The condition of the masses was as deplorable as ever. The Byzantine philosophers who had taken refuge in the Emperor's Court were soon disgusted with what they saw in Iran. Maybe, they were not intellectually detached enough to take an objective view of the customs and practices of an alien people like taking one's own daughter or sister into wedlock or leaving away the dead for the vultures to feed upon. They could not think with the mind of an ethnologist and were disappointed to find things different from what they had expected in the empire of a philosopher-king. But it was not its customs and practices alone that made them turn away from Iran. What really grieved them were the social divisions, the unconquerable distance between the high and the low, the rank misery of the poor and the heartless exploitation of the weak by the strong.[56]

The division of society into castes and classes was not peculiar to Iran. In the Roman Empire the social classifications were no less severe.

Says Robert Briffault:

> When a social structure visibly threatens to topple down, rulers try to prevent it from falling by preventing it from moving. The whole Roman society was fixed in a system of castes, no one was to change his avocation, the son must continue in the calling of his father.[57]

In both empires important jobs were reserved for prominent families which enjoyed great status and the confidence of high officials.

The Peasants of Iran

Ever-increasing taxes had broken the back of the peasantry. Crushed and ruined, and also to save themselves from conscription (for they had no sympathy with the objects for which wars were fought), a large number of peasants had abandoned their fields and taken refuge in temples and monasteries.

> The condition of the peasants was really pitiable. They were tied down to their lands; every kind of forced labour, every type of degrading service was taken from them... large bodies of these poor peasants used to march on foot behind the army, as if they were doomed to eternal serfdom – they received no encouragement, salary, or wages of any kind. The relationship with the landlords was not very different from what obtained between the slaves and their masters.[58]

Extravagance and Luxury

A flood of licentiousness had swept over both Iran and Rome. Sensual enjoyment had become the chief objective in life. Both nations seemed to compete with each other in blind self-indulgence, luxury and extravagance. There was an amazing profusion of the voluptuous embellishments of life and the wares of pleasure and luxury among the ruling circles. Great ingenuity was displayed in these matters. A Parsi historian writes about Khusrau Parvez of Iran that he, "possessed 12,000 women, 50,000 thoroughbred horses and countless palaces, huge amounts of cash and heaps of precious stones and other valuable articles. The grandeur of his court was unique in the world. In sheer splendour no rulers in history can beat the Iranian Emperors."

He also says that "tributes and presents used to pour in upon them from all countries stretching from the Middle East to the Far East. A colossal amount of wealth was left behind by the Iranians when they were ejected from Iraq by the Muslims. It ranged from highly valuable raiments and large vessels of gold to high-class cosmetics and perfumes."[59]

It is stated by Ṭabarī that at the victory of Madā'in, the Arabs came across several Iranian tents which were full of sealed baskets. It was thought that they would contain food but, when the baskets were opened, they were found to be packed with gold and silver vessels.[60]

The Iranian emperors had a carpet, known as the "Carpet of Spring", which was spread out when royal drinking parties were held in the autumn. "It was sixty yards square and could cover about an acre of ground. Its base was of gold in which costly stones and pearls had been set in such a way as to give the impression of a garden. It was divided into several beds of flowering plants and fruit-bearing trees, whose stems and branches were of gold, leaves of silk, buds of gold and silver and fruits of jewels. The border was studded with diamonds. A number of avenues and canals had also been cut in it with jewels. When the Sassanids sat in that ever-blooming garden and drank wine in the autumn, they presented to the world a spectacle it had never seen anywhere before."[61]

Similarly, in Syria the Roman rulers and their Syrian protégés set no limits on the lust of the flesh and its appeasement. Ḥassān ibn Thābit, may Allah be pleased with him, who had spent some years of his pre-Islamic life in the company of rulers of Ghassān, described the pomp and dazzling luxury of the Court of Jabalah ibn Ayham in the following words:

> I saw ten slave-girls there, five of them were Romans, who sang on the harp, and the other five, who sang in the style of the people of Ḥīrah. They had been presented by an Arab chief, Ayās ibn Qubaisah. Other musicians also used to come regularly from Makkah and other Arabian cities. When Jabalah held his bacchanalian parties, jasmine, and other sweet-smelling flowers were spread on the floor, and sweet odoriferous substances like musk and amber were put up in gold containers. Musk of the purest variety was placed in silver salvers. ʿUd[62] was burnt in winter. In the summer, the floor was cooled with ice and hot-weather garments were brought which Jabalah and his friends used to throw over themselves. Furs and other valuable winter clothes were provided in the winter."[63]

This unquenchable passion for amusement, this hideous excess of sensuality were by no means confined to royalty and the aristocracy. The entire society, from the highest to the lowest, had degenerated into scandalous dissipation. Often one individual spent on his dress what could clothe or feed a whole village. The distinguished and the high-born had to maintain fantastic standards of living, or they lost face in society. Shaʿbī says that in Iran, rank in one's tribe was reflected in the headgear. The headgear of some tribal chiefs cost over a hundred thousand *dirhams*.[64] Hurmuz, for instance, being one of fine status, wore on his cap jewels that were worth a hundred thousand *dirhams*. The sole criterion of greatness in Iran was to belong to one of the seven high-class families. Azādia, although he was the governor of Ḥīrah, was generally placed in the second order of nobility and, therefore, his headgear was worth fifty thousand *dirhams*. Rustum's head-dress was worth a hundred thousand *dirhams*.[65]

For the Iranians, frivolous amusement and ostentatious living had become second nature. They could not give up their extravagant habits even in grave circumstances. When Emperor Yezdegerd of Iran had to flee the capital after the fall of Madā'in, he took with him a staggering retinue of 1,000 cooks, 1,000 musicians, 1,000 attendants of panthers and 1,000 falconers, and even this was not considered adequate.[66]

When Hurmuzān came to Madīnah as a vanquished adversary and presented himself before Caliph ʿUmar, may Allah be pleased with him, he asked for a cup of water. But when the water came he refused to drink, as the cup in which it had been brought was coarse and ugly. He declared that he would prefer to die of thirst rather than drink from such a cup. Ultimately another cup was procured for him upon the order of the Caliph.[67]

Rulers or Robbers?

To keep themselves in constant luxury, the rulers extorted money from their subjects with brutal unconcern, and their exactions became heavier day by day. According to the author of *Iran ba ʿAhd-i-Sasanian*: In Iran, "in addition to the regular taxes, there was also the custom known as *ʿA'in'*, of extorting gifts from the people as on the occasion of Nauroz and Mehrgan. The biggest sources of the royal income were, in our opinion, the crown estates and such other items of revenue as were considered to be the exclusive privilege of the crown, such as the gold mines of Armenia, whose entire output was the private income of the Emperor."[68]

In Roman Syria, "people had to surrender one-tenth of their income or produce, apart from paying the tax on principal stock. Then there was the capitation tax. The Romans had also many other important sources of revenue like the octroi [duty], the commercial levy and the mines. Contracts were given for the collection of revenue from the wheat-growing areas and pastures. The contractors were called *ʿashshārīn*. They had organized themselves into corporations and their agents realised much in excess of what was due. Sometimes they sold the tenants as slaves for non-payment of dues."[69]

The Hopeless Plight of the Masses

The population of both Empires was split into two sections. One section comprised the rich and the privileged – princes, noblemen and wealthy landlords and merchants. They enjoyed an abundance of wealth and even adorned the shoes of their horses with jewels and hung brocade and silk on their walls. The other section comprised the common people – artisans, peasants, labourers and small traders. For them life was an unending series of hardships. Caught in an ever-tightening trap of taxes, imposts and exactions, they lived in abject poverty. To make their lives still more wretched, they foolishly yielded to the temptation – a circumstance so common to the underdog – of aping the customs and habits of those occupying the higher rungs of the social ladder. The result was lives full of bitterness and minds full of worry and confusion. They were utterly devoid of either contentment or peace of mind.

The Rich and the Poor

Between the two, the nobler values of life and the precepts of the prophets had been abandoned and ethical standards had become meaningless. The rich were too absorbed in their pleasures to pay heed to religion or the Hereafter. The peasants and labourers were so crushed by the worries of life that they could not afford to look beyond their humdrum daily existence. Thus, material needs and interests had, in one way or another, woven a web around everyone, and made them prisoners.

Remarking on the utter social and moral darkness that had descended on the world during this period of history, Shāh Waliyyullāh Dehlawī,[70] in his outstanding work *Ḥujjatullāh-i'l-Bālighah*, says:

> Centuries of undisputed mastery over large parts of the world, dissipation, irreligiousness and wholesale surrender to the devilish temptations had created among the Romans and the Iranians great fastidiousness of taste regarding comforts of life. They strove hard to outdo one another in the display of crude sensualism and luxury. Accomplished artists and craftsmen, who had collected in Rome and Iran from far and near, employed their skill to

> unite every refinement of convenience, elegance and splendour in the service of the rich. What improvements they introduced in the art of luxurious living gained currency immediately in society. A great value was set on the refinements of material existence. The standard of living had become so inflated that it was considered disgraceful for a nobleman to wear a cap or a waist-band worth less than a hundred thousand *dirhams*. One who did not possess stately mansions, sparkling fountains, gorgeous baths and shady groves and did not maintain an elegant suite of attendants and slaves received little notice in society. It is tiring to dwell further on this state of affairs. The reader can very well understand the situation in those Empires by studying the habits and manners of the rulers of their own country.[71] Luxuries had enlarged themseves into necessities of life. A mortal sickness had come over civilization. It was a terrible affliction that had struck down both the high and the low. Everyone had slipped into a life of extravagance and folly, and in consequence, had involved himself in innumerable cares and worries. The worship of comfort called for a great deal of money, which could be acquired only by fleecing the common people, the peasants, traders and the like. If the latter resisted the exactions, war was waged against them and they were punished; and if they yielded, they were brought into submission like dumb, driven cattle. They toiled day and night. Their woes gave them no respite to turn their minds to think of the good of the Hereafter. Often in a whole country not a single individual could be found with any real solicitude for religion.[72]

In short, those countries under Roman or Iranian domination were in a pathetic state. They were lands of chaos and wretchedness.

Worldwide Gloom

There was, briefly, not one nation in the whole world of the sixth century of the Christian era that could be called healthy in temperament, not one society that was imbued with high ethical ideals, nor a single state that was based on principles of justice, equity and fairness, nor a leadership that possessed knowledge and wisdom, nor a religion that represented the pure teachings of the prophets of God. There was a universal lack of good leadership. The Word of God had become corrupted. The few churches and monasteries that still existed in the thick, encircling gloom could at best be likened to the tiny light of a glow-worm on a dark, rainy night. True knowledge and right action had become so rare, and moral teachers who could guide men along the sublime path of godliness were so scarce that Salmān of Persia,[73] who had forsaken his home and the creed of his ancestors in quest of Truth, could, during the whole course of his journey from his native country to Syria, find only four persons who could provide the soothing balm of faith for his restless soul[74] and who were living according to the way indicated by the Prophets.

The Holy Qur'ān depicts this worldwide darkness and chaos in the following thought-provoking words:

> *Disintegration had appeared on the land and*
> *the sea because of (the deed) that the*
> *hands of men had earned, that (God) might*
> *give them a taste of some of their deeds*
> *in order that they might turn back (from evil)*
>
> al-Rūm 30:41

II

THE ADVENT OF THE PROPHET ﷺ

As humanity lay gasping in the agonies of death, God raised up Prophet Muḥammad ﷺ to bring life back to humanity and deliver it from darkness into light. Says the Holy Qur'ān:

> *A Book which we have revealed unto thee, in order that thou mightest lead mankind out of the depths of darkness into light – by the leave of their Lord – to the Way of (Him) the Exalted in Power, Worthy of all praise!*
>
> Ibrāhīm 14:1

The Prophet ﷺ broke the fetters of ignorance and superstition and invited men to a servitude that released them from all forms of bondage. He restored to them the legitimate comforts of life from which they had deprived themselves under false ethical and spiritual notions. The Book of Islam says:

> *For he commands them what is just and forbids them what is evil; he allows them as lawful what is good (and pure) and prohibits them from what is bad (and impure); he relieves them from their heavy burdens and releases them from the yokes that are upon them.*
>
> al-Aʿrāf 7:157

The Prophet's advent gave to humanity a new life, a new light, a new faith, a new warmth, a new society and a new culture. It was the beginning of a new era in human history, marking the commencement of the real mission of man on earth.

> *The blind and the seeing are not alike, nor are the depths of the darkness and the light; nor are the (chilly) shade and the (genial) heat of the sun; nor are alike those that are living and those that are dead.*
>
> al-Fāṭir 35:19-22

Yawning between Islam and Ignorance, there was a deep and wide chasm. Yet, under the inspired leadership of the Prophet, the world jumped across this chasm and passed from Ignorance to Islam with an alacrity that is without parallel in history. In the following pages we shall see how this glorious miracle was accomplished.

The Era of Ignorance – A Reappraisal

It must be clear from the preceding chapter that the world at the time of the Prophet's advent was like a house hit by a severe earthquake. All that was in it had turned upside down, while large spaces had been bereft of everything and made completely desolate.

In this confusion man had forgotten himself. He had lost his self-respect to the extent that he was shamelessly prostrating himself before stones, trees and water – before all the helpless manifestations of nature. He could not comprehend even simple, everyday truths. His intellect was grounded. He was so confused and his senses had become so perverted that he could not distinguish the real from the unreal, right from wrong, and truth from falsehood.

Vice was seen as virtue. Wolves, so to speak, were appointed to tend sheep; aggressors were allowed to act as arbitrators. The sinful and the wicked lived in peace and enjoyed plenty, while the righteous and the upright were condemned to privation and suffering. Cunning and deceit passed for wisdom and resourcefulness, while wisdom was considered foolishness.

Drinking, gambling, usury and plunder had become the order of the day. Daughters were killed at birth. God's wealth was in the grime of the kings' palms, and human beings their bondsmen. Clergymen had raised themselves to a position of Divinity. They grew fat on the wealth of others whom they deliberately deceived for their own selfish purposes.

Precious qualities which God had bestowed upon man were wantonly misused. Courage and strength had become a means of cruelty and oppression, and wastefulness stood for generosity, arrogance passed for self-respect and artfulness for sagacity. The sole purpose of the intellect was thought to be to plan crimes and invent new ways of hideous debauchery and vulgar extravagance.

For a long time the most valuable of all materials, the human material, had been rotting. It had not had the good fortune to come to the notice of a master-craftsman who should have prepared from it the right mould of civilization. Where there should have been organized communities of men, there were untended flocks of human cattle.

Politics was as unrestrained as a wild animal and power was like a naked sword in the hands of one who had lost his senses on account of heavy drinking and who was using it against himself and against everybody else.

Ineffective Half Measures

Every section of that degenerate society cried out for the undivided attention of a reformer. An ordinary reformer, acting according to his own whims, and without Prophetic Inspiration or Divine Guidance, might have concentrated his energies on correcting a single social pathological condition and, even then, he might not have succeeded. Human nature is complex, abounding in labyrinths and mysterious back doors and, once it is misguided or deflected from its natural course, it cannot be given a new lease of life by removing just one defect. It required a complete overhaul, a thorough reconditioning. If the plant of Godliness was to thrive on human soil, the entire undergrowth of ungodliness had first to be weeded out. There was no other option.

The correction of a single moral defect in human society calls for the dedication of a reformer's entire life. Sometimes many men spend their lifetime combating a moral fault or a social abuse without being rewarded with any measure of success. Take, for example, drinking alcohol. When this habit becomes widespread in a nation, its roots go deep into the collective subconscious, and a whole army of sensuous delights grows along with the habit. Can this be overcome by mere moral exhortation or by punitive legislation alone? No, only a fundamental psychological shift, a radical change in the social and moral outlook of society can eradicate it. Any other course of action will only drive the habit underground and make it more pernicious.

The Difference Between a Prophet and a Leader

Had the Prophet ﷺ been a political leader, the ideal action for him to take would have been to weld Arabia into one country and the Arab tribes into one nation, with himself at their head. Abū Jahl, ʿUtbah and all his other relentless opponents would have readily accepted his leadership. They had already demonstrated their confidence in him by appointing him to arbitrate in Makkah's most dangerous dispute.[75] ʿUtbah had definitely stated that, if he so desired, the Quraysh were willing to make him their king. After he had risen to power in Arabia, he could have led his splendid horsemen into Persia and Rome and brought these Empires under his control. And, in case it was strategically unwise to fight against the Romans and the Iranians simultaneously, what was there to prevent him from overrunning the neighbouring countries of Abyssinia and the Yemen?

However, the Prophet ﷺ had not been raised to substitute one evil for another, to condemn an injustice in one place and condone it elsewhere. He had not been sent to erect the mansion of Arab glory upon the ruins of the hopes and yearnings of other nations, to emancipate men from the subjugation of the Romans and Iranians and to place them under subjugation of the descendants of ʿAdnān and Qaḥṭān.

The Prophet ﷺ was not a political leader. He was a preacher of the Divine Word, a Warner and a Bearer of Glad Tidings. He was the

"Lustrous Lamp". He had come to emancipate men from the worship of their fellow men by calling on them to submit to the One and Real Lord, the Almighty God. He had come to rescue humanity from the dungeon of petty desires by working out its evolution in the boundless spaces of the heavens and the earth; and to deliver it from the tyranny of decayed religions to the bounty of Islam, to check evil and promote good deeds and to prohibit what was dirty and unhealthy and sanction what was clean and wholesome.

He, therefore, did not address himself to any particular country or community, and he made the whole human race his concern. It was only right that he should begin his mission with Arabia as, being the darkest place on earth during the darkest age of human history, it was in dire need of the first rays of light. Besides this, the central place that Makkah occupied on the map of the then known world, together with its tradition of political freedom, made it an ideal base for a movement which stood for Liberty, Peace and Universal Brotherhood. The Arabs also possessed certain inborn virtues that made them fit for being instrumental in spreading the teachings of Islam throughout the world.

The Prophet ﷺ was not one of those reformers who content themselves with striving against a few moral abuses of their age and succeed in eradicating them for the time being, or depart from the world without having accomplished anything at all.[76]

Unravelling the Knot of Human Destiny

The Holy Prophet ﷺ applied the right solution to the problem of human nature. It was the problem which had defied solution at the hands of all reformers before him. He began by entreating men to believe in God and to bring down all false gods from the pedestal of Divinity. "O People," he declared, "Say, 'there is no god but One God' and you shall prosper."

Ignorance About Islam

This thunderous proclamation caused a stir among the ranks of paganism and, in an instant, paganism was up in arms against this simple human truth.

> *And the leaders among them (forthwith) said: 'Go forth and stick to your gods; for this is truly a thing designed (against you).*
>
> Holy Qur'ān, Ṣād 38:6

The ghastly deeds of crime and cruelty perpetrated on the Muslims by the enemies of Truth are preserved in the pages of history. They show that Islam had found its mark and had struck at the very root of unbelief. The citadel of Darkness had been stormed, and the beleaguered forces rushed forth to fight to the bitter end. But the Prophet ﷺ did not waver. In the hurricane of hatred and persecution he stood firm like a rock. He told his uncle who had brought him up since childhood: "O my uncle, if they placed the sun in my right hand and the moon in my left to force me to renounce my work, verily I will not desist until God makes manifest His work or I perish in the effort."[77]

For thirteen years he remained in Makkah, resolute and steadfast, insisting on belief in Divine Unity, his Messengership, Resurrection and the Last Judgement. His faith in his Mission was never shaken, not even for a moment. He did not compromise with untruth. He was convinced that the majestic message that had been vouchsafed to him alone held the answer to all the unsolved problems of humanity.

The First Muslims

The whole of Arabia became hostile to the Prophet ﷺ. It needed the heart of a lion to accept his mission. It meant treading the path of fire and walking into the jaws of death. Yet, some brave souls among the Quraysh responded to the Divine Call. Theirs was not a hurried decision – they knew what they were doing. There were no worldly considerations to prompt them. They deliberately shut the doors to worldly comforts and luxury. They had heard the call to faith, and the world had shrunk for them. Sleep had gone out of their eyes and their soft beds had turned into beds of thorns. Truth had dawned upon them, and now there could be no turning back. They knew in their hearts that there could be no peace for them until they had declared their faith

in God and His Messenger. So they all decided to go to the Prophet ﷺ and accept the faith he preached.

The Prophet ﷺ lived in their part of town, only a short distance away. But the hatred of the Quraysh made the way to him so long and so perilous that to traverse it was like undertaking a long and hazardous journey. It was safer by far to take a trade caravan to Syria or the Yemen, eluding the barbarous highwaymen, than to meet the Prophet ﷺ in Makkah itself. Yet, they did go to him, took at his hand the oath of allegiance to God and His Messenger and pledged their lives to stand by him. They took a tremendous risk. Severe hardships and unsparing trials would inevitably beleaguer their lives, but they were prepared for the worst. They listened to the Holy Qur'ān which said:

> *Do men think that they will be left alone on saying, 'We believe', and that they will not be tested? We did test those before them, and God will certainly know those who are true from those who are false.*
>
> al-ʿAnkabūt 29:2, 3

And they also heard the following Divine Commandment:

> *Or, do ye think that ye shall enter the Garden (of Bliss) without such (trials) as (came to) those who passed away before you? (While) they encountered suffering and adversity and were so shaken in spirit that even the Messenger and those who believed along with him cried out: 'When (will come) the help of God?' Ah! Verily, the help of God is (always) near (at hand)!*
>
> al-Baqarah 2:214

Finally, what they had dreaded happened and the Quraysh emptied the quiver of their wrath. Not one arrow was left unused. But the believers remained steadfast. They said, "*This is what Allah and His Messenger had promised; verily, the Word of Allah and his Messenger is true*" (al-Aḥzāb 33:22); and it reinforced them internally and strengthened them in their resolve. The more they were persecuted, the stronger did their determination grow. From this furnace of trial they emerged as pure as gold.

The Religious and Spiritual Education of the Companions

At the same time the Prophet ﷺ supplied the Companions with the spiritual guidance of the Qur'ān and looked after their religious education. He made them bow, five times a day, before the Creator and the Preserver of the Worlds with cleanliness of body, humility of heart and concentration of mind. Day by day, they increased in stature, morally and spiritually, and rid themselves of shallow, earthly aspirations. Their love for the Lord of the World increased daily. Still, the Companions were tough since war was their old pastime. Their history was full of bloody episodes like those of Basūs and Dāḥis and Ghabrā. The memory of the war of Fijār was still fresh in their minds. But the Prophet ﷺ kept their warlike temperament under control. Their native arrogance had yielded before the sublimity of their Faith. The Prophet ﷺ commanded them to "stay their hands and establish prayer"[78] and they obeyed him. They were like wax in his hands. Without a semblance of cowardice, they passively endured what no people in the world had ever endured. Not a single instance is recorded in the pages of history in which a Muslim raised his arm in the defence of his own person or resorted to retaliation or went back to his old ways of Ignorance.

In Madīnah

When the enmity of the Quraysh exceeded all limits, God allowed the Muslims to migrate to Madīnah where Islam had already found its way.

In Madīnah, the Makkan and the Madinite Muslims fraternized with each other. They had nothing in common except the new Faith. Blood was still dripping from the swords of the Aus and the Khazraj – they had not yet removed from their clothes the stains of blood received in the battle of Buʿāth. In these circumstances, Islam sowed the seeds of affection in their hearts for one another and brought about a brotherhood that would never have been possible among blood brothers. The ties established between the *Anṣār* and the *Muhājirs*[79] were stronger even than the ties of blood.

This new community, which consisted of the emigrants from Makkah and the Helpers from Madīnah, was the nucleus of a splendid Islamic Nation and the Commonwealth of Islam. It was born at a time when the world wavered precariously between life and death. Its birth tipped the scales in favour of life. To strengthen this community was indispensable for the survival of mankind; for this very reason, when God stressed the forging of brotherly bonds between the *Anṣār* and *Muhājirs*, He gave the warning: "*If you will not do so, there will be great corruption and mischief on the earth.*" (Holy Qur'ān, al-Anfāl 8:73).

The Highest Pinnacle of Development

The religious training of the Companions continued in Madīnah under the supervision of the Prophet ﷺ who explained the conception and purpose of religion and fostered among them the virtues of introspection and self-censorship, love of learning and anxiety for the After-life. The Companions were seized by an overwhelming urge for self-effacement in the path of God. So easy had it become for them to turn their backs on worldly attachments that in ten years they set forth more than a hundred times on *Jihād*,[80] twenty-seven times in the company of the Prophet ﷺ.

The verses of the Qur'ān, as revealed through the Prophet ﷺ, brought into force numerous commands with regard to their personal conduct, possessions and families; these were quite new and by no means easy to observe, but the Companions had become so accustomed to surrendering themselves unquestioningly to the Will of God that they experienced no difficulty in complying. Once the Gordian knot of disbelief had been cut, it was easy to unfasten the other knots that bound them. And once the Prophet ﷺ had opened their hearts to Islam, he did not have to struggle at each step to make them reject Wrong and accept Right. They entered into the new faith with heart and soul and submitted themselves without demur to what the Prophet

ﷺ decreed. They unhesitatingly confessed before the Prophet ﷺ such crimes as were not known to anyone except themselves. If they committed any crime, they voluntarily submitted themselves for punishment. Many of them actually had wine-cups in their hands when the Qur'ānic injunction against the use of intoxicants was revealed, but the Word of God came between them and their cups. They threw away the cups at once and broke their wine-barrels so that the drains of Madīnah literally overflowed with their contents.

Thus, when they had attained to the highest pinnacle of moral development and become proof against the inducements of Satan and of their own baser self, when they had learned to prefer the future good to the immediate good and had been transformed into lovers of the Hereafter even while living in this world, when neither poverty could be a barrier in their path nor could riches make them vain, when they had become meek, yet unbending before power, and when they had come to be the dispensers of justice among men even though it might go against themselves, their own kith and kin, God made the whole world subservient to them and appointed them the Defenders of the Faith. The Prophet ﷺ nominated them his successors and went to join the Most High, happy in the triumphant fulfilment of his Mission and in the belief that he had left his charge in hands that would not falter.

History's most Remarkable Revolution

The mighty revolution wrought by the Prophet ﷺ among the Arabs, which through them produced a new and lasting impression on all the nations of the globe, was unique in all respects. It was a most extraordinary event in human history, yet there was nothing about it that could not be explained rationally. Let us study the character, the scope and the influence of this great Revolution on the destiny of the human race.

The Fruits of Faith

During the pre-Islamic era people generally worshipped inanimate objects which could neither help nor grant their petitions and had, in

fact, been created merely to serve their needs. Hence, there was no real moral enthusiasm, no genuine spirituality in their religions. The God of their conception was an artisan who had retired into a corner after finishing His job. They believed that He had bequeathed His kingdom to those whom He had adorned with the mantle of Divinity and now it was they who controlled the affairs of the universe. They lacked any spiritual understanding of God. They did know of Him as the Creator of the universe, and any awareness was akin to the knowledge of a historian who, when he is asked who constructed a certain building, replies that it was built by such-and-such a king, but the mention of the king's name neither inspires awe in his heart, nor makes any solemn impression on his mind. They had no intimate consciousness of the Divine attributes and, consequently, their hearts did not bear the imprint of God's glory or love.

The Greeks had expounded what was largely a negative definition of God. Their definition did not entail the positive virtues connected with His name such as Benevolence, Compassion, Mercifulness and Omniscience. It did prove the First Cause, but divested it of knowledge and will, and set forth such hypothetical premises and theories as were derogatory to Divine dignity. But no system of culture or faith has ever thrived on negative foundations. The Greek philosophers had, accordingly, ended up destroying the spirit of religion and making it a rigmarole of empty ceremonies, sports and festivals.

The Muslims in general and the Arabs in particular rejected this vague and sickly religiousness and attained a Faith which was at once intense and profound and which permeated through every fibre of their existence. They pledged their Faith in God Who has Excellent Attributes, Who is the Most Exalted, the Most Magnificent and the Master of the Day of Judgement. Says the Holy Qur'ān:

> *God is He besides Whom there is no other god; The Sovereign, the Holy One, the Source of Peace (and Perfection), the Guardian of Faith, the Preserver of Safety, the Exalted in Might, the Irresistible, the Supreme; Glory to God (High is*

> *He) above the partners they attribute to Him. He is the Creator, the Evolver, the Bestower of Forms and Colours. To Him belong the Most Beautiful Names; Whatever is in the heavens and on earth, doth declare His Praises and Glory: and He is the Exalted in Might, the Wise.*
>
> al-Ḥashr 59:23, 24

He is the God Who is the Creator and the Preserver of the universe, Who rewards with paradise and chastises with hell, Who swells or shrinks the subsistence of whomsoever He likes, Who is the Knower of all that is hidden in the heavens and the earth, and Who knows the stealth of the eyes and the secrets of the hearts, and is the embodiment of beauty and sublimity, strength and splendour, perfection and beneficence.

This solemn conviction produced a miraculous transformation among the early followers of Islam. Whoever affirmed his faith in the One Transcendent God and testified to '*Lā ilāha illallāh*' experienced a sudden change in himself. The innermost recesses of his soul were lit up with the sublime radiance of God-consciousness, the spirit and the flesh in him ceased to be the enemies of one another; he achieved equilibrium within himself and extraordinary feats of courage, endurance and faith were performed by the believer.

Self-Criticism

This faith was a wonderful source of moral training. It generated among its followers an amazing strength of will, self-criticism and justice, as nothing can help overcome the inducements of the self so successfully as a living faith in the Omnipresence of God.

If anyone succumbed to evil or negative urges and fell into error, even unobserved, he would immediately confess to the Prophet ﷺ and undergo the severest punishment willingly to save himself from Divine Displeasure. A number of such incidents have been handed down to us by reliable historians, such as that of Māʿiz ibn Mālik Aslamī. One day he approached the Holy Prophet ﷺ and said, "O Prophet of God, I have been guilty of adultery, and I beg of you to cleanse me." The Prophet ﷺ sent him away, but he returned the next day and repeated the confession. The Prophet ﷺ again sent him away and inquired from his family whether the balance of his mind had been disturbed. The relatives of Māᶜiz stated that, as far as they knew, there was nothing abnormal in his behaviour. When Māᶜiz came to him for the third time, the Prophet ﷺ again inquired about his mental condition, and his relatives gave the same answer. They would not think of telling a lie to save the life of a relative. Māᶜiz, too, would not shrink back. He appeared before the Prophet ﷺ and confessed his guilt for the fourth time. Then, at last, the Prophet ﷺ ordered him to be stoned to death according to Islamic law.[81]

A similar case was that of a woman named Ghāmidiyyah. She, too, was guilty of adultery and wanted to be "cleansed" so that she might not have to rise with the stain of sin on the Day of Reckoning. When she appeared before the Prophet ﷺ again on the second day, having been sent away on the first, she earnestly said, "Why do you send me away like Māᶜiz? I am pregnant too, and this proves my guilt beyond a shadow of doubt." "Then go away now," the Prophet ﷺ replied. "Come after your child is born." She went away and waited. When the period of waiting was over and she delivered of the child, she again approached the Holy Prophet ﷺ, holding her baby in her arms. "Here is my child," she said. But once more she had to go away, for the Prophet ﷺ commanded her to go away and nurse the child until it was weaned. "Bring it to me," he said, "when it begins to feed other than from the breast." When the child was weaned, Ghāmidiyyah returned to the Prophet ﷺ with her child, the child holding a piece of bread in its tiny hand, proving that it no longer needed to be nursed from the breast. "Here I am, O Messenger of God," the woman declared. "Now I am free. My child is weaned." The Prophet ﷺ then placed the child in the care of a Muslim and ordered that the sentence of death by stoning be carried out. A pit was dug and Ghāmidiyyah was buried in it up to her waist. Then she was stoned. As Khālid ibn al-Walīd hurled a stone at her and blood gushed from her body, some drops of it fell upon his clothes. Recoiling, Khālid uttered uncomplimentary remarks about the woman, which the Holy Prophet ﷺ heard. "No, Khālid, no," the Prophet ﷺ admonished him, "By the One in Whose hand is my life, she has offered such penitence that if the octroi-official[82] did it, even he would be forgiven [by God]." After she was dead, funeral prayers were said over her bier by the command of the Prophet ﷺ and she was buried.[83]

Honesty and Trustworthiness

Virtues such as honesty and trustworthiness developed in the early Muslims as the natural fruits of a sense of living belief in the Omnipresence of the Absolute God. Even when alone and unnoticed, or in any other situation wherein they could easily transgress the bounds of religious conduct, fear of God kept the Muslims under rigid control.

It is related in *Tārikh Ṭabarī* that after the victory of Madā'in, when the Muslims were collecting the booty, one of them brought something he had come across and deposited it with the treasurer. It was so enormously valuable that those who saw it were astounded. They had never seen such a valuable treasure before. They began to question him. "Are you sure you have not held back a part of it?" "By God," he replied, "had I wished I could have misappropriated the whole lot without any of you being the wiser." This straightforward reply made a deep impression and they felt that they were in the presence of an extraordinary man. They begged him to disclose his name, but he declined. "I can't tell you my name," he said, "because you will then start praising me, while all praise is for Allah. I am well content with whatever He bestows as a reward." When he departed, they sent a man after him to find out who he was. Then it was discovered that he was ᶜĀmir ibn ᶜAbd Qays.[84]

The Eschewing of Man-Made Gods

The belief in one God, the Sovereign Lord of the universe, raised the heads of Muslims so high that now they could not be made to bow

before anyone but the Almighty. Mirroring in their hearts, as they did, the glory of the Most Glorious, the glitter of worldly grandeur made no impression.

Abū Mūsā says that when he reached the court of the Negus along with other Muslim emigrants, he found that ᶜAmr ibn al-ᶜĀṣ was sitting on the Emperor's right. ᶜUmārah on his left and the priests were forming a double row in the front. ᶜAmr and ᶜUmārah informed the Emperor that the Muslims would not kneel before him. But the priests insisted that they should do so, upon which Jaᶜfar, may Allah be pleased with him, unhesitatingly said, "We, Muslims, kneel before God alone and before no one else."[85]

Ribᶜī ibn ᶜĀmir was once sent by Saᶜd ibn Abī Waqqās, may Allah be pleased with him, as his envoy to Rustam, the Commander-in-Chief of Iran. Rustam received him in a grand hall which was filled with magnificent carpets. The Commander-in-Chief, wearing a crown and robes which sparkled with gems, sat on a throne. Ribᶜī, in contrast, was very poorly attired. He was dressed in rags and carried a shield too small for his size. His horse was also of a small breed, on which he rode straight towards Rustam, the pony trampling the costly carpets under its hoofs. Approaching the throne, he dismounted, tied the reins of the horse to a bolster and started to walk up to Rustam, still wearing his helmet and arms. The officers of the court remonstrated against him, saying that he should at least take off his helmet before going into the presence of the Commander-in-Chief. But Ribᶜī retorted, "I have come at your request and not of my own accord. I am willing to go back if you do not want me." At this point, Rustam intervened and told his officers to let him come as he wished. Ribᶜī then proceeded, leaning upon his lance, and piercing the carpets with it at each step. The people asked about the purpose of his visit. He said, "We have been sent by Allah to deliver whom He pleases from the overlordship of His slaves (i.e. men) to His own overlordship, and from the narrow confines of this world to the boundlessness of the next and from the oppressiveness of other religions to the fairness and justice of Islam."[86]

Rare Courage

Enthusiasm for the After-life endowed the Muslims with almost superhuman courage. Worldly aims and interests having ceased to have any significance in their eyes, they advanced towards the ultimate goal of paradise with great ardency.

It is reported that as Anas ibn an-Naḍr, may Allah be pleased with him, advanced on the enemy at a critical moment in the Battle of Uḥud, he met Saʿd ibn Muʿādh to whom he said, "By God, Saʿd, I can feel the sweet fragrance of Paradise coming from the direction of the Mount of Uhud." With these words he rushed into the heart of the battle. Saʿd said that when the dead body of Anas was recovered from the battlefield, there were more than eighty wounds on it. The infidels had literally cut him to pieces; as a result, only his sister could recognize his corpse.[87]

In the Battle of Badr the Prophet ﷺ was urging the Muslims on to greater effort. When he said, "March forward to Paradise, the extensiveness of which is as the extensiveness of the heavens and the earth," ʿUmair ibn Ḥamām cried out, "O Prophet of God, is it really that much extensive?" The Prophet ﷺ replied, "Yes. Do you doubt it?" "I doubt not," said ʿUmair, "I only wished that I attained it." "You will," the Prophet ﷺ replied. ʿUmair had taken out some dates and began to eat them. But the opening of the prospect of Paradise before his mind would not let him eat. Was it not foolish to waste one's time on such "trifles" when heaven was beckoning? He flung away the dates and rushed into the thick of the battle. His heart's desire was soon fulfilled.[88]

Abū Bakr ibn Abī Mūsā Ashʿarī narrated that on a certain field of battle his father was recounting how the Prophet ﷺ had said that the gates of Paradise were under the shadow of the sword when a man, his clothes in tatters, stepped forward and asked whether he himself had heard that from the Prophet ﷺ. Abū Bakr's father (Abū Mūsā Ashʿarī, may Allah be pleased with him) replied that it was so. On hearing this, the man went back and took leave of his friends. He unsheathed his sword, broke the sheath into pieces and took the field against the enemy. He was subsequently killed.[89]

ʿAmr ibn al-Jamūḥ, who was lame, had four sons. They used to accompany the Holy Prophet ﷺ whenever he set out on *Jihād*. When the Prophet ﷺ was leaving for Uḥud, ʿAmr wanted to join him, but his sons were opposed to it on account of his physical disability and old age. Finding them adamant, ʿAmr sought the help of the Prophet ﷺ. "My sons dissuade me from going with you," he said, "while it is my desire that I walk in Paradise with my impaired leg." The Prophet ﷺ explained that the *Jihād* was not binding on him. At the same time, he did not like ʿAmr's sons standing in their father's way in the holy cause upon which he had set his heart. So he said to them, "Why don't you let him go? God may grant him martyrdom." The sons agreed and ʿAmr went to join the holy war and was killed.[90]

Shaddād ibn al-Hād says that on a journey a Bedouin came to the Prophet ﷺ and attached himself to his party after embracing Islam. The Prophet ﷺ instructed a Companion to take good care of him. When the campaign of Khayber took place, the Prophet ﷺ gave a share of the booty to the man, but as he was not present – as he was shepperding the cattle of the Muslims – it was kept with a Companion who gave it to him on his return in the evening. The Bedouin took the booty to the Prophet ﷺ and inquired as to what it was. The Prophet ﷺ told him that it was his share of the spoils, upon which he said, "But I did not join you for it," and pointing towards his throat he added, "I joined to be pierced by an arrow here." The Prophet ﷺ replied, "God will fulfil your wish if you are true in your affair with Him." Then another battle took place in which he was killed. When his corpse was pointed out to the Prophet ﷺ, he remarked, "His affair with God was true; so God too made him true."[91]

Implicit Surrender

The unruly Arabs, who were so lawless in their ways, surrendered themselves so absolutely to the guidance of the Faith that it was impossible for them to infringe the Divine Law. They accepted the Sovereignty of God in its fullest sense. In peace and in war, in joy and in sorrow, in every relationship of life, at each turn of affairs and in the minutest details of their concerns they looked to His guidance and help and carried out His commands without the slightest demur.

They had known paganism, having been born and brought up in it. They could, therefore, fully appreciate the value of Islam and understand that Islam meant the replacement of one mode of life by another, leaving the anarchy of desire for the rule of God. Before Islam, they were at war with God; now they were His willing slaves. There could be no room for one's personal opinion after the Word of God had come. To disobey the Prophet ﷺ, to dispute with him, to take one's case to a court other than the one in which the law of God was dispensed, to give priority to one's family tradition over Faith – these things were out of the question. They rejected paganism *in toto* and entered wholeheartedly into a new and fuller existence.

Faḍālah ibn ʿUmair al-Laythī once planned to assassinate the Prophet ﷺ during the *Ṭawāf*[92] of the Kaʿbah. As Faḍālah drew near him, the Prophet ﷺ inquired, "Is it you, Faḍālah?" "Yes, it is I, O Prophet of God," he replied. "Tell me," the Prophet ﷺ asked, "with what intention have you come?" "There is nothing to tell," replied Faḍālah, "I was only remembering God." The Prophet ﷺ smiled and placed his hand over Faḍālah's heart. The peace of Faḍālah's heart was restored. He, afterwards, would say that as soon as the hand was lifted, the Prophet ﷺ appeared to be so handsome, as if God had not created anything in the world more beautiful than he. On his return, Faḍālah met his mistress who invited him to chat, but he declined. He said that there could be no scope for such a thing after one had submitted to Islam.[93]

True Knowledge

The prophets had imparted to man the true knowledge of God's existence and His attributes and actions. They had laid the foundations upon which man could erect the binding of his own spiritual conduct without getting involved in fruitless metaphysical discussions on "being" and "knowing". But man heeded not. Instead of being grateful for Divine guidance, he allowed his thoughts to drift aimlessly. He behaved like an explorer who, setting aside the geographical charts, tries to scale every height, fathom every depth and measure every distance on his own. The result of such endeavours can at best be a few sketchy notes and incomplete, random hints. So when the people tried to reach God with the help of reason alone and without the light of the Prophet's teachings, their knowledge of God consisted of little else besides random thoughts, conflicting theories and haphazard conclusions.

The Companions of Prophet Muḥammad ﷺ were twice blessed in this respect because, by giving themselves up to his guidance, they were spared the pointless quest of speculative theology regarding the existence and nature of God and were left free to devote their energies to productive learning. They served as the guardians of the Revealed Word. Consequently, they were able to retain the substance of faith while others only skirted its shadow.

A Single Humanity

The Islamic concept of God as the Creator, Nourisher and Sustainer of all peoples and nations and the universal scope of the ministry of Prophet Muḥammad ﷺ demolished all barriers of blood, colour and geography between man and man and welded mankind into one family. In Islam all men formed, as it were, a single humanity. They were members of the same family, being the children of the same father: Adam. An Arab had no superiority over a non-Arab and a non-Arab had no superiority over an Arab. The most honoured was the most righteous.

The Prophet ﷺ said emphatically, "O people, Verily, God has removed from you the blemish of ignorance and the pride of birth. There are but two classes of men: those who are righteous and God-fearing and honourable in the eyes of God; and those who are wicked and sinful and dishonourable in His eyes."[94]

Typical of his teachings was the advice he gave to Abū Dharr, may Allah be pleased with him: "Look here, you are neither greater than, nor superior to, anyone except, of course, in case you excel him in virtue."[95]

Typical also was the affirmation he used to repeat to his Creator daily during the late night prayers: "I testify that all men are brothers."[96]

Everything that tended to divide humanity into factions and groups was severely condemned by the Prophet ﷺ: "He who lives in factionalism is not one of us. He who dies in factionalism is not one of us. He who fights for factionalism is not one of us."[97]

Once, on the battlefield, a *Muhājir* slapped an *Anṣārī*, upon which the *Anṣārī* cried out, "O *Anṣār*". Following his example, the *Muhājir*, too, shouted, "O *Muhājir*". The Prophet ﷺ at once checked them. "Leave these parochial slogans," he said, "these are filthy."[98]

The Prophet ﷺ abolished the old tribal notion of kinship that demanded one remain loyal to one's brother whether he was the oppressor or the oppressed. In his view, "helping a kinsman in an unjust cause was like trying to hold back by the tail a camel determined upon jumping into the well."[99] He succeeded in establishing a classless society in which the high and the low, the rich and the poor, the white and the coloured were united in one single brotherhood. All sections of the people readily co-operated and stood like one man in the hour of need. Women were the trusts of God in the hands of men; wives had their rights over husbands, as husbands had their rights over wives.

Social Responsibility

The Muslims were charged with a strong sense of responsibility. Their minds had matured and they conducted themselves as responsible members of their families, their professions, their Faith and the entire society.

They were the helpers of truth; they acted by mutual consultation; they obeyed the head of the State, the Caliph, wholeheartedly and overtly as well as covertly, but only as long as he remained loyal to the Divine Commandments. "There is no loyalty unto the created which involves disloyalty unto the Creator,"[100] was an essential dictum of their polity. The revenues of the State, which until then filled the private purses of the rulers, were confided in God and spent as approved by Him. The position of the Caliph was like that of an orphan's guardian; he took from the public funds only what was necessary for his sustenance in case he did not have an income of his own, otherwise he accepted no payment or reward. Ownership of land, too, was vested in God and they believed that they would be called upon to answer before Him for every inch of it held by them.

A Civic Conscience

Centuries of ignorance and oppression had brought the common folk down to the level of animals, who mutely submitted to the many social wrongs to which they were subjected. In the righteous and democratic environment of Islam the civic sense of the people was aroused, and the Islamic society came to possess a social conscience. Social responsibility was hammered into human consciousness by Islam as a religious demand.

The Real Purpose of Love

The noble instinct of love, to whose credit lie many outstanding achievements in history, had, before Islam, been rendered dormant. Things had come to such a state that it was now understood only in the context of the transient manifestations of beauty. For many years, there had not appeared anyone who could, by the appeal of his personality and the exquisiteness of his character, claim the unqualified devotion of his fellow men and then divert it into the right channel. The world found such a man in Prophet Muḥammad ﷺ, in whom God had assembled all that was adorable in a human being.

Eyewitness accounts reveal that whoever came into the presence of the Holy Prophet ﷺ was instantaneously overawed, while those who came to know him were bewitched. His admirers reported that they had not seen the like of him anywhere in the world. Hearts were drawn to him as if they had been waiting all their lives to be drawn by the magnetism of his personality. History cannot provide a single instance of anyone meeting with such love, obedience and respect as he inspired in his people.

Exceptional Devotion

Cited below are some instances which illustrate the exceptional devotion of the Prophet's Companions.

One day Abū Bakr, may Allah be pleased with him, was assaulted by the enemies of the Faith at Makkah. ᶜUtbah ibn Rabīᶜah, in particular, beat him so severely that his face swelled until it became difficult to recognize him. He was carried home in an unconscious condition by Banū Taym. But so ardent was his love for the Prophet ﷺ that the first thing he did on regaining consciousness towards the evening was to inquire about the Prophet's welfare. "How is the Prophet of God?" he asked through his swollen lips. His attendants felt greatly piqued and they began to scold him for showing so much concern for one who, in their opinion, was the sole cause of his misfortune. But he persisted in his inquiry, and when his mother, Umm Khair, brought him nourishment, he refused to accept it until he had received news about the Prophet ﷺ. Umm Khair assured him that she knew nothing about his friend. He then asked her to go and inquire from Umm Jamīl, the daughter of Khaṭṭāb, but the latter was so terrified that she would not admit that she knew the Prophet ﷺ. "I do not know who is Muḥammad ibn ᶜAbdullāh or Abū Bakr," she declared, "but I am willing to accompany you to your son if you like." Umm Khair replied that she would like nothing better. When Umm Jamīl came to Abū Bakr's house and saw his condition, she began to curse his assailants. She said, "I swear by God that the community that has done this is a community of shameless heathens. God will surely punish it for its sins." But Abū Bakr had no patience for such things. "Tell me," he said, "how is the Prophet?" Umm Jamīl cautioned him that his mother was listening. When Abū Bakr assured her that it was not necessary to observe secrecy in the presence of his mother, she disclosed that the Prophet ﷺ was safe at the house of Ibn Arqam. Abū Bakr, thereupon, declared that he would neither eat nor drink until he had joined the Prophet ﷺ. They waited for the darkness of the night to deepen and, when it was safe enough Abū Bakr was taken to the Prophet ﷺ by his mother and Umm Jamīl. Alone, he then took his meal.[101]

During the Battle of Uḥud, as the news circulated that the Prophet ﷺ had been seriously wounded, a woman whose brother, father and husband had been killed in the battle that very day forgot her own sorrow and rushed to the battlefield shouting, "How is the Prophet?" People assured her that by the grace of God he was safe, but she refused to be comforted until she had actually seen him. She was taken to him. When she saw him, she said: "No calamity is a calamity if you are safe."[102]

Khubaib, may Allah be pleased with him, when about to be put to death by his persecutors, was asked, "Don't you wish now that Muḥammad were in your place?" He cried out, "I would not like to be released on the condition that he may be given even a pinprick."[103]

On the battlefield of Uḥud, the Prophet ﷺ dispatched Zayd ibn Thābit to convey his greetings to Saᶜd ibn Rabīᶜ and inquire how he was feeling. Zayd made a long search among the dead and the wounded and came upon Saᶜd just in time, for he was dying. He had received about seventy wounds. Zayd hastily delivered the Prophet's message. Saᶜd replied, "Pay my respects to the Prophet and tell him that I am smelling the sweet smells of Paradise, and to my community of Anṣār say that if anything happened to the Prophet while even one of them lived, they would not escape Divine wrath." Upon saying this he died.[104]

Again on the battlefield of Uḥud, there was an occasion when the Prophet's life was greatly endangered. Without a moment's hesitation, Abū Dujānah exposed his back to shield him; arrows pierced his body but he did not flinch.[105] The Prophet's wounds were sucked clean by Mālik al-Khūdrī. The Prophet ﷺ told him to spit out the blood, but he declined, saying, "By God, I am not going to spit it (on the ground)."[106]

Abū Sufyān, when he came to Madīnah, went to meet his daughter, Umm Ḥabībah, who was married to the Prophet ﷺ. He was about to sit on the Prophet's bed when she hastily rolled it up. Abū Sufyān was taken aback at this treatment and sarcastically remarked, "Daughter, I could understand whether I was not worthy of the bed or the bed was not worthy of me." "No," his daughter explained, "the thing is that it is the Prophet's bed and you are an unclean infidel."[107]

The love and reverence shown to the Prophet ﷺ by his followers is also apparent from the statement made by ʿUrwah ibn Masʿūd Thaqafī before his brethren Quraysh on his return from Ḥudaibiyyah. He said, "I have seen many monarchs. I have been in the courts of Caesar, Khusrau and Negus. I can swear that I have not seen any king held in greater respect by his subjects than Muḥammad is by his Companions. By God, when he gives an order, they all rush to carry it out; when he performs the *wuḍū'*,[108] they nearly come to blows in the scramble for the water he has used for it; when he speaks, a hush overtakes them. So excessively do they revere him that they dare not raise their eyes in his presence to obtain a full view of him."[109]

Unprecedented Obedience

Because of their unprecedented devotion to the Holy Prophet ﷺ, the Companions never spared themselves in his service. The declaration made by Saʿd ibn Muʿādh on behalf of the Ansār just before the Battle of Badr illustrates beautifully the boundless loyalty of these worthy Muslims.

"I declare unequivocally," it reads, "on behalf of the Anṣār, that you may stay wherever you wish, establish or break relations with whomsoever you like, and take away from our possessions whatever it pleases you to take away and leave whatever it pleases you to leave. What you will take away will make us happier than what you will not. We shall not deviate from the path of loyalty, come what may. We shall follow you even if you march up to Burk Ghamdān, and were you to plunge your horse into the sea, by God, we, too, shall jump into it."[110]

Such obedience did his word command among his people that when he proclaimed the social boycott of the three Muslims, who had held themselves back from the Battle of Tabūk without valid reason, the whole of Madīnah at once turned into a dead city for them. One of the defaulters, Kaʿb, gives the following account of the incident.

"The Prophet had prohibited social intercourse with us. People began to avoid our company; their entire attitude towards us was changed. The very earth seemed to have shrunk upon us. It was no longer the place we knew. When things became unbearable, I, one day, betook myself to Abū Qatādah's garden by jumping over its wall. Abū Qutādah was my cousin, my uncle's son, for whom I had the greatest affection. I greeted him, but he did not return my greeting. Then I asked him, 'Tell me, for the sake of God, don't you know that I love God and the Prophet?' He remained silent. I implored him in the name of God to answer my question, but again there was no reply. On being pressed by me for the third time for a reply, he said, 'God and the Prophet know better.' Tears welled up in my eyes at this answer and I jumped over the wall and came out of the garden."

Another incident in Kaᶜb's life is worth mentioning here. While the Holy Prophet ﷺ was enraged on some account, a messenger brought Kaᶜb the Prophet's order that he was to stay away from his wife. "Shall I divorce her?" asked Kaᶜb. "No," the messenger replied, "only keep away from her." Kaᶜb sent his wife away to her parents to wait there until the final settlement of the matter by the Almighty.

During his social boycott, Kaᶜb received a letter from the ruler of Ghassān, which read as follows: "We have come to know that your Master has withdrawn his favours from you. God surely did not send you into the world to suffer disgrace and be left to rot. Come to us. We shall treat you with great honour."

Kaᶜb did not hesitate. After he had read it, he said, "It is also a part of my trial," and threw it into the fire. That was the end of it.[111]

The spirit of loyalty infused by the Prophet in his followers enabled them to overcome the most deep-rooted evils in their midst. A word from him was sufficient to enforce total prohibition. It is related by Abū Burdah from his father who says, "We were having a drinking party. I rose up and left for the Prophet's place to pay my respects to him. On the way I learnt that the following verses had been revealed, announcing total abstinence:

> *O ye who believe, intoxicants and gambling, (dedication of) stones, and (divination by) arrows, are an abomination – of*

> *Satan's handiwork; avoid such (abomination), that ye may prosper. Satan's plan is (but) to excite enmity and hatred among you with intoxicants and gambling, and hinder you from the remembrance of God and from prayer. Will ye not then abstain?*
>
> Holy Qur'ān, al-Mā'idah 5:90-1

"I returned to my friends and recited the verses to them up to, 'Will ye not then abstain?' Some of them were holding glasses in their hands which had been partly emptied. They stopped at once. The wine that had passed through the lips (but had not yet been swallowed) was spat out."[112]

All the loyalties of family, friends and tribe faded before this loyalty. It is stated that the Prophet ﷺ once summoned ʿAbdullāh, son of ʿAbdullāh ibn Ubayy, and spoke to him thus: "Do you know what your father says?" ʿAbdullāh replied, "May my father and mother be a sacrifice unto you! O Prophet of God, what does he say?" "He says," said the Prophet ﷺ, "that if I returned to Madīnah, he who was honourable would turn out him who was debased." On hearing this, ʿAbdullāh exclaimed, "He is right. You are honourable and he is debased. You come to Madīnah by all means. It is well known there that no son is more obedient to his father than I, but if it be the wish of God and His Prophet that I sever my father's head, I am ready to do so." The Prophet ﷺ bade him not to do so.

On reaching Madīnah, ʿAbdullāh positioned himself at the city gate, sword in hand, to await his father's arrival. As soon as ʿAbdullāh saw his father, he roared: "Was it you who said that if the Prophet ﷺ returned to Madīnah, he who was honourable would turn out him who was debased? You will soon learn who is honourable and who is debased. By God, you cannot live in Madīnah now without the permission of God and His Prophet."

ʿAbdullāh ibn Ubayy was stunned when he heard these words from his son, and he began to wail. "Do you hear, O men of Khazraj, my son hinders me from returning to my home! Do you hear, O men of Khazraj, my son hinders me from returning to my home!" But his son did not relent. "As surely as I believe in God," he said, "you cannot enter Madīnah unless the Prophet allows you." People tried to intercede, but in vain. At last the Prophet ﷺ was informed. He sent word to ʿAbdullāh to let his father come in. Then ʿAbdullāh yielded, saying, "Now that the Prophet's permission has come, he can enter."[113]

New Men – A New *Ummah*

Thus it was that the most stupendous change in human history was brought about. The Prophet ﷺ had uncovered rich treasures of human material that had been lying dormant under the mass of Ignorance since the beginning of creation and imparted to them the light of genius which was to hold the world spellbound through ages to come. He had made into men what until then were mere herds of dumb-driven cattle. He had aroused their innate possibilities; he had released the fountains of their real life and elevated them to be the standard-bearers of light, learning, Faith and culture in the world. Within a short span of time the desert of Arabia threw up mighty personalities whose names illuminate the pages of history to this day.

ʿUmar, who used to graze his father's camels, suddenly rose to dazzle the world with the sublimity of his character and grandeur of his achievements. He humbled the empires of Caesar and Chosroes and perfected the foundations of a dominion which spread over both and was vastly superior to them in governance and organisation. Nothing need be said of his widely-known moral sense, justice and righteousness.

Another example is Khālid ibn al-Walīd. He was an enterprising young Qurayshite who, having earned some renown in local feuds, was held in high esteem by the tribal warlords but enjoyed no distinction in the peninsula, for he had no great achievements to his credit. But after embracing Islam he shone in the world as the Sword of Allah. This Sword fell upon Rome like lightning and his brilliant conquests are recorded in history.

Abū ʿUbaidah commanded small detachments of Muslims in the early wars. He then assumed supreme command of the Islamic forces and ejected Heraclius forever from the land of Syria. Heraclius cast a parting glance at it and said, "Adieu, Syria, we shall not meet again."

ʿAmr ibn al-ʿĀṣ was noted among the Quraysh for his sagacity – he travelled to Abyssinia to plead with the Negus to hand back the Muslim emigrants to their tormentors. He is known as the conqueror of Egypt.

Saʿd ibn Abī Waqqāṣ was unknown as a soldier before he became Muslim. He then captured the keys of Madā'in, annexed Iran and Iraq to the Islamic Dominion and is recorded in history as the conqueror of ʿAjam.[114]

Salmān the Persian, the son of a village priest, left his home and suffered many trials and tribulations until he reached Madīnah and embraced Islam. He then returned to the country of his birth as its Governor. But this high honour made no difference to the simplicity of his nature. He still lived in a modest cottage and was often seen carrying loads on his head.

Bilāl, the Abyssinian slave, acquired such eminence that even Caliph ʿUmar addressed him as his Master.

Zayd ibn Ḥārithah commanded the Muslim army in the Battle of Mūtah. The army included men of the merit and valour of Jaʿfar ibn Abī Ṭālib and Khālid ibn al-Walīd. His son led another army which had in it such outstanding men as Abū Bakr and ʿUmar.

Abū Dharr, Miqdād, Abū Dardā', ʿAmmār ibn Yāsir, Muʿādh ibn Jabal and Ubayy ibn Kaʿb, after embracing Islam, became renowned ascetics and excellent scholars.

ʿAlī ibn Abī Ṭālib, ʿĀ'ishah, ʿAbdullāh ibn Masʿūd, Zayd ibn Thābit and ʿAbdullāh ibn ʿAbbās ascended to the highest pinnacle in the world of learning through sitting at the feet of the Prophet ﷺ, a man who had not been tutored by any mortal. They became fountainheads of knowledge and wisdom. The world now listens to these "sons of the desert".

A Well-Blended Body of Men

Indeed never before had a more harmonious body of men appeared on the stage of history. They were equipped with every requisite for success in both worlds. These men produced the blueprint of a culture and a dominion which, within a remarkably short time, rose to be highly influential over three large continents. It was a mine of talent which sent forth an endless stream of men of quality and ability, including wise rulers, honest administrators, impartial judges, prayerful leaders, pious army commanders and God-fearing scientists.

Owing to the peculiar mental upbringing of the Muslims and the ceaseless propagation of Islamic ideals among them, the Islamic Commonwealth was steadily supplied with earnest and God-fearing servants. The responsibilities of the government were vested in those who preferred the dissemination of Truth to the collection of revenue, and who possessed a correct understanding of the organic relationship between religion and life, and knew how to co-ordinate the world of faith with the world of practical affairs in such a way as to make life full and righteous. Under the stewardship of these men the civilization of Islam unfolded in its full majesty and the blessings of the Faith sprang into life in a manner never witnessed before.

The Holy Prophet ﷺ applied the key of Messengership to the lock of human personality and it opened up, laying before the world all the rich treasures with which God had endowed man. He cut asunder the mainsprings of ignorance and brought its power to dust. He forced, with Divine power, the then benighted world to march on a new highway of life. He inaugurated a fresh era in the annals of mankind – the Islamic era which will shine for ever in human history.

III

THE ERA OF MUSLIM GLORY

Characteristics

Once the Muslims were inspired, they quickly burst the bounds of Arabia and threw themselves zealously into the task of the fuller mission of human destiny. Their leadership held a guarantee of light and happiness for the world; it gave the promise of turning humanity into a single, divinely-guided society. Some of the characteristics of Muslim leadership were as follows.

The Muslims had the unique advantage of being in possession of the Divine Book (Qur'ān) and the Sacred Law (*Sharīʿah*). They did not have to rely on their own judgement regarding the vital questions of life, and were thus saved from the manifold difficulties often inherent in such a course. The Divine Word had illumined for them all the avenues of life and had enabled them to progress towards a destination which they clearly envisaged. It was not merely a case of trial and error. Says the Holy Qur'ān:

> *Can he who was dead, to whom We gave life and a Light whereby he can walk amongst men, be like him who is in the depths of darkness from which he can never come out?*
>
> al-Anʿām 6:122

They were to judge men on the basis of the Revealed Word; they were not to diverge from the dictates of justice and equity; their view was not to be blurred by enmity, hatred or the desire for revenge.

O ye who believe, stand out firmly for God as witnesses to fair dealing, and let not the hatred of others to you make you swerve to wrong and depart from justice. Be just; that is nearer to piety; and fear God, for God is well-acquainted with all that ye do.

al-Mā'idah 5:8

They did not suddenly leap to power from the abysmal depths of degradation through just their own efforts. The Qur'ān had already moulded them into shape. They had been brought to a high level of nobility and purity by the Prophet ﷺ through long years of unremitting care. The Prophet ﷺ had conditioned them to a life of austerity and righteousness; he had instilled into their hearts the virtues of humility and courageous self-denial; he had purged them clean of greed and of striving after power, renown or wealth. It was laid down by him as a fundamental principle of Islamic polity that: "We shall not assign an office under the government to anyone who makes a request for it, or shows his longing for it in any other way."[115]

The Muslims were as far removed from falsehood, arrogance and mischief as white is from black. The following words of the Holy Qur'ān had not been ground into them night and day in vain:

That Home of the Hereafter We shall give to those who intend not high-handedness or mischief on earth; and the End is (best) for the righteous.

al-Qaṣaṣ 28:83

Instead of aspiring to positions of authority and trust, they accepted them with great reluctance and when they did accept an official position they accepted it as a trust from God, to whom they would have to render a full account of their sins of omission and commission on the Day of Judgement. Says the Holy Qur'ān:

> *God doth command you to render back your trusts to those to whom they are due; and when ye judge between man and man, that ye judge with justice.*
>
> al-Nisā' 4:58

> *It is He Who hath made you (His) vicegerents on the earth. He hath raised you in ranks, some above others; that He might try you in the gifts ye receive; for thy Lord is quick in punishment; yet He is indeed Oft-Forgiving, Most Merciful.*
>
> al-Anʿām 6:165

Further, the Muslims were not agents of any particular race or country, nor did they want to establish Arab Imperialism. Their mission was a universal mission of faith and freedom. They were happily free from all the sickly obsessions of colour and territorial nationality. All men were equal. The Holy Qur'ān pointedly said:

> *O mankind, We created you from (a single pair of) a male and a female; and made you into nations and tribes, that ye may know each other (not that ye may despise each other). Verily the most honoured of you in the sight of God is (he who is) the most righteous of you. And God has full knowledge and is Well-Acquainted (with all things).*
>
> al-Ḥujurāt 49:13

Once the son of ʿAmr ibn al-'Āṣ, the Governor of Egypt, struck an Egyptian commoner with a whip. The matter was brought to the notice of Caliph ʿUmar. The Caliph did not show the least regard for the high status of the offender's father, and ordered the Egyptian straightaway to avenge himself for the harm done to him. To the offender's father he administered this telling rebuke, "Why have you made them slaves while they were born free?"[116]

The Arabs were not mean-spirited in making the benefits of faith, culture and learning available to non-Arabs. They did not care for the nationality or family connections of the recipients when it came to the conferment of high honours and positions in the State. They were, so to speak, a cloud of bliss that rained ungrudgingly over the entire world, and from which all peoples, everywhere, freely profited according to their own capacity.[117]

The Arabs allowed a free and equal partnership to all nations in the establishment of a new, socio-political structure and in the advancement of mankind towards a fuller and richer moral ideal. There were no national divisions, no apartheid, no vested interests, no priesthood and no hereditary nobility in the Islamic Commonwealth. No special benefits were reserved for anyone. There was nothing to prevent the non-Arabs from surpassing the Arabs in the various fields of life. Even as doctors of *Ḥadīth*[118] and *Fiqh*[119] a number of non-Arabs attained to distinction for which the Muslims in general and the Arabs in particular feel proud. Ibn Khaldūn writes: "It is an amazing fact of history that though their religion is of Arabian origin and the Law that the Prophet had brought had an Arab complexion, with a few exceptions, all eminent men of learning in the Muslim *Millat*, in the field of theological as well as secular sciences, are non-Arabs. Even those who are Arabs by birth are non-Arabs by education, language and scholarship."[120] During the later centuries, too, non-Arab Muslims continued to produce leaders, statesmen, saints and scholars of exceptional merit. This would obviously not have been possible had the Arabs been mean or prejudiced in sharing their opportunities with the people of other nationalities in the Islamic world.

Humanity has many sides: physical, emotional, social, moral, mental and spiritual. We cannot neglect one for the benefit of another. Humanity cannot progress to its highest level unless every human instinct is brought into play. It would be futile to hope for the establishment of a healthy human society until an intellectual, material, moral and spiritual environment is created in which a man is able to develop his latent potential in harmony with God's plan of creation.

We learn from experience that this goal must remain a dream so long as the reins of civilization are not held by those who attach due importance to both the material and the spiritual yearnings of life, and can, besides having a high moral and spiritual sense, fully appreciate the claims of flesh and blood upon man and the inter-relationship between the individual and society.

Any defect in the integration of the material and spiritual elements in the inner nature of a people should be displayed inevitably in its entire social outlook and organization. Thus, if a community which believes only in one side of life – material progress – and is unaware of its spiritual side and the transcendental realities such as resurrection and futurity, acquires ascendancy over the world, civilization will manifest itself in material objects such as brick, stone, paper, cloth, steel and lead; it will revolve around law-courts, battlefields, factories, ball-rooms, hotels, clubs and theatres and flourish and grow rich there. But on the domestic side, and in the domain of morality and the other spheres of human life, there will be no difference between man and beast. In short, civilization will be like the corpulent body which may give the impression of well-being at first sight, but, in reality, is the victim of innumerable ailments.

Similarly, if a community which repudiates temporal interests and stands for the negation of the self, cherishing only the things of the spirit, comes into power, the natural potential of man will be stunted and civilization will wither away. Under its influence, people will renounce the world and become hermits. They will prefer celibacy to matrimonial life, and the life of caves and forests to that of towns and cities. Self-torture will become the highest form of religious exercise, so that the hold of the body over the soul might weaken, and the spirit of man might be "purified". Death will gain superiority over life as through it mankind would be saved from the tumult of the "world of matter" and gain access to the tranquillity of the "world of spirit" and complete their spiritual progress.

This philosophy of life being opposed to the natural scheme of things, whenever such a society comes into being, the spirit of man does not fail to react violently against it soon after the first flush of enthusiasm is over, and to avenge itself by rushing madly towards the other extreme of vulgar material enjoyment and debauchery.

Very few communities that had the privilege to act as the torch-bearers of civilization during the various epochs of history could succeed in establishing a harmonious equilibrium between the temporal and the spiritual, between the body and the spirit, between the mind and the senses. Generally speaking, they were either crudely materialistic or plainly hermit in their mental and spiritual attitudes, and this kept mankind deviating most of the time between the two opposite ends of materialism and monasticism.

Uniqueness of the Companions

The Companions of the Holy Prophet ﷺ were unique in the sense that religion, morality, social dynamism, politics, (i.e. all the diverse requirements of a civilized society) were mirrored in the most beautiful colours in their lives. There was no schism, no corroding lack of integration in their souls. Because of this, they were ideally suited to operate as stewards of humanity. We, consequently, find that no period in the recorded history of the human race has been more auspicious in its true sense than what is known among the Muslims as *Khilāfah Rāshidah* (i.e. the reign of the first four Caliphs). During this epoch, all the material, moral and spiritual resources of man were brought into use to make him an ideal citizen of an ideal State. The Government was judged by the yardstick of morality, and morals were judged by their utility to lift humanity in permanent values and establish justice in human society. Though the Islamic Commonwealth was the richest and the most powerful State of its time, the popular heroes and ideal personalities in it were drawn from among those who possessed not earthly glory, but purity and nobility. There was no disparity between power and morality. Material advancement was not allowed to overrun moral progress – that is why in the Islamic world the incidence of crime was very low in spite of the abundance of wealth and the great heterogeneity of its population. In short, this epoch was the most beautiful springtime mankind has experienced to this day.

All this was due to the moral strength of faith, excellence and the training of those who were at the helm of affairs in the Muslim State. In whatever capacity they served the State, they conducted themselves as the most perfect models of Islamic morality. Whether as administrators or petty officials, or as soldiers or policemen, they performed their duties with exemplary modesty, justice and piety.

The sterling character and qualities of the Muslim soldiers were once praised by a Roman officer in these words: "At night you will find them prayerful; during the day you will find them fasting. They keep their promises, order good deeds, suppress evil and maintain complete equality among themselves."[121]

Another testified thus: "They are horsemen by day and ascetics by night. They pay for what they eat in territories under their occupation. They are first to salute when they arrive at a place and are valiant fighters who just wipe out the enemy."[122]

A third said: "During the night it seems that they do not belong to this world and have no other business than to pray, and during the day, when one sees them mounted on their horses, one feels that they have been doing nothing else all their lives. They are great archers and great lancers, yet they are devoutly religious and remember God so much and so often that one can hardly hear talk about anything else in their company."[123]

It was because of this moral training that when the fabulous Crown and the "Carpet of Spring" of the Chosroes of Iran fell into the hands of Muslim soldiers after the victory of Madā'in, they promptly delivered them to their Commander, who dispatched them to the Caliph at Madīnah. When the latter saw those articles, he was filled with admiration for the great integrity of the soldiers who had handed them over to their leader intact and for those who had brought them safely all the way to Madīnah.[124]

The Islamic View of Life

Islam alone, of all religions, embraces life in all its aspects. It does not stand as a barrier between man and his legitimate desire for a full life. It does not regard man's earthly existence as a collection of gloomy sorrows or a punishment for some original or inherited sin. At the same time, it does not look upon this life as a fleeting opportunity for material satisfaction or a place for sensuous delight. Islam proclaims life to be a Divine gift so that man may attain nearness to God and attain perfection by making full use of the possibilities of his body and spirit. It is an opportunity for action to make the best of oneself; there is not going to be another opportunity after it. Says the Holy Qur'ān:

> *He Who created Death and Life, that He may try which of you is best in deed.*
>
> al-Mulk 67:2

> *That which is on earth We have made but as a glittering show for it in order that We may test them – as to which of them are best in conduct.*
>
> al-Kahf 18:7

The Companions of the Prophet ﷺ considered this universe as the domain of God in which He had raised them in the first instance as human beings and then as Muslims to serve as His Vicegerents and the guardians of those who dwelt in it. The Holy Qur'ān says:

> *I will create a Vicegerent on earth.*
>
> al-Baqarah 2:30

> *It is He Who hath created for you all things that are on the earth.*
>
> al-Baqarah 2:29

> *We have honoured the sons of Adam; provided them with transport on land and sea; given them for sustenance things good and pure; and conferred on them special favours, above a great part of Our Creation.*
>
> al-Isrā' 17:70

God has promised to those among you who believe and
work righteous deeds, that He will, of a surety,
grant them in the land, inheritance (of power),
as He granted it to those before them; that He
will establish in authority their religion – the one
which He has chosen for them; and that He will change
(their state), after the fear in which they (lived),
to one of security and peace; they will worship Me
(alone) and associate none with Me.

al-Nūr 24:55

God had granted mankind the right to enjoy the resources of the earth without being foolish, vain or wasteful:

Eat and drink – but waste not by excess, for God
loveth not the wasters.

al-Aʿrāf 7:31

Say: who hath forbidden the beautiful gifts of God,
which He hath produced for His servants, and the things,
clean and pure, which He hath provided for sustenance?
Say: they are, in the life of this world, for those who
believe, (and) purely for them on the Day of Judgement.

al-Aʿrāf 7:32

The Muslims have been appointed the shepherds of mankind. It is their religious duty to keep humanity on the straight path, to remove imperfections from human society, to defend the weak and to establish justice and peace on the earth. Says the Holy Qur'ān:

Ye are the best people raised up for mankind,
enjoining what is right, forbidding what is wrong,
and believing in God.

Āl ʿImrān 3:110

> *O ye who believe, stand out firmly for justice and*
> *be the witnesses of God to fair dealing.*
>
> al-Nisā' 4:135

Muhammad Asad admirably summed up the Islamic concept of life as a well-balanced harmonious totality, which cannot be divided nor separated into the physical and spiritual: "...If Islam does not share the gloomy aspect of life as expressed by Christianity, it teaches us, nonetheless, not to attribute an exaggerated value to the earthly life as the modern Western civilization does. The Christian outlook is: The earthly life is a bad business. The modern West – as distinct from Christianity – adores life in exactly the same way as the glutton adores his food; he devours it, but has no respect for it. Islam, on the other hand, looks upon the earthly life with calmness and respect. It does not worship life, but regards it as a passing stage on our way to a higher existence. But just because it is a stage, and a necessary stage, too, man has no right to despise or even to underrate the value of his earthly life. Our travel through this world is a necessary, positive part in God's Plan. Human life, therefore, is of tremendous value; but we must never forget that it is a purely instrumental value. In Islam, there is no room for the materialistic optimism of the modern West which says: "My kingdom is of this world alone" – nor for the life-contempt of the Christian: "My kingdom is not of this world." Islam goes the middle way. The Holy Qur'ān teaches us to pray:

> *Our Lord, give us the good in this world and the good*
> *in the Hereafter.*
>
> al-Baqarah 2:201

"Thus, the full appreciation of this world and its goods is in no way a handicap for our spiritual endeavours. Material prosperity is desirable, though it is not a goal in itself. The goal of all our practical activities always ought to be the creation and maintenance of such personal and social conditions as might be helpful for the development of moral stamina in men. In accordance with this principle, Islam leads man towards a consciousness of moral responsibility in everything he does, whether great or small. The well-known injunction of the gospel: 'Give Caesar that which belongs to Caesar, and give God that which belongs to God' – has no room in the theological structure of Islam, because Islam does not allow of a differentiation between the moral and the practical requirements of our existence. In everything there can be only one choice: the choice between Right and Wrong – and nothing in-between. Hence, the intense insistence on action as an indispensable element of morality. Every individual Muslim has to regard himself as personally responsible for all happenings around him, and to strive for the establishment of Right and the abolition of Wrong at every time and in every direction.

"The sanction for this attitude is to be found in the verse of the Holy Qur'ān:

> *Ye are the best people raised up for mankind, enjoining what is right, forbidding what is wrong, and believing in God.*
>
> Āl ʿImrān 3:110

"This is the moral justification of the aggressive activism of Islam, the justification of the early Islamic conquests and its so-called 'Imperialism'. For Islam is 'Imperialist', if we must use this term; but this kind of Imperialism is not prompted by love of domination; it has nothing [to do] with economic or national selfishness, nothing [to do] with the greed to increase our own comforts at other people's cost, nor has it ever meant the coercion of non-believers into the belief of Islam. It has only meant, as it means today, the construction of a worldly frame for the best possible spiritual development of man. Moral knowledge, according to the teachings of Islam, automatically forces a moral responsibility upon man. A mere Platonic discernment between Right and Wrong, without the urge to promote the Right and to destroy the Wrong, is a gross immorality in itself. In Islam, morality lives and dies with the human endeavour to establish its victory upon earth."[125]

The Effects of the Rise of Muslim Power

The rise of Muslim power and the coming of age of the Islamic civilization during the first century of the *Hijrah* were events of unequalled significance in man's moral and social development. These events confronted the "World of Ignorance" with a crisis of unprecedented magnitude. So far Islam was no more than a religious movement, but henceforth it emerged as a complete civilization – refined, progressive and full of energy and life.

Henceforth, there were two opposite systems in the world: one a comprehensive, easy-to-understand, practical, revealed Faith; the other a rigmarole of rigid formalism, conjecture, superstition and myth.

The superior society of Islamic ideology was envisaged and brought to life on solid spiritual foundations. Its real emphasis was not on material prosperity but on the development of moral stamina in men and on the metaphysical orientation of life. The soul of man was, as such, free from contradictions within its framework. It was content. There was no greed, no insatiable longing for worldly power or riches. The government stood firmly for equity and equality and held itself as much responsible for the moral and spiritual prosperity of its people as for the protection of their lives and property. Its governors and administrators were also the finest citizens of the Islamic State; the most exalted ascetics were often found among those who had the greatest opportunities of indulging in comfort and luxury of all kinds.

In contrast with the social soundness and spiritual vigour of the Islamic World was the avarice, confusion, and vulgarity of the "World of Ignorance", where everyone in authority seemed desperately resolved upon taking full advantage of their position of power.

Islam and Humanity

This being the case, people felt no hesitation in leaving the realm of Ignorance for the Light of Islam. They stood to lose nothing, and there was everything to be gained. Islam offered to them the balm of belief, the sweetness of faith, the membership of a democratic, cosmopolitan society – a society without any kind of distinction – and the protection of a powerful State. The expansion of the frontiers of Islam was, quite naturally, very rapid.

The effects of the growth of Islamic power were extremely far-reaching. The path of Godliness became easy to take. Until recently to obey the commands of God was a most perilous thing; now the reverse was true. It was no longer necessary to preach the message of faith in secret. Says the Holy Qur'ān:

> *Call to mind when ye were a small (band) despised through the land, and afraid that men might despoil and kidnap you; but He provided a safe asylum for you, strengthened you with His aid, and gave you good things for sustenance that ye might be grateful.*
>
> al-Anfāl 8:26

The Revival of Humanity

Those who had entered the fold of Islam could now exert themselves more effectively for the moral and spiritual revival of humanity. They could establish right and prohibit wrong with much greater success. The rejuvenating currents of Islam ran through the world, infusing men everywhere with a new life and an unparalleled enthusiasm for progress. The lost values of life had been rediscovered. Paganism became a sign of reaction, while it was considered progressive to be associated with Islam. Even nations that did not come directly under the influence of Islam benefited profoundly, though unconsciously, from the freshness and vitality of the new creative impulses released by its impact on large parts of the world. Numerous aspects of their thought and culture bear evidence to the magic touch of Islam. All the reform movements that arose in their midst owed their origin to Islamic influences.

A universal gift of Islam to humanity was the re-establishment of man's belief in the Unity of God. So uncompromisingly and so energetically did the Muslims espouse the doctrine of Monotheism that even the Trinitarians and the worshippers of idols had to offer apologies and excuses for their ideas on religion and for their modes of worship.

Islam and Christianity

Formerly, Christians used to be shocked at mention of the idea of Divine Unity and exclaim:

> *Has he made the gods all into one God? Truly this is a wonderful thing!*
>
> Holy Qur'ān, Ṣād 38:5

Now they took pains to explain that their beliefs and practices did not contravene the belief in the Oneness of God. There appeared a number of sects among the Christians who denied the Divinity of Jesus and explained the doctrine of Trinity in a way that brought them within the orbit of Monotheistic teachings. The belief that clergymen acted as intermediaries between man and God was also severely criticized by Christian reformers and ultimately given up. A movement was started in Europe in the eighth century against the practice of making confessions before priests. It was asserted that man should address himself directly to his Maker, without the aid of an intercessor. In addition, a feeling of revulsion was created throughout Christendom, with the support of powerful Roman Emperors such as Leo III, Constantine V and Leo IV, against paintings and statues in churches. Emperor Leo III issued a decree in 726 CE prohibiting the adoration of images. In 730 CE he proclaimed the arts of painting pan sculpture to be the remnants of Paganism. This new development in the very heart of the Graeco-Roman cultural zone was indisputably an echo of the message of Islam that had reached Europe through Spain. Claudius, one of the pioneers of the movement, had been born and brought up in Muslim Spain.[126] It was his custom to set fire to any image or painting that was found in his diocese. The Reformation itself, in spite of all its shortcomings, was inspired by Islam.

Islam and Europe

It was not, however, in the field of religion alone that Islam imparted a new glow of life to Europe. There is not a single area of European revival that is not indebted to Islamic thought. As Robert Briffault said:

> For although there is not a single aspect of European growth in which the decisive influence of Islamic civilization is not traceable, nowhere is it so clear and momentous as in the genesis of that power which constitutes the permanent distinctive force of the modern world and the supreme source of its victory – natural science and scientific spirit.[127]

> Science is the most momentous contribution of Arab Civilization to the modern world...It was not science only which brought Europe back to life. Other and manifold influences from the civilization of Islam communicated its first glow to European life.[128]

Islam and India

The contribution of Islamic civilization to the culture of the different people of India has also been of great importance. Many progressive features in the socio-cultural structure of the different Indian communities, such as respect for women and their rights, can be traced to the influence of Islam through various channels. It can be safely claimed that after the dawn of Islam no cultural or religious system in the world can honestly deny its indebtedness to Islam and Muslims.

Islam's Influence in Times of Decadence

Several characteristics of the Muslim faith and civilization continued to operate even after the huge Islamic social structure had begun to disintegrate, one of these being belief in God. Islam had planted the idea of God so firmly in the minds of its followers that the passage of time could do no harm to it. The followers of Islam could indulge in immorality – as they wholeheartedly did during the period of their decline – but it was just not possible for them to shake off their belief in God. The moral sense of right and wrong, faith in the Omnipresence of the Almighty, and the solicitude for the After-life would pinch their hearts in the midst of their follies and, sometimes, it would instantly transform their lives. Not infrequently did it happen that people abandoned their wicked ways and took to a life of piety in response to a sudden call of the conscience. A simple heavenly warning would in a moment stir princes to renounce their kingdoms and turn into ascetics, while we see daily that warnings a thousand times more severe fail to make any impression on spiritually frozen hearts. Often, on hearing a Qur'ānic verse like the following, the people suddenly felt that they had woken up to a new life:

> *Has not the time arrived for the Believers that their*
> *hearts in all humility should engage in the remembrance*
> *of God and of the Truth which has been revealed (to them),*
> *and that they should not become like those to whom was given*
> *Revelation aforetime, but long ages passed over them and their*
> *hearts grew hard, for many among them are rebellious*
> *transgressors?*
>
> al-Ḥadīd 57:16

Such incidents were common in the seminaries of religious leaders in Baghdad, even when that city had slipped into moral stupor. It has been reported by Ibn Jubair al-Andalusi that people used to weep during the sermons of Shaikh Raḍiyyuddīn Qazwīnī and they swarmed around him to ask about God's forgiveness of their sins.

During the sermons of Ḥāfiẓ Ibn al-Jawzī, "people cried and fainted and had to be carried away. They would give their forelocks in his hands (a sign of submission) and he would caress their heads".[129] According to his own estimate, around a hundred thousand people repented at his hand.[130] At the sermon assemblies of Shaikh Ismāʿīl Lahorī, an Indian Traditionist of the 5th century AH, it is stated that thousands embraced Islam.[131] Ibn Baṭūṭah has enumerated numerous incidents of a like nature in connection with the achievements of Muslim missionaries in India.

To conclude, the language of Islam had gained free currency in the language of the world. Modes of expression peculiar to Islam were widely used by non-Muslims. Many non-Muslim scholars learnt the Qur'ān by heart. Abū Isḥāq the Sabian, one of the most celebrated non-Muslim calligraphists and literateurs of his age, is reputed to have observed the Ramaḍān fasts.

People travelled from one end of the Islamic world to the other, across forests, mountains and rivers, in search of spiritual guides. The saints and those of the spiritual path were the refuge of the world. Their dwelling places were overcrowded with devotees and sparkled with life more than the palaces of the high dignitaries of the State. The sermon assemblies of Shaikh ʿAbdul Qādir Jīlānī inspired greater awe than the courts of the ʿAbbāsid Caliphs.

IV

MUSLIM DECADENCE

The Beginnings

A certain writer has remarked that there are two happenings in human life, the exact time of which one can never tell. One is related to the individual, the other to collective existence; one is the coming of sleep, the other is the decline or fall of a nation. No one can tell exactly when a person passes from wakefulness to sleep, nor at what point a nation begins to decline. With the Islamic Empire, however, it was different. If we have to draw a line between its ascent and decline, we can do it easily: the time between the *Khilāfah Rāshidah* and the emergence of Arab Imperialism.

The Caliphate was primarily a religious institution, and its political character was subsidiary. The Caliphate retained its spiritual orientation during the regime of the first four Caliphs because the men who then guided its destiny were what may be described as the living miracles of the Prophet Muḥammad ﷺ. They were the true specimens of the comprehensiveness of faith. They were ascetics, imāms, preachers, judges, law-givers, chancellors of the exchequer, generals, administrators and statesmen. On this account all power in the Empire – spiritual and temporal – was vested in one man, the Caliph, who surrounded himself with a body of advisers, moulded and modelled by the same Master-craftsman who had trained the Caliph. The Caliph acted in consultation with his advisers, and the spirit of these ideal pupils of the Prophet ﷺ pervaded the entire life of the *millah*, leaving no room for a clash between the spiritual and the temporal spheres of its activity.

Jihād and *Ijtihād*

There being no separate realms of "God" and "Caesar" in Islam, the Muslim Caliphate or *Imamah* calls for a large variety of human qualities. A caliph or imām should, in addition to possessing a high degree of personal virtue, be keenly alive to the needs of *Jihād* and *Ijtihād*. *Jihād*, in Islamic terminology, means to strive to one's utmost for what is the most noble object on earth. There can be nothing more noble for a Muslim than the earning of God's Pleasure through complete submission to His Will. For this a long and sustained inner struggle is required against the false deities that may lay claim to his spiritual allegiance, as well as against all those whims and desires that may try to lure him away from the fold of goodness and piety. When this has been attained, it becomes his moral responsibility to exert himself for the improvement of his fellow beings and the establishment of Divine sovereignty over the world around him. It is a privilege as well as a necessity, for it often becomes impossible to remain true to God even in one's individual capacity in an ungodly environment. This latter circumstance has been described in the Qur'ān as *Fitnah*, meaning calamity, sedition, treachery, sin, temptation and seduction.

It is true that everything that exists in the world – animals, plants or minerals – bows to the sovereignty of God and is subservient to His Will. Says the Holy Qur'ān:

> *While all creatures in the heavens and on earth have,*
> *willingly or unwillingly, bowed to His Will, (accepted Islam),*
> *and to Him shall they return.*
>
> Āl ʿImrān 3:83

> *Seest thou not that to God bow and worship all things*
> *that are in the heavens and on earth – the sun, the*
> *moon, the stars, the hills, the trees, the animals; and*
> *a great number among mankind? But a great number are (also)*
> *such as are fit for Punishment.*
>
> al-Ḥajj 22:18

But this has nothing to do with human endeavour. All created things are subject to the unfailing laws of nature. They, in due course, pass through the different phases of birth, growth and decay that have been ordained for them. The Law for the enforcement of which the Muslims are required to strive is the one which was brought into the world by the Prophets. Opposition to this Law will not cease as long as the world endures. There will always be some force or other to resist and to reject it. *Jihād* is, therefore, an eternal phase of human life. It may take various forms, one of which is war, which may sometimes be the highest form to take, the object of which is to crush the forces of evil which pull in the direction of unbelief and involve people in the highly hazardous spiritual tussle of having to choose between Truth and Untruth. Says the Holy Qur'ān:

> *And fight them on until there is no more tumult or oppression, and there prevail justice and faith in God.*
>
> al-Baqarah 2:193

It is essential for those who take part in *Jihād* to be well-versed not only in the teachings and practices of Islam, but also in the philosophy and ways of unbelief, so that they may be able to recognize unbelief in whatever disguise it may manifest itself. It was said by ʿUmar, may Allah be pleased with him, "I am afraid, he who has been brought up in Islam and has no knowledge of *jāhiliyyah* [un-Islamic culture and philosophy], may become an instrument disintegrating Islam unknowingly."[132] It is, however, not possible for every Muslim to acquire an intimate understanding of the ways of *jāhiliyyah* (un-Islamic culture and philosophy); however, he who directs and controls the affairs of the Islamic State should be better informed in this respect. The Muslim leaders also should build up their strength to the best of their capacity and to hold themselves constantly in readiness to meet the challenge of their enemies and of the enemies of faith. It is a command of God, as the Holy Qur'ān says:

> *Against them make ready your strength to the utmost of your power, including steeds of war, to strike terror into (the hearts of) the enemies of God and your enemies and others besides them, whom ye may not know, but whom God doth know. Whatever ye shall spend in the cause of God shall be repaid unto you, and ye shall not be treated unjustly.*
>
> al-Anfāl 8:60

Ijtihād means the ability to cope with the ever-changing pattern of life's requirements. It calls for a deep insight into the soul of Islam, and a thorough knowledge of the basic principles of Islamic jurisprudence. It also includes the ability to use the treasures of nature in the service of Islam instead of letting them fall into the hands of the unbelieving materialists who use them for spreading arrogance and mischief in the world.

The Umayyads and the ʿAbbāsids

Unfortunately, those who succeeded to the Caliphate after the first four Caliphs were greatly lacking in these qualities. They did not have the moral or spiritual calibre one would expect of Muslim leadership. They were not able to wear down the pagan attitudes and habits of their race. None of the Umayyad and the ʿAbbāsid Caliphs, with the solitary exception of ʿUmar ibn ʿAbdul Azīz (d. 101 AH), came fully up to the standard of Islam.

The Evils of Monarchy

As a result, there soon occurred a rift between the Church and State in the religio-political order of Islam. The Caliphs, not being proficient or interested enough in religion, addressed themselves solely to political and administrative matters and disregarded their religious duties. When a religious need arose, they turned to the *ʿUlamā'* for advice, but accepted only that which suited their purpose. Thus, secular activity became independent of religion. The *ʿUlamā'*, except those few who succumbed to the worldly advantage gained by joining the Imperial

Court, arrayed themselves against it and initiated revolts within the Empire from time to time, or they quietly withdrew into religious establishments and devoted their energies to individual improvement and reform.

As the hold of religion weakened, the standards in morality also deteriorated rapidly among Muslims. The perverse influences of the demoralized attitude of the Caliphs, who were far from being models of Islamic morality (some were positively the reverse), was inevitably to adversely affect the moral structure of society as a whole. The Qur'ānic injunction regarding "the enjoining of Right and the forbidding of Wrong" ceased to have any meaning in practice, since it did not enjoy the backing of the State and, the vigilance of religion having ended, the un-Islamic tendencies began to affect the followers of Islam, ruining the rugged simplicity of their faith. The Muslims settled down to a life of ease and pleasure. They became lazy and self-indulgent. In such circumstances it was futile to expect that they would discharge their duties as true followers of the Prophet and carry forward the message he had bequeathed to them.

The fine impression that Islam had made on non-Muslims during the earlier days was nullified owing to the moral degeneration of its followers. The non-Muslims naturally attributed the failings of the Muslims to their faith. They lost confidence in Islam. A European writer remarked – and correctly – that the decline of Islam began when people started to lose faith in the sincerity of its representatives.

Philosophical Mind Games

From the natural sciences Muslim thinkers drifted towards metaphysics and the theology of the Greeks, which was, in fact, merely a revised version of their mythology. The Greeks had ingeniously imparted a scholastic look to their mythology by dressing it up in philosophical garb. Their philosophy was purely speculative. The spirit of the Qur'ān, on the other hand, is anti-classical. The Muslims, in fact, had no need to enter into theoretical disputes regarding the Being and the Attributes of God after the concrete knowledge the Qur'ān had placed in their hands. But they did not appreciate its worth and, instead of concentrating on solid spiritual and material welfare which would have paved the way for the universal expansion of Islam, they wasted their energies in profitless metaphysical discussion.

Religious Innovations

Thus, pagan beliefs and practices infiltrated into Muslim society. The superiority the Muslims had over others flowed solely from their religion and the secret of the greatness of their religion lies in it being the Revealed Law. This Law is the creation of God and, says the Holy Qur'ān:

> *(Such is) the artistry of God who disposes of all things in perfect order.*
>
> al-Naml 27:88

If this Divine Law becomes polluted with human intervention, it will cease to be what it should be – a guarantee of success in this world and the next. Neither the human intellect will submit to it nor will the mind of man be won over.

Revival and Restoration

So far, however, the basic values of religion remained intact and free from distortion. They remained absolutely free from all kinds of innovation, interpolation, misconstruction and suppression. Islam did not close its eyes to the lapses of its followers. It was always on the alert, correcting, mending, admonishing. The Qur'ān and the *Sunnah* were continually there – intact and unpolluted – to guide and to judge on occasions of doubt and dispute. They kept alive the spirit of defiance against the libertinism of the ruling classes and against other un-Islamic influences. The whole course of Islamic history is alight with the crusading endeavours of conscientious, determined, brave-hearted men who, like the true successors of the Prophets, faced the challenges of the time and restored, revived and kept on moving the *Millah* by resorting to *Jihād* and *Ijtihād*. These two principles, which embody the dynamism of Islam, never caused a vacuum in its structure. They remained always active in the body of Islam as living factors, holding aloft the torch of religious endeavour in the midst of the severest tempests. Thus it was that darkness was never allowed to spread over the whole World of Islam.

Similarly, at every critical turn of its history, some mighty man of action, some inspired defender of the Faith invariably burst upon the scene to beat off whatever threatened the existence of the *Millah*. Two of the many such outstanding personalities produced by the undying spirit of Islam to defend itself were Nūruddīn Zangī and Ṣalāḥuddīn Ayyūbī.

The Crusades and the Zangī Dynasty

Europe had been harbouring evil designs against the followers of Islam ever since they annexed the eastern wing of the Roman Empire, including all the Christian holy places. But, as the Muslims were then strong enough to defy all incursions, the Christian nations of Europe could not bring themselves to challenge them. Towards the end of the 11th century, however, the situation underwent a change, and great armies of Crusaders were organized all over the European continent to attack the Muslim countries of Palestine and Syria. The Crusaders regained possession of Jerusalem in 1099 (492 AH) and took over the greater part of Palestine. Describing their invasion, Stanley Lane-Poole says:

> The Crusaders penetrated like a wedge between the old wood and the new, and for a while seemed to cleave the trunk of Muhammedan Empire into splinters.[133]

Of the unspeakable cruelties perpetrated on the helpless Muslims by the Christians on their entry into Jerusalem, one Christian historian writes:

> So terrible, it is said, was the carnage which followed that the horses of the Crusaders who rode up to the mosque of Omar were knee-deep in the stream of blood. Infants were seized by their feet and dashed against the walls or whirled over the battlements, while the Jews were all burnt alive in their synagogue.[134]

The conquest of Jerusalem by the Christians was a momentous event. It exposed the rot that had started in the lands of Islam. Besides that it announced the awakening of Europe after the Dark Ages which had followed the decline of Rome. It threw the entire Muslim world into jeopardy. The spirits of the Christians rose so high after it that Reginald, the master of Krak, began to dream of laying his hands on the holy cities of Makkah and Madīnah.

The most calamitous hour in the history of Islam since the Tragedy of Apostasy[135] was at hand. However, at that moment there arose, from an unexpected quarter, a new star on the horizon of Islam. This was the Zangī dynasty of Mosul, two members of which, ᶜImāduddīn Zangī and Nūruddīn Zangī, repeatedly defeated the Crusaders and drove them out of almost every town in Palestine except Jerusalem. Nūruddīn holds a high place in the history of Islam for his administrative merit, piety, humility, justice and zest for *Jihād*. A contemporary chronicler, Ibn Athīr al-Jazarī, while speaking of Nūruddīn, observes, "I have studied the lives of all the former Sultans. I can say that but for the first four Rightly-Guided Caliphs and ᶜUmar ibn ᶜAbdul ᶜAzīz, none among them was more religious, just and clement than he."[136]

When Nūruddīn died, Ṣalāḥuddīn became the spearhead of Muslim resistance. Fighting battle after battle, he inflicted a crushing defeat on the Crusaders at Ḥiṭṭīn, Palestine, on July 4, 1187 (Rabīᶜ II 14, 583 AH). The hopes of the Christians were dashed to the ground and their armies were so totally demoralized that:

> A single Saracen was seen dragging some thirty Christians he had taken prisoners and tied together with ropes. The dead lay in heaps, like stones upon stones, among broken

crosses, severed hands and feet, whilst mutilated heads strewed the ground like a plentiful crop of melons".[137]

Ṣalāḥuddīn then proceeded to retake Jerusalem. The fire that had been blazing in the breasts of the Muslims since that city had fallen into the hands of the Christians was at last quenched. Qāḍī Ibn Shaddād, an intimate friend and counsellor of the Sultan, described the stirring spectacle of the victory of Jerusalem in these words:

> On all sides prayers were being offered; from all sides the cries of '*Allāh-u-Akbar*' could be heard. After ninety years the *Jumuᶜah* prayers were offered in Jerusalem. The cross, which the Christian soldiers had mounted on the Dome of the Rock, was pulled down. It was a wonderful spectacle. The grace of the Almighty and the triumph of Islam were visible everywhere.[138]

The generosity, the magnanimity and the high sense of Islamic morality, which Ṣalāḥuddīn displayed in that hour of his triumph, have been universally applauded by historians. Says Stanley Lane-Poole:

> If the taking of Jerusalem were the only fact known about Saladin, it were enough to prove him the most chivalrous and great-hearted conqueror of his own and perhaps of any age.[139]

Europe was furious at these reverses. In desperation, Crusaders from every European country converged on Syria and another series of bitter battles was fought between the Christians and the Muslims. Once again Ṣalāḥuddīn stood gallantly against the storm of concentrated Christian fury. After five years of relentless fighting, a truce was signed at Ramla in 1192 CE. The Muslims retained Jerusalem and all the other towns and fortresses they had captured, while the Christians only reigned over the small state of Acre. Thus, at last, the task which Ṣalāḥuddin had set himself, or rather, the mission God had charged him with, was accomplished. Lane-Poole observes:

> The Holy War was over; the five years' contest ended. Before the great victory at Hittin in July 1187, not an inch of Palestine west of the Jordan was in the Muslims' hands. After the Peace of Ramla in September 1192, the whole land was theirs except a narrow strip of coast from Tyre to Jaffa. Saladin had no cause to be ashamed of the treaty.[140]

Ṣalāḥuddīn was a man of extraordinary ability and energy. His capacity for organization and leadership was astounding. After hundreds of years he had succeeded in uniting the various nations and tribes among Muslims under the banner of *Jihād*, by making them forget their feuds and jealousies for the sake of Islam:

> All the strength of Christendom concentrated in the Third Crusade had not shaken Saladin's power. His soldiers may have murmured at their long months of hard and perilous service year after year, but they never refused to come to his summons and lay down their lives in his cause...
>
> Kurds, Turkmans, Arabs and Egyptians, they were all Moslems and his servants when he called. In spite of their differences of race, their national jealousies and tribal pride, he had kept them together as one host – not without difficulty and, twice or thrice, a critical waver.[141]

The Death of Ṣalāḥuddīn

Ṣalāḥuddīn, the faithful son of Islam passed away on March 4, 1193 CE (Safar 27, 598 AH). His selfless, crusading spirit had made the Muslim world safe from the tyranny of the West for a long time to come. But the Christians had derived immense benefit from these wars and they busied themselves at once in preparing for a new assault. Their turn came in the 19th century. The Muslims, however, wavered again and allowed the ground to slip from under their feet. They began to fight among themselves. Unfortunately, they were no longer blessed with a leader possessing the iron purpose, glowing enthusiasm and unflinching sincerity of Ṣalāḥuddīn.

Muslims Still an Obstacle in the Path of Ignorance

Even with all their failings, the Muslims were nearer to the path of the prophets than any other people. For this reason, whatever of their former power and prestige was left, continued to serve as a deterrent to Ignorance. They were still a force in the world, commanding respect from near and far. But, internally, they were steadily declining. This fact could not be concealed for very long from the outside world. The façade of their strength was finally broken towards the middle of the 13th century, when they were attacked by wave after wave of savage nations and hostile powers and Islamic lands fell into the hands of their enemies.

The Tartar Invasion

The fiercest among the barbarian invaders were the Tartars. They emerged from their steppe homelands and spread like locusts over the Islamic world. It was a dreadful calamity which left the Muslims breathless with fear and frustration. Ibn Athīr says:

> This disaster was so terrible that for long I could not decide whether to mention it or not. Even now it is with extreme reluctance that I do so. Who, indeed, can have the heart to relate the tragedy of the death of Islam and of the followers of Islam or the story of its humiliation and disgrace? Would that I had not been born or that I were dead and forgotten before this catastrophe occurred. But friends prevailed upon me to write about it. I, too,

> thought that no useful purpose would be served by ignoring this tragedy.
>
> It is a disaster without parallel in history. It affects the entire human race in general and the Muslims in particular. If anyone were to claim that there has been another event like it from the time of Adam to this day, it would be incorrect, for history cannot produce a single instance that could be compared with it, nor, perhaps, will anything like it happen again till Doomsday (except the appearance of Gog and Magog). The savages took pity on none. They slaughtered men, women and children ruthlessly. They ripped up the abdomens of pregnant women and killed the children in the wombs. ('To God do we belong and to Him do we return. There is no fear or power but with God'.) It was a world-consuming tragedy. It rose like a storm and swept over the whole world.[142]

The victorious Tartars made their entry into the capital city of Baghdad in 650 AH, and turned it into a mass of rubble. Ibn Kathīr gave the following account of the sacking of Baghdad:

> Death and destruction reigned supreme in Baghdad for forty days, after which this most beautiful city of the world was left crushed and ruined to the extent that only a handful of persons were to be seen in it. Dead bodies were piled in the streets in heaps as high as a ridge. It rained and the corpses decomposed. Their stench filled the air and a virulent epidemic broke out which spread as far as Syria, taking a very heavy toll of life wherever it raged. Famine, pestilence and death stalked the land.[143]

The Egyptians Push Back the Tartars

When they had overrun Iraq and Syria, the Tartars turned their attention towards Egypt. The Egyptian Sultan, Saifuddīn Qaṭaz, decided that attack was the best form of defence and, instead of waiting for the Tartars to arrive, he took the initiative and marched against them with a large army. A tremendous battle took place at ʿAin Jālūt in which, contrary to past experience, the Tartars were routed.

After the death of Saifuddīn the good work was continued by his successor, Baibars, who completely shattered the myth of the invincibility of the Tartars by inflicting successive defeats upon them until the whole of Syria was again in Muslim hands.

The Conquerors of Muslims Become the Captives of Islam

However, the Tartars still ruled over a vast stretch of Islamic territory from Iraq to Iran. The seat of the Islamic Caliphate, Baghdad, was in their hands. It was a cruel irony that such an uncultivated race should be in possession of the nerve-centre of Islamic culture. It affected the entire intellectual and cultural life of the Muslims. But they could do nothing about it. They were powerless.

Now, when all seemed lost, the spiritual power of Islam came to the fore to accomplish a wonderful miracle of conquest. A few unknown and sincere Muslim preachers and courtiers commenced the work of the propagation of Islam among the ruling circles of the Tartars and Islam's magic did the rest. The conquerors of the Muslims became the captives of Islam. Writing about this glorious event, Ibn Kathīr says:

> In this year (694 AH) Kāzān, the great grandson of Chengiz Khān, sat on the throne, and embraced Islam publicly at the hand of Amīr Tauzūn (may the blessings of Allah be on his soul!). With him nearly all the Tartars became Muslims. Gold, silver and pearls were given away in charity on the day of the Sultān's conversion. The Sultān adopted 'Mahmud' as his Muslim name and attended the congregational Friday prayers. Many temples were demolished. *Jizyah*[144] was imposed. Confiscated

> properties were restored in Baghdad and other places to their rightful owners and justice was dispensed. People saw rosaries in the hands of the Tartars and extolled the Bountifulness and the Glory of God.[145]

The Impact of the Tartar Invasion on the Muslim World

The Muslim World suffered a grave setback as a result of the Tartar invasion. Its intellectual progress was arrested and a general feeling of pessimism was created among the Muslims about the future of Islam. Overwhelmed by it, the *ʿUlamā'* and Muslim intellectuals closed the door of *Ijtihād*. Stagnation crept over them and they believed that the safety of Islam lay in rigidly containing everything in its existing state.

It was exceedingly unfortunate for the stewardship of the world to have passed into the hands of a people who had just stepped out of a barbaric condition. Though the conversion of the Tartars had made it possible for Muslims to live in peace and had reinstated Islam as the religion of the Empire, the Tartars were greatly lacking in the qualities of the Islamic *Imāmah*. It would have taken those qualities a long time to develop in them and the Islamic world, in such circumstances, could ill afford to wait. What the Muslims urgently needed was an ardent and energetic nation which could instil new life into them and discharge the function of their leadership with the dedication of an inspired people.

The Advent of the Ottoman Turks

Within a short time, in the 15th century (9th century AH) the Ottoman Turks made their debut on the stage of history. They shot to the notice of the world in 1455 CE (853 AH) when their twenty-four-year-old Sultan, Muḥammad the Conqueror, took Constantinople, the hitherto impregnable capital of the Eastern Roman Empire. This victory which had eluded the Muslims for eight hundred years, in spite of repeated attempts, thrilled the entire Muslim world and revived its spirits. The Muslims felt they could pin their hopes on the Ottoman Turks as the potential leaders of a Muslim revival; they could be trusted with the leadership of the Islamic world. They had sufficient endurance, foresight and strength and had given ample proof of their ability in the pursuit of their ideals. Baron Carra de Vaux rightly observed:

> The victory of Muhammad the Conqueror was not a gift of fortune or the result of the Eastern Empire having grown weak. The Sultan had been preparing for it for a long time. He had taken advantage of all the existing scientific knowledge. The cannon had just been invented and he decided to equip himself with the biggest cannon in the world and for this he acquired the services of a Hungarian engineer, who constructed a cannon that could fire a ball weighing 300 kilogrammes to a distance of one mile. It is said that this cannon was pulled by 700 men and took two hours to be loaded. Muhammad marched upon Constantinople with 300,000 soldiers and a strong artillery. His fleet, which besieged the city from the sea, consisted of 120 warships. By great ingenuity the Sultan resolved to send a part of his fleet by land. He launched seventy ships into the sea from the direction of Qāsim Pāshā by carrying them over wooden boards upon which fat had been applied (to make them slippery).

The Sultan had struck so much fear into the heart of Europe that, when he died, the Pope ordered continuous thanksgiving for three days throughout Christendom.[146]

Advantages Enjoyed by the Ottomans

The Ottomans enjoyed a number of distinct advantages which destined them for the leadership of the Muslim world:

(i) They were a vigorous, big-hearted and enterprising race, charged with a crusading zeal. Used to a nomadic existence, they were free from the lazy and voluptuous habits that had been the ruin of the Eastern Muslims.

(ii) They possessed great military strength and could be relied upon to safeguard the spiritual and temporal interests of Islam and defend the Muslim world against its enemies. Their rule extended over three continents – Europe, Asia and Africa. The Muslim world from Iran to Morocco was in their possession. Asia Minor they had subjugated, and in Europe they had advanced as far as the walls of Vienna. They were masters of the Mediterranean Sea. A trusted friend of Peter the Great wrote to him from Constantinople, saying that the Ottoman sultans regarded the Black Sea as their private lake in which they allowed no foreigners. The Turkish navy was so powerful that the combined maritime strength of Europe could not compete. In 1547 (945 AH), the combined fleets of Rome, Venice, Spain, Portugal and Malta were badly beaten. During the reign of Sulaimān the Great, the Ottoman Empire stretched over an area of 400,000 square miles – from the river Sāva in the north to the mouth of the Nile in the south and from the Caucasus in the east to Mount Atlas in the west. Every important city of the ancient world, with the exception of Rome, was included. The Ottoman fleet consisted of 3,000 ships.[147] Many Christian monarchs sought the favours of the Ottoman sultans and even church bells would be silenced as a mark of respect.

(iii) The Ottomans occupied a place of vital strategic importance on the world map. Their capital, Istanbul (Constantinople) was unrivalled in its geographical and strategic situation. It stood at the meeting-point of Europe and Asia, from where the Ottomans could control all three continents of the Old World. It was said by Napoleon at a later date, that if a world government was ever established, Constantinople would be the ideal capital.

The Ottomans were established in Europe, which was to acquire great importance in the near future and was already beginning to throb with a new life. They had a glorious opportunity of stealing a march on Christian Europe in heralding the New Age and guiding the world along the path of enlightened progress that Islam had chalked out for it before Europe emerged to lead it to its doom.

The Decline of the Ottoman Turks

But, to their misfortune, and to the misfortune of the entire Islamic world, the Turks surrendered to the temptations of ease and luxury; their morals deteriorated and their rulers became tyrannical. Internal feuds and dissensions began, and provincial governors and Army generals became corrupt and disloyal.

The greatest error the Ottomans made was that they allowed their minds to become static. In the sphere of warfare and military organization, they utterly ignored the Divine injunction, reproduced earlier, enjoining them to preserve their strength to the utmost in order to strike terror into the hearts of their enemies. Slowly they allowed their magnificent fighting machine to rust and decay.

Again, the advice of the Prophet ﷺ, that "Wisdom is the lost property of a Muslim – wherever he finds it, it is his," failed to influence them. Placed as they were in the midst of the hostile nations of Europe, it was expected that they would permanently keep before them the wise advice ᶜAmr ibn al-ᶜĀṣ had given to the Egyptians: "Don't forget that you are eternally in danger. You are standing at an outpost of vital importance. Therefore, be always vigilant and ready with your arms. You are surrounded by enemies whose covetous eyes are on you and your country."[148] But the Ottomans became complacent. While the European nations were making rapid progress, the Turks remained at a standstill.

As the well-known Turkish scholar, Halide Edib, said in her book, *Conflict of East and West in Turkey*: "As long as the world remained scholastic, [the] Moslem Religious Body did its duty admirably, and the Sulemānieh and the Fātiḥ Medressehs were the centres of learning and of whatever science there was at that time. But when the West broke the chains of scholasticism and created a new learning and science, the effects of which were to change the face of the world, the Moslem Religious Body failed very badly in its educational function. The ᶜUlamā took it for granted that human knowledge had not grown beyond what it was in the thirteenth century, and this attitude of mind persisted in their educational system down to the middle of the last century.

"The complacence of the ʿUlamā in Turkey particularly and in the Moslem world generally had nothing to do with their loyalty to the teachings of Islam, for scholastic philosophy and theology – Christian or Moslem – is Hellenic. It is more or less Aristotelian, the teaching of a Greek, a pagan philosopher. And for this reason a brief comparative review of the Christian and Islamic teachings seems necessary here.

"The Qur'ān does not set out to explain the creation of the material universe in detail. It emphasizes much more the moral and social side of the human life. It is concerned with '*Ḥusn*' and '*Qubḥ*', that is, the beautiful and the ugly, which is nothing more than the good and the evil. Hence its law. Nor is the metaphysical and spiritual side of Islam at all complicated. It is based on the recognition of Unity – a single creative Force of One Allah. Hence, the simplicity of Islam and the comparative freedom of Moslems to accept the new interpretation of the material world. But this admirable simplicity and open-mindedness, which could accommodate new knowledge of matter, did not last long among the Moslems. In the ninth century, not only Islamic law, but also theology was definitely put into rigid frames by the great Moslem thinkers – the *Mutakallimūn*; the philosophy of Aristotle was incorporated in the new Moslem theology, and the door of *Ijtihād* was closed.

"Now Christian doctrine, which is the teaching of St. Paul and the Church Fathers rather than that of Christ, contains a detailed explanation of the material universe. This had been accepted as a revelation and its truth had to be accounted for. As Christian theologians could not prove everything by observation, they tried to do so by reasoning. They had recourse to Aristotle, for the reason that he is almost a magician in his logical capacity.

"When the West began to study nature by observation, by analysis and experiment, the Christian Church was shocked. When the analytical methods led to great discoveries, the Church thought that meant the end of its authority. Hence in the West we behold an age of suffering and martyrdom for the scientist and the honest seeker after truth about the material universe.

"After a bloody conflict between Science and Christianity, the Christian Church took up a realistic attitude, and scientific knowledge was gradually incorporated in the instruction given in colleges as well as the primary schools. The universities, which were like the *Madrasas* of the *ᶜUlamā*, evolved into centres of new learning and science, without losing their hold over Theology and Metaphysics. The consequence was that the Christian Church preserved its authority over some section, at least, of the intelligentsia; the Catholic and the Protestant priests could discuss problems of every kind with the new youth, and could be reckoned among the scientifically-educated elite.

"The position of the Ottoman *ᶜUlamā'* was quite different. They never persecuted new learning or new truth about matter. But in the first place there was nothing in the way of new thought to persecute. As long as they were the supreme educators of the Moslem nation, nothing new could infiltrate; they saw to that, and their learning stagnated. Further, during the age of decline, they were so occupied with politics that it seemed by far the easiest thing to stick to Aristotle, to reasoning on the basis of knowledge, rather than venture on observation and analysis. Therefore, the *Madrasas* remained, until the end of the last century, what they were in the 13th century. The '*Wakf*' or Mosque Schools, which were the sole organization for primary education, remained similarly unchanged."[149]

Intellectual Sterility throughout the Muslim World

Intellectual sterility and the inefficiency of the educational system were not peculiar to Turkish life, but were common to the entire Muslim world. Muslims, universally, had grown inert both mentally and spiritually. If we do not, for the sake of caution, trace this stupor back to the 14th century CE, the 15th century was definitely the last to reveal any real intellectual life among the followers of Islam. It was during this century that Ibn Khaldūn wrote his *Prolegomena*. In the 16th century indolence of mind, slavish pedantry and blind imitation became complete. One does not find even one in a hundred among the *ᶜUlamā'* of the last four centuries who may, with justice, be called a genius or who may have produced anything to set beside the bold and noble intellectual activities of the earlier centuries. Only a few were above the low intellectual level of their age and, incidentally, they all came from India. One of these eminent personalities was Shaikh Aḥmad Sirhindī Mujaddid Alf Thānī (17th century CE) who left a lasting impression on the whole Muslim world. His *Letters* made a valuable contribution to Islamic religious thought.

Another prominent figure was Shāh Waliyyullāh Dehlawī (18th century CE). His *Ḥujjatullāh-i'l-Bālighah*, *Izālat-ul-Khifā'*, *al-Fauz-ul-Kabīr* and *al-Inṣāf* were unique works in their particular fields. The third prominent person was his son, Shāh Rafīᶜuddīn Dehlawī who, in the 19th century, wrote *Takmīl-ul-Adhhān* and *Asrār-ul-Maḥabbat*. Also outstanding was Shāh Ismāᶜīl Shahīd, whose *Manṣab-i-Imāmat* and *'Abaqāt* remain to this day works of great merit. Similarly, the *ᶜUlamā'* of Farangī Mahal and of some of the educational centres of the Eastern areas, who were worthy of note for their high degree of learning and scholarship, did much to improve the educational standards of their time. But their talents were confined largely to scholastics, the only exception being Shāh Waliyyullāh who wrote on ethics, politics, economics, mysticism, history and sociology.

Excessive conservatism and servility to tradition also robbed poetry and literature of its freshness. Language became heavy with embellishments. Even personal letters, official notes, memoranda and royal edicts were not free from this defect. The *Madrasas* and other institutions of learning were afflicted with an inferiority complex which degraded literature and thought. Classics were gradually expelled from the syllabi, and their place taken by the compilations of latter-day writers who lacked originality of thought and were merely blind imitators or interpreters of the old masters. Classical texts written by early scholars were replaced by annotations and commentaries, in the compilation of which the authors practised extreme economy and reduced them to mere notes.

Eastern Contemporaries of the Turks

Along with the Ottoman Empire were two important Muslim Empires in the East, one of which was the Moghul Empire of India. Founded in 1526 by Bābur, it had the rare good fortune to be ruled, one after the other, by a number of wise and powerful Emperors, the last of whom was Aurangzeb who will always be remembered in the history of Islam in India for the purity of his personal character, religious ardour and wide conquests. He ruled for about half a century. After his death in the first half of the 18th century, the Moghul Empire declined and his successors proved weak, inefficient and utterly unworthy. Simultaneously, this was the time of Europe's resurgence. Not to speak of protecting the World of Islam against the hostile intentions of the West, the Moghals could not save their own Empire from falling prey to the onslaught of the West and became, on account of their weakness and incapability, the stepping stone for England's boundless prosperity[150] and the enslavement of the Muslim world.

The other was the Safavid Empire of Iran. In its earlier days, it was a very enlightened and progressive state, but exaggerated Shīᶜism and senseless quarrelling with Turkey sapped its energy and rendered it ineffective.

Both these Empires isolated themselves completely from the outside world. They lost touch with time and shut their eyes to the numerous changes that were taking place around them. Europe was a far cry, and even the developments in adjoining Muslim countries did not excite any interest.

Individual Efforts

The ability of Islam to sustain itself when everything appears to have conspired against it runs through the whole course of its history. In various Muslim lands there arose men of strength and vision who tried to reverse the process of history. In India, the lion-hearted Tipū Sultān made a heroic attempt to win back his country from the foreigners. A little later, Sayyid Aḥmad Shahīd dreamt of founding a state extending up to Bukhārā on the lines of *Khilāfah Rāshidah*. He encouraged thousands of earnest and noble-minded preachers and fighters who, through their religious enthusiasm, sincerity and selflessness, revived the memories of the first centuries of Islam. But collective degeneration had become so extensive that individual exertions could not arrest the march of decay.

Europe's Scientific and Industrial Progress

Europe, meanwhile, was making colossal scientific and industrial progress. Europeans were conquering hidden forces of matter, unveiling new secrets of nature and discovering "unknown" lands. During the 16th and 17th centuries, Europe produced a large number of outstanding men in all fields of creative activity. Scientists such as Copernicus, Bruno, Galileo, Kepler and Newton revolutionized the world of physics, while Columbus, Vasco da Gama and Magellan discovered the New World and many other lands and sea routes.

The destiny of mankind was being re-cast in the West and the world was changing at a breath-taking pace. He who lost a moment in idleness lost a great deal. The Muslims, alas, neglected not minutes but centuries, whereas the European nations realized the value of time and covered the distance of centuries in years.

The Turks lagged so far behind in the field of industry that ship-building was not started until the 16th century. The printing press, health services and the defence academies were introduced in Turkey only in the 17th century. Towards the end of the 18th century, when a balloon was seen flying over Constantinople the Turks thought it was a magic trick.

With Imperial Turkey lagging so far behind, what could have been the plight of those Muslim countries that were under its suzerainty? They did not possess even minor industries. A French traveller, Volney, who travelled in Egypt in the 18th century and stayed for four years in Syria, wrote that: "this country (Syria) is so backward in the matter of industry that if your watch goes wrong here, you will have to go to a foreigner to get it mended".[151]

In their heyday the Turks were unmatched in the world for military proficiency. But now, even in this area, the Europeans had surpassed them. In 1774, the Ottoman Empire suffered a crushing defeat at the hands of Europe. The shock of this defeat helped somewhat to open the eyes of the Turks to the ugly realities of their situation and some efforts were made by them to improve things. Military re-organization was taken in hand with the help of foreign experts. The real work of national reconstruction was, however, undertaken by Sultān Salīm III who had, incidentally, been brought up outside the palace. He opened new-fashioned schools including an Engineering College in which he himself taught. He also laid the nucleus of a modern army called the "New Order" and introduced political reforms. But stagnation had become so firmly entrenched in Turkey that before any substantial headway could be made, the old army rebelled against the Sultan and he was slain. After him, Mahmūd II and his successor, ʿAbdul Majīd I, devoted themselves to the task of nation-building and the country took some steps forward during their reigns.

But these few attempts at reconstruction were nothing compared to the mighty strides of Europe. The fate that befell the Muslims in Morocco, Algiers, Egypt, India, Turkestan and elsewhere in the 18th and the 19th centuries could easily have been predicted in the 16th and 17th centuries.

V

THE RISE OF THE WEST AND ITS CONSEQUENCES

With the decline of the Turks, international leadership passed from the Muslims to the non-Muslim nations of the West, which had been preparing for this for a long time and were now left without a rival. By virtue of conquest, or cultural, economic or political penetration, their influence quickly spread throughout the globe.

The History of Western Civilization

Western civilization is not of recent origin. Its roots go back thousands of years to ancient Greece and Rome. The Western outlook on life and ethics can be traced directly to the ancient Greek and Roman civilizations.

The Western nations kept cultivating the spirit, the philosophy, the sciences, the literature and the ideas of the Greek and Roman cultures until the 19th century when they created a new façade. It is possible to be deceived by the splendour of the new façade, but the fact remains that its substance was made up of Greek and Roman materials. The Greek civilization was the first clear manifestation of the Western mind. It was the first civilization to be built exclusively on Western intellectual and ethical ideals and aspirations.

Greek Civilization

The intellectual fundamentals of Greek civilization may be summed up as follows:

(i) Disregard of transcendental truths;
(ii) Want of religious feeling and spirituality;
(iii) Worship of material comfort; and
(iv) Exaggerated patriotism.

Greek civilization was purely materialistic. The Greeks could not even conceive of God without giving Him physical forms and shapes, and making images for His Attributes and installing them in their temples so as to lend a visible aspect to their devotions. They had a god of sustenance, a god of benevolence, a god of fury, and so on. All the attributes of physical existence were ascribed to these gods. Even abstract concepts such as beauty and love were symbolized as separate deities. The logical lists on ten kinds of predication and nine heavens in the 'categories' of Aristotle were also but the products of materialistic rationality from the effects of which the Greek spirit could never free itself.

A brilliant interpretation of ancient Greek civilization was once given by Dr Haas, a German scholar, in three lectures he delivered in Geneva on "What is European Civilization?" He held that the first stage for European civilization was set by Ancient Greece where: "the aim was to develop man harmoniously. The supreme measure was a beautiful body. It clearly emphasized the senses. Physical education – games and dancing – and mental education – poetry, music, drama, philosophy, even the sciences – were kept in proportion so as to develop the mind but not at the expense of the body. Its religion had no spirituality, no theology, no mysticism."[152]

Many Western writers have similarly drawn attention to the spiritual ineffectiveness of the religion and the lack of moral enthusiasm and dignity in the religious practices and festivals of the Greeks. Lecky, for instance, says: "The Greek spirit was essentially rationalistic and eclectic; the Egyptian spirit was essentially mystical and devotional... 'The Egyptian deities,' it was observed by Apuleius, 'were chiefly honoured by lamentations and the Greek divinities by dances'...The truth of that last part of this very significant remark appears in every page of Greek history. No nation has a richer collection of games and festivals growing out of its religious system; in none did a light, sportive and often licentious fancy play more fearlessly around the popular creed, in none was religious terrorism more rare. The Divinity was seldom looked upon as holier than man, and a due observance of certain rites and ceremonies was deemed an ample tribute to pay to him."[153]

There was nothing incomprehensible in this sorry state of affairs for, apart from the general Western conception of life as a purely utilitarian proposition, the basic structure of the theological metaphysics of the Greeks was such that it left very little room for the development of the spirit of religious reverence and awe. The denial of the Attributes of God and of His personal control over the universe, and the replacement of Him as the Creator and the Sustainer of the worlds by a self-supposed Active Intellect, could only lead to the destruction of spiritual enthusiasm. Why would one adore God with his body and spirit and address one's prayers and petitions to Him if one did not have faith in His Beneficent Care and Dispensation?

Thus, Greek civilization was utterly agnostic. The Greeks did not strictly deny God, but they had no place for Him in their practical scheme of things. They supposed that He had, after having brought forth the Active Intellect, retreated into seclusion. Naturally enough, they did not look upon Divinity as more holy than man. We read about so many inventors in history, but do they inspire a feeling of reverence?

The worship of idols, the exaggeration of emphasis on material comfort, the devotion to idols and pictures, music and the other fine arts, the extravagant notion of individual liberty and the excessive indulgence in games, sports and festivals had a harmful effect on the Greek mind and morals. Hideous excesses of unnatural lust and unending protests and revolts against all forms of authority gradually became the order of the day; vulgarity received a charter and greed became rampant. The description of the democratic young man given by Plato is not dissimilar to what happens in our own times. He writes:

> ...he will not receive or suffer within the ramparts the true reasoning of anyone who asserts that some pleasures spring from the desires that are good and noble, but others from those evil, and that the former should be fostered and honoured, and the latter disciplined and enslaved. To all such remarks, he shakes his head, and says that all are alike and deserving of equal honour.
>
> Day after day he gratifies the pleasures as they come – now floating down the primrose path of wine, now given over to teetotalism and hunting; one day in hard hunting, the next slacking and idling, and the third playing the philosopher. Often he will take to politics, leap to his feet and do or say whatever comes into his head; or he comes to admire military people and inclines to their way of life; or he would look jealously at a man of business and take to his profession. He, in short, takes this life as pleasant and free and blessed and leads his life like this right up to the end.[154]

Another major characteristic of the Western spirit is its narrow nationalism. Nationalism is much more intense in Europe than in Asia. This is due, partly, to geographical reasons. In Asia, the natural regions are extensive, with a wide range of physical, climatic and ethnological diversities. The land is more fertile and can support life with greater ease. The tendency in India has always been, therefore, towards large, multi-racial states and the world's most extensive empires were established on the subcontinent. Europe, on the contrary, is split up into a large number of small territorial units, segregated from each other by formidable natural barriers like high mountains and deep rivers. The population in these areas is dense, the pressure on land is heavy and the means of subsistence are scarce. The struggle for existence is very acute. All these factors have contributed to the creation of a strong national sentiment, particularly in Central and Western Europe where the idea of a political community could not extend beyond the bounds of a city-state.

The entire civilization of the Greeks was built around their city-states. Lecky says that the state occupied a predominance in the Greek mind and virtue was firmly connected with patriotism. The cosmopolitanism of Socrates and Anaxagoras had made little impression upon the Hellenes. Aristotle's system of ethics was based on differentiation between the Greeks and the non-Greeks. According to him, the Greeks had no more obligations to barbarians (foreigners) than to wild beasts. In fact, when a philosopher declared that his sympathies extended beyond his own state and included all the people of Greece, he caused great astonishment among his own people.

Roman Civilization

The Greeks had developed a brilliant literature, philosophy and civilization, while the Romans had only just emerged from a military stage. In these circumstances, it was only natural for the Romans, when they conquered Greece, to become imbued with the intellect and manners of the Greeks.

> It is also evident that the Greeks, having had for several centuries a splendid literature, at a time when the Romans had none, and when the Latin language was still too crude for literary purposes, the period in which the Romans first emerged from a purely military condition would bring with it an ascendancy of Greek ideas. Fabius Pictor and Cincius Alimentus, the earliest native historians, both wrote in Greek…After the conquest of Greece, the political ascendancy of the Romans and the intellectual ascendancy of Greece were alike universal. The conquered people, whose patriotic feelings had been greatly enfeebled by the influences I have noticed, acquiesced readily in their new condition, and notwithstanding the vehement exertions of the

> conservative party, Greek manners, sentiments, and ideas soon penetrated all classes and moulded all forms of Roman life.[155]

The Roman religion had never been a source of moral enthusiasm. Being wholly paganish and superstitious, it was altogether incapable of checking the progress of scepticism and unbelief among its followers. Consequently, as the Romans advanced culturally, they grew openly contemptuous of their faith. They had already decided that their gods had nothing to do with the management of the practical affairs of this world. Cicero reports that when lines declaring that the gods took no care of the things of man were read in theatres, the audiences responded with loud applause.[156] St Augustine and other Fathers long after ridiculed the pagans who satirized in the theatres the very gods they worshipped in their temples.[157] The spirit of religious reverence had, indeed, become so weak that when the fleet of Augustus was wrecked, he solemnly degraded the status of Neptune, the sea-god. At the death of Germanicus, people freely stoned and overthrew the altars of the gods.[158]

Religion in Rome was, in truth, nothing more than a social tradition and a utilitarian formula. To quote Lecky once again: "...(the Roman religion) was purely selfish. It was simply a method of obtaining prosperity, averting calamity, and reading the future. Ancient Rome produced many heroes, but no saints. Its self-sacrifice was patriotic, not religious. Its religion was neither an independent teacher nor a source of inspiration..."[159]

A natural corollary of the naked materialism of the Romans was Imperialism and exploitation of the weaker nations for selfish motives. This, too, has been inherited *in toto* by modern Europe. According to Muhammad Asad:

> ...the underlying idea of the Roman Empire was the conquest of power and the exploitation of other nations for the benefit of the mother country alone. To promote

> better living for a privileged group, no violence was for the Romans too bad, no injustice too base. The famous 'Roman Justice' was justice for the Romans alone. It is clear that such an attitude was possible only on the basis of an entirely materialistic conception of life and civilization – a materialism certainly refined by an intellectual taste, but nonetheless foreign to all spiritual values. The Romans never in reality knew religion. Their traditional gods were a pale imitation of Greek mythology, colourless ghosts, silently accepted for the benefit of social convention. In no way were the gods allowed to interfere with real life. They had to give oracle through the medium of their priests if they were asked; but they were never supposed to confer moral laws upon men.[160]

During its closing years the Roman Empire was transformed into a sea of corruption and evil. The original military discipline of the Romans and the simplicity of their ethical code were swept away by the avalanche of wealth and luxury. John William Draper gives the following excellent portrayal of the conditions that prevailed in Rome at that time:

> When the Empire in a military and political sense had reached its culmination, in a religious and social aspect it had attained its height of immorality. It had become thoroughly epicurean; its maxim was that life should be made a feast, that virtue is only the seasoning of pleasure, and temperance the means of prolonging it. Dining-rooms glittering with gold and encrusted with gems, slaves and superb apparel, the fascinations of feminine society where all the women were dissolute, magnificent baths, theatres, gladiators – such were the objects of Roman desire. The conquerors of the world had

> discovered that the only thing worth worshipping was Force. By it all things might be secured, all that toil and trade had laboriously obtained. The confiscation of goods and lands, the taxation of provinces, were the reward of successful warfare; and the emperor was a symbol of Force. There was a social splendour, but it was the phosphorescent corruption of the Ancient Mediterranean world.[161]

Christianity Spreads Across the Roman Empire

The establishment of Christianity as the official religion of the Roman Empire, which was made possible by the ascension of Constantine to the throne of the Caesars in 305 CE, was an event of revolutionary importance. Christianity, thereby, came to possess an Empire which it would not otherwise have dared dream of. As Constantine's victory was the outcome of the heroic sacrifices of his Christian supporters, he duly rewarded them with a generous share in the affairs of the Empire.

The Paganization of Christianity

In reality, however, this was a most inauspicious moment for Christianity. The religion did gain an Empire, but lost its soul. The Christians had won on the field of battle, but they were completely routed in the realm of faith and morality. The pagans and, what was more the Christians themselves, wrenched the Christian creed out of shape, and in this unfortunate development Constantine himself played no small part. Says Draper:

> Place, power, profit – these were in view of whoever now joined the conquering sect. Crowds of worldly persons, who cared nothing about its religious ideas, became its warmest supporters. Pagans at heart, their influence was soon manifested in the paganization of Christianity that ensued forthwith. The Emperor, no better than they, did nothing to check their proceedings.

> But he did not personally conform to the ceremonial requirements of the Church until the close of his evil life, AD 337.[162]

> Though the Christian party had proved itself sufficiently strong to give a master to the Empire, it was never sufficiently strong to destroy its antagonist, paganism. The issue of struggle between them was an amalgamation of the principles of both. In this, Christianity differed from Mohammedanism which absolutely annihilated its antagonist and spread its own doctrines without adulteration.[163]

> To the Emperor – a mere worldling – a man without any religious convictions, doubtless it appeared best for himself, best for the Empire, and best for the contending parties, Christian and pagan, to promote their union or amalgamation as much as possible. Even sincere Christians do not seem to have been averse to this; perhaps they believed that the new doctrines would diffuse most thoroughly by incorporating in themselves ideas borrowed from the old, that Truth would assert herself in the end and the impurity be cast off.[164]

The amalgamation of paganism with Christianity, from which its soul and beauty had departed, could not bring about an improvement of the moral conditions of the Romans. On the other hand, it produced a great outburst of monasticism, which was perhaps a more painful era in the moral history of mankind than the former extravagance of sensuality. This atrocious and sordid routine of self-torture played a large part in the spread of materialism and irreligiousness in Europe and we will, therefore, study it here at some length.

The Progress of Monasticism

It is difficult today even to imagine the intensity and rapidity of the progress of the monastic movement in Europe. On account of the extreme inaccuracy of the historians of the movement, it is not easy to speak confidently of the actual number of hermits. The following facts may, however, be helpful in obtaining an idea of its great popularity.

It is stated that in the days of St Jerome, nearly 50,000 monks used to assemble at the Easter festivals; that there were, in the 4th century, nearly 5,000 monks under a single abbot; that St Seraphim had 10,000 monks under him; and that towards the close of the 4th century the monastic population in a great part of Egypt was nearly equal to the population of the cities.

For two hundred years the maceration of the body was considered to be the highest proof of moral excellence. St Macarius of Alexandria is said to have slept for six months in a marsh, exposing his body to the stings of venomous flies. He would carry around with him eighty pounds of iron. His disciple, Eusebius, carried one hundred and fifty pounds of iron, and lived for three years in a dried-up well. Another famous saint, named John, is said to have stood in prayer for three years, leaning occasionally on a rock to rest his weary limbs. Some hermits discarded their clothes and crawled on all fours like beasts covered only by their matted hair. Some lived in the deserted dens of wild beasts; others preferred dried-up wells; others dwelt among the tombs. One sect of monks lived solely on grass. Cleanliness of the body was regarded as pollution of the soul, and the saints who were most admired became a hideous mass of filth. St Anthanasius related how St Antony had never, until extreme old age, been guilty of washing his feet. St Abraham, who lived for fifty years after his conversion to Christianity, scrupulously avoided washing either his hands or his feet from that date. Abbot Alexander used to say, looking mournfully back at the past, "Our fathers never washed their faces, but we frequent the public baths."

Hermits, disguised as religious teachers, roamed about from place to place seducing children for their order. The control of parents over their children was broken. Those children who forsook their parents and became monks were held in high public esteem. What was lost in obedience by the father was gained in prestige by the priest. The eloquence of St Ambrose is reported to have been so seductive that mothers used to lock up their children to guard them against his charisma.

The inroads made by monasticism into the family domain were exceedingly damaging. Social ties were rent apart and the foundations of family life shaken. Domestic virtues were cast into discredit. It is hard to visualize the hard-heartedness of the hermits towards those who were bound to them by the closest earthly ties. The saints broke the hearts of their mothers with ingratitude and abandoned their own wives and children. Their business was to save their own souls; they were not concerned with what befell their families. The hermits ran away from the shadow of a woman. It was sinful to converse even with one's mother, wife or sister. Their life-long penances were all for nothing if they happened to meet a woman in the street or let her shadow fall upon them.

This undoing of domestic life had a disastrous effect on people's character. Personal virtues such as courage, generosity, frankness and cordiality were discouraged and sometimes utterly destroyed.

The Consequences of Monasticism

It would be foolish to assume that such excessive asceticism and self-denial succeeded, in any measure, to counteract the grotesque licentiousness and materialism of the Romans. The moral and religious history of mankind does not warrant such optimism. It is opposed to human nature. Experience shows that only an ethical or spiritual system which is not opposed to innate human aims and instincts and which, instead of crushing them, succeeds in disciplining them and elevating them from the bestial to the noble, can tame arrogant materialism and convert it into a healthy social force.

This is the method of Islam, the way of the Prophet Muḥammad ﷺ. We have noticed how the Arabs were both chivalrous and warlike in temperament. The Prophet ﷺ did not attempt to tone down or suppress their valour. He diverted it from mutual warfare and senseless blood-feuds to *Jihād* in the way of Allah. Similarly, the Prophet ﷺ did not try to stifle their inborn generosity and high-mindedness. He put these virtues to their best advantage by advising his followers to employ them for bringing relief to the needy and the forlorn instead of allowing them to branch out towards ostentation and self-conceit. He wove the indigenous characteristics of the Arabs into the fabric of Islam. He taught his religion as a new theory of life, giving to mankind something more wholesome and more divine for whatever he took away from it. He even allowed for times of amusement and recreation. As the great Muslim scholar, Ḥāfiz Ibn Taimiyah, has said, "Man agrees to give up a thing only when he is provided with a substitute thereof";[165] and that, "Prophets are raised up to evolve and to improve human nature, and not to change it."[166]

These truths are underlined in the teachings of the Prophet Muḥammad ﷺ by innumerable instances. When the Prophet arrived in Madīnah, he found that the Madinites had two festivals a year in which they indulged in merrymaking. He inquired about the nature of the festivals and was told that the Madinites had been celebrating them from very early times. Then he said, "God has given you better festivals than these, ʿĪd al-Aḍḥā and ʿĪd al-Fiṭr."[167]

ʿĀ'ishah, may Allah be pleased with her, relates: "On an ʿĪd day two Anṣār girls were singing the songs of the Battle of Buʿāth at my house. They were not professional singers. Abū Bakr, may Allah be pleased with him, chanced to pay us a visit at that moment. 'What!,' he exclaimed, 'the Devil's songs in the Prophet's house?' Thereupon the Prophet ﷺ said to him, 'Abū Bakr, every community has its ʿĪd (day of rejoicing). It is our ʿĪd today'."[168]

Roman Christianity, on the contrary, took upon itself the utterly hopeless task of trying to alter human nature and tried to work out a system that was beyond human endurance. In the beginning people accepted it as a sort of recoil from the abundant materialistic inclinations of pre-Christian Rome, but they soon tired of it with the consequence that there came to exist in the Christian world two parallel and diametrically opposed movements of licentiousness and asceticism. There was no scarcity of moral enthusiasm, but it was drawn away into the desert, and the cities presented a scene of depravity and degradation that has seldom been surpassed. Says Lecky:

> ...the level of public men was extremely depressed. The luxury of the court, the servility of the courtiers, and the prevailing splendour of dress and of ornament had attained an extravagant height. The world grew accustomed to a dangerous alternation of extreme asceticism and gross vice and, sometimes, as in the case of Antioch, the most vicious and luxurious cities produced the most numerous anchorites [hermits]. There existed a combination of vice and superstition which is eminently prejudicial to nobility, though not equally detrimental to the happiness of man. Public opinion was so low that very many forms of vice attracted little condemnation and punishment, while undoubting belief in the absolving efficacy of superstitious rites calmed the imagination and allayed the terrors of conscience. There was more falsehood and treachery than under the Caesars, but there was much less cruelty, violence and shamelessness. There was also less public spirit, less independence of character, less intellectual freedom.[169]

Corruption of the Clergy

Gradually, the corruption of the monastic movement reached classes and institutions which appeared the most holy. The agape, or love-feasts, which were regarded as symbols of Christian unity, became scenes of drunkenness and riot until they were finally suppressed by the government in the seventh century. The commemoration of martyrs degenerated into scandalous waste. High prelates were charged with flagrant breaches of morality. St Jerome complained that the banquets of many bishops eclipsed in splendour those of the provincial governors. Religious offices were obtained by intrigue; benefices, dispensations, licenses, absolutions, indulgences, and privileges were bought and sold like merchandise. "Pope Innocent VIII pawned the Papal tiara. Of Leo X it was said that he squandered the revenues of three Popes: he wasted the savings of his predecessor, spent his own income, he anticipated that of his successor..."[170] It was affirmed that all of the revenues of France were insufficient to meet the expenditures of the Popes.

In short, the history of the Church and the Papacy was the detailed elaboration of the following Qur'ānic verse:

> *O ye who believe! Lo! many of the (Jewish) rabbis and the (Christian) monks devour the wealth of mankind wantonly and debar (men) from the way of Allah.*
>
> al-Tawbah 9:34

The Struggle between the Church and the State

In the 11th century there ensued a bitter and most uninspiring struggle between the Church and the State. The Pope had the better of the Emperor during the initial rounds of the encounter, and the power of the Church was so greatly increased that, in 1077, Pope Hilderbrand ordered King Henry IV to come and submit to him, and Henry, realizing the Pope's enormous power, felt obliged to undertake the journey all the way to Canossa in bitter cold and in the most humiliating circumstances. Barefoot, and clad in the penitent's shirt, he knocked at the castle gate and it was only after much persuasion that the Pope condescended to let him in and beg forgiveness.

After this, fortunes fluctuated between the Church and the State – sometimes the Pope won and sometimes the Emperor – until, after hundreds of years of confusion and bloodshed, the Church conceded defeat. During this period of conflict, the people in the whole of Christendom were forced to endure the double tyranny of religion and politics, of the Church and the State.

Misuse of Power by the Church

The Church, during the Middle Ages, enjoyed far more power than the Roman Emperors and had it wanted it could have contributed emmensely to the cause of European civilization.

> Had not the sovereign pontiffs been so completely occupied with maintaining their emoluments and temporalities in Italy, they might have made the whole continent advance like one man. Their officials could pass without difficulty into every nation, and communicate without embarrassment with each other, from Ireland to Bohemia, from Italy to Scotland. The possession of a common tongue gave them the administration of international affairs with intelligent allies everywhere, speaking the same language.[171]

But the guardians of the Church failed in their duty. They misused their power and opportunities and allowed things to deteriorate from bad to worse. The well-being of countries is generally portrayed in the variations of their populations. Judging from this, we find that in five hundred years the population of England could scarcely double itself, while the population of Europe, as a whole, could not do so even at the end of a thousand years. This was, no doubt, due, to some extent, to the practice of celibacy but, in the main, it was the result of bad food, wretched clothing, inadequate shelter, personal uncleanliness, absence of physicians and the popularity of shrine-cures, in which society was encouraged by the clergy to put its trust. It was the policy of the Church to discourage the physician and his art, for the Church profited from the gifts it received and the profits of the shrines. Consequently, epidemic diseases were permitted to spread over the Continent unchecked.

Aeneas Sylvius, who travelled in Britain in 1430, left a graphic description of the all-pervading ignorance, superstition, poverty and want that held sway over that country.

Pollution of the Scriptures

The biggest and most fatal error the clergymen committed was that they incorporated in the holy Scriptures all the prevailing notions of geography and physics. Those notions were by no means the limits of human knowledge which is essentially progressive. Perhaps the clergymen did so in good faith – to raise the merit of the Scriptures in popular estimation, but its consequences were most certainly disastrous. That started a violent conflict between Christianity and science in which Christianity, which had already suffered in its purity through dogmatic corruption, was overcome and the prestige of the clergymen was undermined forever. Christianity in Europe fell into disfavour, never to rise again in public estimation. Worst of all, Europe turned atheist.

The Church, having established itself as the sole depository and controller of knowledge, was always ready to resort to civil power to compel obedience to its decisions. Thus, there evolved, under the name of Christian topography, a complete system of geography which had no divine sanction, and those who refused to accept it were declared heretics.

The Struggle between Religion and Science and Tyranny of the Church

Meanwhile, owing to Islamic and Muslim scientific influences, the volcano of knowledge erupted in Europe. Its thinkers and scientists broke the chains of intellectual slavery. They boldly refuted the religious theories, which were based on preposterous evidence, and proclaimed the results of their own investigations. The Church authority reacted ruthlessly. It established the Inquisition: "to discover, and bring to book, the heretics lurking in towns, houses, cellars, caves and fields". This institution performed its duty with such savage alacrity that a Christian theologian exclaimed that it was hardly possible for a man to be a Christian and die in his bed. It is estimated that between 1481 and 1801 the Inquisition punished three hundred and forty thousand people, nearly thirty-two thousand of whom were burnt alive, including the great scientist, Bruno, whose only crime was that he taught the plurality of the worlds. Bruno was delivered to the secular authorities to be punished, "as mercifully as possible, and without the shedding of blood", which, in fact, was the horrible formula for burning a prisoner at the stake. Galileo, another scientist of no less worth, was remorselessly punished till he died in prison for having held the view that, contrary to the "Scriptures", the earth moved around the sun!

The Revolt

At last, the patience of the genius of Europe was exhausted and it openly rose in revolt against the representatives of Christianity and its traditions. Provoked by the intellectual stagnation of the clergy, and the heinous atrocities perpetrated by the Inquisition, the enlightened sections among the Europeans developed a strong aversion to all knowledge, morality and truth associated with the Church and religion in general. They could not help connecting religion with all the misdeeds of the Papacy and the brutal sufferings of the secular scholars. A dismal disbelief crept over the Continent. Freed from their former serfdom under Christianity, the peoples of Europe began to exhibit a definite intolerance of every kind of spiritual control. Thus, what had originally started as a tussle between Christianity and secular knowledge, flared up into an all-out contest between Religion and Progress. It was concluded arbitrarily by the intelligentsia of Europe that Religion and Science were altogether incompatible and, consequently, for the advancement of Science it was necessary to discourage religion. It was no doubt a mistaken notion to pitch Science against Religion in general instead of against Christianity alone, but there were attenuating circumstances for this mistake.

Precipitancy of the Intellectuals

The intellectuals did not have either the patience nor the understanding to distinguish between true religion and its self-appointed leaders. They did not care to ponder, calmly and impartially, on who really was responsible for the tragedy, the teachings of religion or the ignorance and bigotry of the priests; and if it were the latter, how far justifiable it was to condemn religion for the sins of its so-called officials.

They also did not possess the broadmindedness and the genuine thirst for truth which might have led them to a dispassionate study of Islam, although it had, by that time, grown to be the faith of a number of powerful neighbouring nations. Islam could have easily provided a straight and simple answer to their intellectual and spiritual difficulties by breaking the gloom of scholastic theology of the Middle Ages and liberating their spirit from the shackles of darkness. It could have announced the dawn of better things by granting full freedom to the natural urges and legitimate cravings of the mind and body without, for a moment, failing to prohibit what was base and wicked. Says the Holy Qur'ān:

> *For he (the Prophet) commands them what is just and forbids them what is evil; he allows them as lawful what is good (and pure) and prohibits them from what is bad (and impure); he releases them from their heavy burdens and from the yokes that are upon them.*
>
> al-Aʿrāf 7:157

The racial prejudice of the Europeans also stood in the way. The barriers of hatred erected by the Crusades between the Christians and the Muslims, and the resulting ill-will of the Christian missionaries did a lot to entrench the antagonistic attitude of the West towards Islam. Part of the blame should, however, also be laid at the door of Muslim preachers, for they sadly neglected the opportunity of making such an important continent as Europe acquainted with the message of Islam, though all the resources of mighty Empires were at their disposal.

Western Materialism

In this spiritual vacuum, Europe took a tragic turn. It descended by degrees into the depths of materialism. Its social thinkers and scientists investigated the nature of the world and of life as if there were no absolute power which created them and ruled over them according to some plan and purpose without itself being subject to any laws. They interpreted the material universe and its manifestations along mechanical lines and called it objective and scientific method, rejecting as slavery to tradition whatever was based on belief in the existence of God. One by one, they disowned everything that existed apart from matter and energy, everything that was not realizable in experience, or could not be weighed and measured.

For a long time the Europeans did not openly reject the notion of God – all Europeans are not atheists, even today – but the intellectual and moral position they had adopted definitely precluded all claim of religion upon life. Attempts were made after the Renaissance to produce a reconciliation between Religion and Science, as some sort of religious arrangement was thought necessary to preserve the tranquillity of society by influencing the social relations of men. But the pace set by materialistic civilization was so hot that religion could not stand it. It also entailed a good deal of inconvenience to keep materialism in harmony with transcendental truths. As decades and centuries advanced, the ceremony was waived, and much of Europe took unconditionally to the worship of matter.

Significantly enough, there appeared at that time a number of outstanding social and political writers and teachers who indiscriminately sowed the seeds of materialism in the minds of people and laid emphasis on the sensuous enjoyment and the mechanistic views of morality. Machiavelli paved the way by divorcing politics from ethics and prescribing a dual standard of morality, one private and the other public. If religion must exist, he taught, let it be confined to the personal sector of life. It was none of its business to intrude into politics. The State was a law unto itself. The subject matter of Christianity was the other world; it had nothing to do with the world in which man lived. The State had no use for the religious, for their religiousness often acted to its detriment and prevented them from disregarding the basis of morality in the hour of its need. Princes and officials of the State, it was believed, should be ready to take recourse to deceit, falsehood and treachery in the pursuit of national objectives.

These philosophers and writers played havoc with the standards and values of religion. They made fun of the ancient notions of religious morality and, after presenting sin in a highly fascinating light, invited people to give free rein to their appetites. Western civilization reverted to its origins. It became merely a new edition of the pagan civilizations of ancient Greece and Rome. All the aspects of these ancient civilizations, that were subdued under the influence of Oriental Christianity, were revived by the cultural craftsmen of the 19th century. The same lack of spiritual feeling, the same inability to believe that characterized the religions of the Greeks and the Romans, is apparent in the religious make-up of the modern West. The same extravagance of sensuality that was prevalent in the cultural fabric of Greece and Rome is exhibited fully in Western civilization today. The soul of the modern Western young man is no different from the soul of the democratic young man of ancient Greece as portrayed by Plato in his *Republic*, in so far as he regards himself entitled to indulge in the gratification of his desires.

Christianity or Materialism?

The real religion of the West today, the religion that rules over its mind and spirit, is not Christianity but Materialism. Says the author of *Islam at the Crossroads*:

> No doubt, there are still many individuals in the West who feel and think in a religious way and make the most desperate efforts to reconcile their beliefs with the spirit of their civilization, but they are exceptions only. The average Occidental – be he a Democrat or a Fascist, a Capitalist or a Bolshevik, a manual worker or an intellectual – knows only one positive 'religion', and that is the worship of material progress, the belief that there is no other goal in life than to make life continually easier

> or, as the current expression goes, 'independent of nature'. The temples of this 'religion' are the gigantic factories, cinemas, chemical laboratories, dancing halls, hydro-electric works; and its priests are bankers, engineers, film-stars, captains of industry, finance magnates. The unavoidable result of this craving after power and pleasure is the creation of hostile groups armed to the teeth and determined to destroy one another whenever and wherever their respective interests come to a clash. And on the cultural side the result is the creation of a human type whose morality is confined to the question of practical utility alone, and whose highest criterion of good and evil is material success.[172]

Professor C.E.M. Joad cites the following incident as symptomatic of the growing malady of religious disbelief among the young men and women of Europe:

> I recently asked a group of twenty students, young men and women for the most part in their early twenties, how many of them were, in any sense of the word, Christian. Only three said that they were; seven had never thought about the matter one way or the other, while the remaining ten were belligerently anti-Christian. I saw no reason to suppose that the proportion of believers to non-believers indicated by these replies is untypical. Yet fifty or even twenty years ago it would assuredly have been different. Canon Barry's conviction that a Christian revival on a large scale can save the world seems, then, to be shared by a diminishing number of persons, and I can see no reason why Canon Barry should think his opinion to be true, except such as is afforded by his *wish* that it may be true. Now wishes may father thoughts, but they do not breed evidence. I return, then, to the opinion

expressed at the beginning of this article that, so far as present indications go, the Christian Church in this country will, in another hundred years, be to all intents and purposes, dead. Since Christianity is our theme, it will be well to conclude with a parable. I take it from the daily paper:

> 'A fortune is being made by a man of seventy-seven who, after sixteen years of self-imposed poverty, living on £2 a week, has invented and patented a method of turning old Bibles into gun-cotton, artificial silk, cellulose, and expensive note-paper. His machinery has already been installed at a Cardiff factory and at eight others in various parts of the country where modern armaments are being made from ancient Testaments. He that hath ears to hear may hear.'[173]

In another book, Joad says:

> For centuries England has been dominated by the gospel of acquisition. 'Money talks', and the desire for it, has for two hundred years past been a greater spur to effort than all other incentives added together. For money buys possessions, and by the number and grandeur of his possessions a man's merit is chiefly estimated. Politics, literature, the cinema, the radio, even on occasions the pulpit, have poured forth year after year a stream of propaganda devoted to convincing their readers and seers and listeners that a society in which acquisitiveness is the most highly developed of the instincts is a civilized society. The worship of money assorts oddly with our profession of a religion which assures us not only that poverty is good and riches are evil, but that a rich man has as poor a chance of eternal happiness as the poor man

has a good one. Nevertheless, though the dictates of prudence no less than the exhortations of religion unite in recommending poverty to those who would serve God and go to heaven, people have shown no disposition to act as if the exhortations of religion were true, and have been willing and eager to barter their chance of celestial bliss in the future for a sufficiency of worldly goods in the present. Perhaps they have believed that they could make the best of both worlds, and by the timeliness of a death-bed repentance, secure for themselves as much consideration in the next world as their bank balances have obtained for them in this one. Implicitly their view would seem to be that expressed by Samuel Butler in his Note-Books. 'It is all very well for mischievous writers to maintain that we cannot serve God and Mammon. Granted that it is not easy, but nothing that is worth doing is ever easy.'

Whatever we may be in theory, most of us demonstrate by our practice that we are convinced Butlerians. So strong indeed is our addiction to wealth, so confirmed our belief that it is wealth which, above all other things, confers merit upon a man and greatness upon a State, that it has succeeded in inspiring two theories of the greatest historical importance with regard to the nature of the motive force which makes the wheels of the world go round. One of these, *laissez faire* economics, dominated in the nineteenth century. It asserted that men would always act in the way which they considered would conduce to their greatest economic advantage; that, in short, they were inspired by a hedonism not of the passions, but of the pocket. The other, which bids fair to dominate the early part of the twentieth century, is Marx's theory of economic determinism, which insists

> that the way in which, at any given moment, a society organizes its economic system to satisfy its material needs, determines its arts, its ethics, its religion, and even its logic, no less than its form of government. Both these theories derive their greatest plausibility from the value which men and women demonstrably place upon wealth as a criterion of merit in individuals and a sign of greatness in States.[174]

God-Forgetfulness

In the Qur'ān it is said of idolaters and polytheists that they cry out to God for help in adversity. But the godless materialists of the West have lost themselves so completely in material self-satisfaction that it would be futile to expect any such thing from them. In the words of the Holy Qur'ān:

> *And most surely We sent (Apostles) to many nations before thee and We afflicted them with suffering and adversity that they might learn humility. When the suffering reached them from Us, why did they not then practise humility? On the contrary, their hearts became hardened and Satan made their (sinful) acts seem alluring to them.*
>
> al-Anʿām 6:42-3

> *And most surely We inflicted punishment on them, but they humbled not themselves to their Lord, nor did they submissively entreat (Him)!*
>
> al-Mu'minūn 23:76

In times of deep crisis or distress as, for example, in a war, one does not find any trace of religious fear or respect. The intellectual and moral leaders of the West exult in this and call it courage and resoluteness. In the eyes of a Muslim, however, it is sheer spiritual apathy.

An Indian in London in 1940-41, when the Nazi air-offensive was at its peak, painted a graphic picture of the air-raids of those days under the caption "A Night in London" in the following words:

> Being tired of persistent air-raids during the last several days and nights, we were engaged that night in making preparations for a rather lavish Indian-English dinner. The landlady had generously placed the kitchen at our disposal, and the big room on the upper storey had been converted into a ball-room. There were about twenty-five of us in all, both men and women. We did the cooking together. After the meal was over, we began to dance. Then, all of a sudden, the air-raid siren was heard. At first a hush fell over us. 'What now?' one of us asked without interrupting his dance. 'Carry on,' a girl said. And we carried on till, not to speak of the house, the whole locality began to ring with our songs and laughter.[175]

Later in the book he says:

> After a few days, it became a regular practice that the siren went up at about 7 or 8 p.m., the drone of the enemy planes was heard, the searchlights wove a blazing pattern in the sky and the guns began to boom. If a cinema-show happened to be in progress, it used to be stopped for a while and it was flashed on the screen that 'The air-raid has started, but the picture will continue. For those who wish to take shelter, the passage to the left goes down into the basement.' But no one moved from his seat, and the picture was resumed.

Apart from the modern West, such things could only happen in ancient Greece and Rome. It is said that when the city of Pompei was destroyed by the volcano, Vesuvius, it was daytime and the citizens were enjoying gladiatorial games in the amphitheatre when clouds of wet ashes and lava began to descend. Many of them were burnt to death in their seats, and many more were killed in the stampede that followed. Only those were saved who were lucky enough to get away in boats in time. The city lay buried under its lava bed for 1800 years. It was dug out by excavators in the 19th century to serve as a warning to the world. Says the Holy Qur'ān:

> *Or else, did the people of the towns feel secure against the coming of Our wrath in broad daylight while they played about (carefree)?*
>
> al-Aʿrāf 7:98

How different is the case in such situations of God-fearing people can be imagined from the following verse:

> *O ye who believe, when ye meet a force, be firm, and call God in remembrance much (and often) that ye may prosper.*
>
> al-Anfāl 8:45

The Companions of the Holy Prophet ﷺ related that, whenever a distressing circumstance confronted the Prophet, he at once stood up for prayer. When the Battle of Badr was fought, the Prophet ﷺ marshalled his troops, and then he retired to his camp and gave himself up to prayer. "O God," he exclaimed again and again, "O God, if these Believers are destroyed, no one will be left on the earth to worship Thee."[176]

An Easterner's View

One Eastern writer and scholar, ʿAbd-ur-Raḥmān Kawākibī, made a penetrating character-study of Western men in the following passage:

> The Westerner is stubborn, hard-hearted and materialistic. He is malicious, selfish and vindictive. It would appear that nothing of the lofty idealism of Oriental Christianity is now left with him. Take, for instance, the German. You will find him dry and rude. He believes that the weak has no right to exist. Power is the sole criterion of greatness with him, and the source of all power is wealth. Learning he does value, honour he does admire, but only for the sake of the wealth they bring in. The Greek and the Italian are selfish and libertine by nature. With them, intellect means freedom, life means shamelessness and prestige means the capacity to show off and to domineer.[177]

Materialism in Spiritualism

Materialism has so ceaselessly absorbed the attention and the will of Western people that even their spiritual activities are tinged with it. The modern movement for investigating the spiritualistic phenomena and holding communication with the dead is wholly materialistic in its conception. It is being worked out as a material science and an industrial enterprise. Unlike Islamic spiritualism or Eastern mysticism, it has nothing to do with spiritual uplift – with things like self-purification, piety and preparation for the After-life.

All the endeavours in the West, thus, are guided solely by considerations of power, pride and glory. The idea of Divine approval has no place in their calculations, while it is the very basis of a Muslim's thought and action. A civilization of the Western type can only be a deadly poison for those human values held dear by a Muslim. A thing to be proud of in the West is something to be shunned by a follower of Islam. Says the Holy Qur'ān:

> *Say: 'Shall we tell you of those who lost most in respect of their deeds – those whose efforts have been wasted in this life, while they thought their works to be an achievement? They are those*

who deny the Signs of their Lord and the fact of their having to meet Him (in the Hereafter). Vain will be their works, nor shall We, on the Day of Judgement, give them any weight.
al-Kahf 18:103-5

And We shall turn to whatever deeds they did (in this life), and We shall make such deeds as floating dust scattered about.
al-Furqān 25:23

Once the Prophet ﷺ was asked who among the following three persons would be considered a fighter in God's way – a man who fought under the impulse of his strength, or the one who fought in defence of his honour, or the other who fought for fame? The Prophet replied that a war in God's way is the one which is waged to make God's Word dominant. Those who were conscious of the real importance of this took great pains to conceal their virtuous and kindly deeds from public knowledge and even then they were haunted by a constant fear of hypocrisy. It was a favourite prayer of ʿUmar, may Allah be pleased with him: "O God, make all my acts pure; let them be for Thy sake alone; and allow not anyone beside Thee to have a share in them."

Economic Pantheism

Karl Marx is one example of the total immersion of the Western mind in materialism. He developed the doctrine of class struggle to maintain that all history was merely the result of economic conditions, under whose influence all other life-phenomena had received form and imprint. He recognized only the economic aspect of human existence, denying the validity of other factors such as religion, ethics, soul and intellect. All wars of history, he said, all insurrections and revolutions, were nothing but the endeavours of the smaller and the emptier stomach to have its revenge on the larger and the fuller one. Even religious wars, one could justifiably conclude from this, were caused by economic motives and those who waged them were moved by no higher sentiment than to establish a better order of production and distribution of wealth. This economic "pantheism" recognizes no holy wars, no religious endeavours and no spiritual movements.

Nothing Exists Except Sex and Hunger

The outlook on life in the East being basically spiritualistic, there have been instances of mystics raising the cry of "nothing exists but God" in moments of spiritual ecstasy. The spirit of the West is dominated by materialism. When its thinkers are in an exalted state, they reject everything that does not have a direct bearing on economic materialism and cry out: "Nothing exists but sex and hunger." The mystics of the East regarded man as the "Shadow of God upon earth". Overwhelmed by this notion some declared: "I am God." Conversely, the materialists of the West do not credit man with anything higher than an animal existence.

The Darwinian Theory of Evolution

In the 19th century, conclusions were arrived at in Europe which encouraged an animal approach to human problems. In 1859, Charles Darwin published his *The Origin of Species* to show that man was an evolved animal who had attained his present form after passing through various stages, including those of the amoeba on the lowest and of the ape on the other end of the scale in the long process of life's evolution. The book caught the attention of the whole of Europe. It revolutionized the scientific approach to man's problems, and gave powerful support to the view that the universe was functioning without the direction or supervision of a supernatural power, there being nothing behind its visible framework except the soulless law of Nature. In the words of C.E.M. Joad:

> It is difficult for us to realise the sense of shock with which the publication of Darwin's *Origin of Species*, and the evidence upon which his conclusions were based, affected our fathers. Darwin had shown, or at least was

> thought to have shown, that the process of life's evolution upon this planet had been continuous from its earliest beginnings in the amoeba and the jelly-fish right up to its most highly developed forms. We were its most highly developed forms. Therefore the process of development from the amoeba to ourselves was continuous and unbroken. Now the Victorians had been led to believe that man was a special creation, that he was, in fact, a degenerate angel; whereas if Darwin were right, he was only a promoted ape.[178]

In spite of the awkward predicament in which the Darwinian theory placed mankind, and its conceptual and historical fallacies, it made a deep impression on the Western mind, probably because the Western mind had already been brought into a receptive state. Nudism and other Western movements for a return to nature are all the direct consequences of the view that man is, after all, an elevated animal.

The Growth of Nationalism

It has already been pointed out that a narrow national feeling, racial prejudice and an exaggerated regard for geographical division are the characteristics of the Western mind which has been transmitted steadily from one generation to another. Although by the time Christianity arrived in Europe, when the teachings of Jesus Christ had become changed, they still bore the imprint of the great master and carried within them the characteristics of a revealed religion. No religion, however debased it may be, can ever allow the barriers of race or colour to be erected within the organic unity of humanity. It had, therefore, striven to unite the different nations of Europe into a single family under the protection of the Church. But when Martin Luther started the Reformation in the 16th century and unscrupulously made use of German nationalism as a major weapon in his fight against the Church, the unifying force that held together the various peoples in Christendom was broken and they began to be increasingly separated from one another. The weaker the hold of Christianity became, the stronger grew the influence of Nationalism in Europe, as if Christianity and Nationalism were the two sides of a balance: the more one of them went up, the more the other came down. As Lord Lothian stated:

> Europe once had the same kind of cultural and religious unity as India in the earlier days of Christianity. But when in the 15th century the new learning of the Renaissance and the new movement for religious reform known as the Reformation began, because it had no constitutional unity, Europe fell into pieces and has since then remained divided into those national sovereign states whose strife and wars are not only the ruin of Europe itself, but the principal threat to the peace of the world.

Furthermore, he says:

> The decline in the authority of religion, the indispensable guide of man, the one source which can give more purpose and nobility and meaning to life of man, explains, at least in part, why the Western World has given its allegiance in the recent decades to new political gospels based on race or class, or has pinned its faith on a form of science which admittedly is almost wholly concerned with advance in the material plane, with making life more rather than less expensive and complicated. And it explains, also in part, why Europe finds it so difficult to attain to that unity in spirit and life which would enable it to rise above the spirit of exclusive and militant nationalism which is its principal bane today.[179]

Immediately, then, Europe built a barrier between itself and the rest of the world, with the nations that fell on its side of the barrier constituting the elite of humanity. It was completely in conformity with the practice of the ancient Greeks and Romans who regarded only themselves as civilized and everybody else, and particularly those living to the east of the Mediterranean, as barbarians.

Separate Worlds

The nationalist states of Europe have organized themselves into many separate "worlds", walled in by the frontiers of politics, race and geography. They have made gods of themselves and demanded the same adoration and loyalty from their citizens as is due to the Creator alone. They are above and beyond everything. All living and dying must be for them alone. If need be, lives must be blindly sacrificed at their altars. To every nationalist his own state is God's most noble creation on earth and all else is rubbish.

Nationalism brings forth the same fruit everywhere. It is impossible for a people to be imbued with nationalism and not have an aggressive nature. The leadership of such peoples invariably passes into the hands which know of no religious or moral control and have no object before them other than the enhancement of national prestige. In such states the recollection of vanished glory and past greatness is shamelessly employed to feed the nation's conceit; and philosophy, literature and even the physical sciences are converted into instruments for strengthening the national will.

Hatred and Fear

Hatred and fear are the essential ingredients of modern nationalism. To arouse the national sentiment in a people it is necessary to provide them with something they can hate and someone they can fear. Joad analysed this so beautifully in the following passage:

> Now the emotions which most men have in common and which are, therefore, the most easily aroused, are those of hatred and fear. It is by such emotions and not by compassion, charity, generosity, or love that great masses of men are most easily moved...those who wish to

> rule the nation for whatever purpose, will do well to find something to hate, somebody to fear. If I really wanted to unite the nations of the modern world, I should invent for them an enemy in some other planet, or possibly on the moon.
>
> It is not surprising, then, that the Nationalist states of the modern world should be chiefly guided by the emotions of hatred and fear in their dealings with their neighbours, since it is upon these emotions that their governors thrive, and by them that unity is strengthened.[180]

Islam is against the philosophy of national separatism and selfishness as it has no regard for truth and stands bluntly for "my nation, right or wrong". In the structure of the Qur'ānic thought, considerations of descent or national adherence have no place. Islam rejects every alignment, friendship or loyalty which has its source in national or party spirit. To illustrate this principle the Prophet ﷺ very pointedly said:

> He is not one of us who proclaims the cause of tribal partisanship; and he is not one of us who fights in the cause of tribal partisanship; and he is not one of us who dies for the sake of tribal partisanship.[181]

He who dies fighting for a national or partisan cause dies a heathen's death,[182] and is reported to have been declared by the Holy Prophet ﷺ to be outside the pale of Islam. In another *ḥadīth* the Prophet is reported to have declared: "Whoever fights under a flag in support of a partisan cause or in answer to a call of a partisan cause or to help a partisan cause and is then killed, his death is a death in the cause of Ignorance."[183] Similarly, "He who is killed (while fighting) under a flag supporting a partisan cause, or is killed in a fight in support of a partisan cause, is not one of my people."[184]

Islam recognizes only two broad divisions of mankind, one

comprising those who are the true servants of God and the champions of Truth, and the other comprising those who are followers of the Devil and the champions of falsehood. Islam declares itself to be at war with all those who form the latter division, no matter to what nationality or race they belong, as enmity or warfare in Islam is not governed by national or political considerations, but by the considerations of truth and righteousness.

The Weaker Nations

The supporters of nationalism promote the sentiment of nationalism in the smaller and weaker nations until they begin to burst with national pride. Such nations develop on nationalist lines with no extra-territorial alignments. Ultimately, these nations are devoured by a greater power while the world looks on. The story of the destruction of the Central European nations in the last war is well known. It is much regretted that the countries of the Islamic world, which possess a message that cuts across the conventional divisions of politics and blood and is universal in its scope and possesses an ideology which is far more dynamic, are also being overcome with national feeling. It is doubtful if, weak and ill-equipped as these countries are, they will be able to survive an onslaught from outside.

National Prestige

The prestige of the modern nationalist states requires that they should hold under their sway large parts of the world, possess extensive sources of revenue and be in a position to enforce their will on neighbouring states and to terrorize and overawe their rivals. In such states faithful citizens feel a false sense of pride in the superiority of their own culture and traditions and they develop a contempt for the cultures and traditions of all other nations, and are ready and willing at all times to commit the most detestable crimes and barbaric acts at the bidding of their leaders. The moral calibre of such a nation may be extremely low, its citizens may be utterly devoid of moral sense and human dignity and may not be following any moral code, yet such a nation is deemed fit to be respected as a great nation. Joad observed that:

> ...national greatness and prestige mean in effect the wielding of sufficient power to enable one, if necessary, to enforce one's will upon others. The fact that the prestige of a nation has no relation to moral qualities should in itself constitute a sufficient condemnation of the ideal which nationalism enshrines. If a country merely tells the truth, its prestige is low. Prestige, in fact, depends upon what Mr Baldwin has called 'the strength to command respect and attention', in other words, on high explosives and incendiary bombs and the patriotic loyalty of the young men who will be willing to drop them on cities and civilian populations. Thus the prestige for which a nation is admired stands for precisely the reverse of the qualities for which an individual is admired. This being so, the possession of prestige should, I suggest, disqualify a power from being considered civilized in proportion to the amount of prestige possessed. It is not admirable to be able to command respect by the power of blackmail.[185]

Enlightenment or Trade

Godless states are, in fact, trade societies or cartels whose real job is to extort, not to confer, benefits. They have no spiritual roots, no ethical ideals, and they are supremely unconcerned with the inner selves of their peoples and the welfare of humanity at large. Their attention is focused only on material gain. Whenever there is a clash between morality and economic gain, these states will always give preference to the latter.

Vulgar and immoral practices are not criminal offences in such states. The duty of their law is to regulate evil, not to check it. Prostitution is, for example, a legal trade; usury is practised by governments; gambling flourishes under respectable names; alcohol is freely available and the industry is extolled as a source of national wealth. Radio, cinema and television function solely as an instrument of entertainment. Instead of educating the masses and refining them morally, it perverts their tastes and makes them frivolous. Official censorship is extremely sensitive where political or administrative interests are involved, but when it comes to ethical and moral questions, it becomes lethargic and accommodating. Pornographic and other worthless literature invades and plagues the public mind but the machinery of government moves only rarely against it. Along with its morals, the health of the nation also plummets. Shops are flooded with spurious sex-stimulants, "pick-me-ups", preservers of youthful vigour and restorers of lost vitality. Their manufacturers remain at liberty by bribing government officials or by making lavish contributions to the funds of the party in power. All this happens because the pivot of state activity in these countries is not religion, but material prosperity.

On the other hand, those states which have as their goal the teachings of the prophets of God operate as organizations for enlightenment and moral uplift. It is worth remembering that when a complaint was made to Caliph ʿUmar ibn ʿAbdul ʿAzīz that the revenues of the Empire had decreased as a result of the reforms he had introduced, he retorted that the Holy Prophet ﷺ had been sent into the world as a guide and not as a tax-collector. In that brief sentence, the Caliph summed up the entire philosophy of a religious state.

In a religious state the stress lies on the moral and spiritual welfare of the people. Taxes and imposts have their value, but only as a means of promoting the true development of citizens and keeping the machinery of the state in good order. They have no other value. In such states political and economic questions are examined from the standpoint of religion and no second thoughts are entertained about subordinating material interests to spiritual needs. Usury, gambling, adultery, fornication and other perverse and shameless acts, along with their incentives and inducements, have no chance of making an appearance within their frontiers. All items of individual gain which are harmful to the larger interests of society are prohibited, regardless of the loss it may entail for the state coffers. Programmes of reform in such states have an eye not only on the improvement of the outward conduct and on raising the standard of living of the people, but also on improving their inner thoughts and impulses, because it is utterly impossible to improve the standards of behaviour in a people and to create real happiness among them without inculcating proper moral sentiments. Thus, religious states place restrictions on all things that encourage unhealthy desires and condemn those as public enemies who incite licentiousness and sinfulness through art or industry. This is so because these states regard themselves not as policemen but as the guardians of people's morals and well-being. Says the Holy Qur'ān:

> *(They are) those who, if We establish them in the land, establish regular prayer and give regular charity, enjoin right and forbid wrong; with God rests the end (and decision) of (all) affairs.*
>
> al-Ḥajj 22:41

The Difference Between Trade and Ethics

The modern "get-rich-quick" age has inspired a fierce race for money-making with the result that shops and stores are filled with fancy goods and gadgets irrespective of the purchasing capacity of the consumers or the social and moral effects on them. The shops present a brilliant spectacle of garments, shoes and luxury goods of the latest designs. Then, suddenly, these things go out of fashion and their place is taken by new arrivals, most of which are, in fact, the same goods with a few alterations. Standards of prosperity and elegance change from day to day. The material amenities of life keep on increasing, but this does not increase ease or happiness in life, as the cost of living, too, increases with greater speed. What was a comfortable income yesterday is totally insufficient today. Contentment has become a meaningless word. The soul of man is unhappy. The existing social environment demands everyone to consider it a religious obligation to attain the highest standard of living. Modern man plunges into the task with all his heart but when, after a lifetime of struggle, the goal seems to have come within the range of realization, it rises to a higher level. This has reduced life to an absurd enterprise. The spirit of man is decaying. There is little lasting happiness or peace in the world. Homes which could have been havens of peace are virtual hell-spots on earth due to the lack of this or that imaginary requisite of happiness. Is the above picture any different from that of ancient Rome?

Scientific Progress

There has been stupendous scientific and technological progress in modern times. We propose now to examine this progress from a different point of view – from the point of view of man – and see how far the environment which science and technology have succeeded in creating for him is suited to his genius.

The Islamic View

Muslims believe that the real purpose of science is to remove obstacles in the way of true development of man's personality by using the latent forces in nature in such a way as to broaden life and make it rich in all its aspects.

In pre-historic times man travelled on foot. Then he learnt to make use of the beasts of burden; later he invented the cart. But man has a restless soul. He is never satisfied with his situation and is always striving to make himself more and more comfortable. As his needs multiplied, his standards of comfort and pace of life also changed. Better and quicker modes of transport were devised till the steamship replaced the sailing vessel on the sea and marvels of speed and efficiency were invented for travel by land and air. If these inventions are used as a means to a good life, they are a blessing of God. The Holy Qur'ān has described as "a bounty from our Lord" the advantage man enjoys over other creatures in travel:

> *And cattle He has created for you (men); from them ye derive warmth, and numerous benefits, and of their (meat) ye eat. And ye have a sense of beauty in them as ye drive them home in the evening, and as ye lead them forth to pasture in the morning.*

And they carry your heavy loads to lands that ye could not (otherwise) reach except with souls distressed; for your Lord is indeed Most Kind, Most Merciful. And (He has created) horses, mules, and donkeys for you to ride and use for show; and He has created (other) things of which ye have no knowledge.

al-Naḥl 16:5-8

We have honoured the sons of Adam; and We have provided them with transport on land and sea; and We have given them for sustenance things good and pure; and We have conferred on them special favours, above a great part of our creation.

al-Isrā' 17:70

And He it is that has created pairs in all things, and has made for you ships and cattle on which ye ride, in order that ye may sit firm on their backs, and when so seated, ye may celebrate the (Kind) Favour of your Lord, and say, 'Glory to Him Who has subjected these to our (use), for we could never have accomplished this (by ourselves), and to our Lord, surely, must we turn back.'

Zukhruf 43:12-14

And to Sulaiman (We made) the wind (obedient); its early morning (stride) was a month's (journey) and its evening (stride) was a month's (journey).

Sabā' 34:12

Then We subjected the Wind to his power, to flow gently to his order, withersoever he willed.

Ṣād 38:36

There is a profound difference between the approach of a believer and that of a non-believer to these gifts. When a believer makes use of them, he does so with a strong feeling of humility, because he knows that it is only the Mercy of God that has enslaved the free, high-spirited animals and the inert steel and wood to his will; otherwise, he himself was helpless. Says the Holy Qur'ān:

> *In order that ye may celebrate the (Kind) Favour of your Lord, and say, 'Glory to Him Who has subjected these to our (use), for we could never have accomplished this (by ourselves).'*
>
> Zukhruf 43:13

The believer also knows that there will come a day when he will be called on to answer for the uses to which he put his powers and opportunities. "*And to our Lord, surely, must we turn back*" (Holy Qur'ān, Zukhruf 43:14).

The words of the Prophet Sulaiman عليه السلام are:

> *This is by the Grace of my Lord; to test me whether I am grateful or ungrateful; and if any is grateful, truly his gratitude is (a gain) for his own soul; but if any is ungrateful, truly my Lord is free of all needs, Supreme in Honour.*
>
> Holy Qur'ān, al-Naml 27:40

A believer makes the most appropriate use of his own capabilities and the power of nature. He uses them in the path of Faith, Righteousness and Truth which is the true purpose of their creation:

> *And We sent down Iron in which is (material for) mighty war, as well as many benefits for mankind that God may also test who it is that will help Him, and His Apostles, Unseen, for God is Strong, Mighty.*
>
> Holy Qur'ān, al-Ḥadīd 57:25

He who has faith in God and fears Him can never be a supporter of wrong. In the words of Moses: "*O my Lord, for that Thou hast bestowed Thy Grace on me, never shall I be a help to those who sin*" (Holy Qur'ān, al-Qaṣaṣ 28:17).

In short, true Faith alone teaches man not to be conceited or wasteful by impressing upon him that he is only the trustee and not the owner of the treasures that are lying scattered everywhere in the universe, the Creator and Lord Sovereign of them all being God alone, to whom he is responsible for the way he exploits and makes use of them.

The Holy Qur'ān mentions a number of instances to emphasize the different attitudes adopted by godly and ungodly people in respect of worldly wealth. On the one hand, there is the Prophet Yusuf عليه السلام bursting into lofty words of gratitude at the height of his worldly glory:

> *O my Lord, Thou hast indeed bestowed on me some power, and taught me something of the interpretation of dreams and events. O Thou Creator of the heavens and the earth, Thou art my Protector in this world and in the Hereafter. Take Thou my soul (at death) as one submitting to Thy Will (as a Muslim) and unite me with the righteous.*
>
> Yūsuf 12:101

And when Sulaiman عليه السلام beheld his own resplendent majesty, the following words of thanksgiving sprang spontaneously from his pious lips:

> *O my Lord, so order me that I may be grateful for Thy favours, which Thou has bestowed on me and on my parents, and that I may work the righteousness that will please Thee; and admit me, by Thy Grace, to the ranks of Thy righteous servants.*
>
> al-Naml 27:19

On the other hand, those who were devoid of Faith were so overcome by their own power and wealth that they insolently refused to acknowledge anyone as superior to or more powerful than themselves:

> *Now the ᶜĀd behaved arrogantly through the land against (all) truth and reason, and said: 'Who is superior to us in strength?' What! Did they not see that God, Who created them, was Superior to them in strength? But they continued to reject Our Signs!*
>
> Fuṣṣilat 41:15

One such man was Qārūn (Korah), who was one of the richest men of ancient times. When his people said to him:

> *Exult not, for God loveth not those who exult (in riches). But seek, with the (wealth) which God has bestowed on thee, the Home of the Hereafter, not forgetting thy portion in this world; but do thou good, as God has been good to thee, and seek not (occasions for) mischief in the land; for God loveth not those who do mischief.*
>
> al-Qaṣaṣ 28:76, 77

He replied that his riches were the fruits of his own labour and intelligence and he was not indebted to anyone.

The consciousness of one's own powers and the haughty denial of the Eternal, the Supreme, as having authority over man and nature alike breed a madness which no canons of morality and no considerations of humanitarianism can control or cure. It is really and truly essential to the growth of peace and happiness that knowledge, power and wealth should be rigidly kept under the ceaseless control of religion.

The Disparity Between Power and Morality

Since the Renaissance the conquest of the material world has been extremely rapid, and the spiritual world has fallen into oblivion with an almost equal rapidity. This has given rise to a generation that looks almost superhuman insofar as its power over matter is concerned, but is not very much superior to the beasts when judged with reference to its own inner state. With all the means of a good life at its command, it does not know how to live. It is narrow and selfish. It cannot distinguish between the primary and the secondary qualities of things, and is unworthy of the power it has come to acquire over matter. In the words of Joad, "Science has given us powers fit for the gods, and to their use we bring the mentality of schoolboys and savages."[186] Joad says further:

> This contrast between the marvels of our scientific achievements and the ignorance of our social childishness meets us at every turn. We can talk across continents and oceans, wire pictures, install television sets and satellite dishes in homes, listen in Ceylon to Big Ben striking in London, ride above and beneath the earth and the sea. Children can talk along wires, typewriters are silent, teeth-filling painless, liners have swimming-baths, crops are ripened by electricity, roads are made of rubber, X-rays are the windows through which we view our insides, photographs can speak and sing, murderers can be tracked down by wireless, hair is waved by electric current, submarines go to the North Pole, aeroplanes to the South…Yet, we cannot, in the midst of our enormous cities, provide a little space where poor children might play in comfort and safety…As an Indian philosopher once said to me: "…Yes, you can fly in the air like birds and swim in the sea like fishes; but how to walk upon the earth you do not yet know."[187]

Commenting in the same vein on the catastrophic results of the enormous advantages gained by the sciences of inanimate matter over those of living things, another Western writer, Alexis Carrel, the Nobel prize-winning French Surgeon, observes:

> In truth, modern life has set them [people] free. It incites them to acquire wealth by any and every means,

> provided that these means do not lead them to jail...It allows them to frequent excitation and the easy satisfaction of their sexual appetites. It does away with constraint, discipline, effort, everything that is inconvenient and laborious.[188]

And again:

> Modern civilization seems to be incapable of producing people endowed with imagination, intelligence and courage. In practically every country there is a decrease in the intellectual and moral calibre of those who carry the responsibility of public affairs. The financial, industrial and commercial organizations have reached a gigantic size. They are influenced not only by the conditions of the country where they are established, but also by the state of the neighbouring countries and of the entire world. In all nations, economic and social conditions undergo extremely rapid changes. Nearly everywhere the existing form of government is again under discussion. The great democracies find themselves face to face with formidable problems – problems concerning their very existence and demanding an immediate solution. And we realise that, despite the immense hopes which humanity has placed in modern civilization, such a civilization has failed in developing men of sufficient intelligence and audacity to guide it along the dangerous road on which it is stumbling. Human beings have not grown so rapidly as the institutions sprung from their brains. It is chiefly the intellectual and moral deficiencies of the political leaders, and their ignorance, which endanger modern nations.[189]

Thus, it appears that the environment, which science and technology have succeeded in developing for man, does not suit him because it has been constructed at random, without regard for his true self.[190]

The environment born of our intelligence and our inventions is adjusted neither to our stature nor to our shape. We are unhappy. We degenerate morally and mentally. The groups and nations in which industrial civilization has attained its highest development are precisely those which are becoming weaker and whose return to barbarism is the most rapid. But they do not realise it. They are without protection against the hostile surroundings that science has built around them. In truth, our civilization, like those preceding it, has created certain conditions of existence which, for reasons still obscure, render life itself impossible. The anxiety and the woes of the inhabitants of the modern city arise from their political, economic and social institutions but, above all, from their own weakness. We are the victims of the backwardness of the sciences of life over those of matter.[191]

No advantage is to be gained by increasing the number of mechanical inventions. It would perhaps be as well not to accord so much importance to discoveries of physics, astronomy and chemistry...What is the good of increasing the comfort, the luxury, the beauty, the size and the complications of our civilization, if our weakness prevents us from guiding it to our best advantage? It is really not worthwhile to go on elaborating a way of living that is bringing about the demoralization and the disappearance of the noblest elements of the great races. It would be far better to pay more attention to ourselves than to construct faster steamers, more comfortable automobiles, cheaper radios or telescope for examining

> the structure of remote nebulae...There is not the shadow of a doubt that mechanical, physical and chemical sciences are incapable of giving us intelligence, moral discipline, health, nervous equilibrium, security and peace.[192]

Misuse of Scientific Inventions

Scientific inventions are in themselves neither good nor bad. They are rendered good or bad by the use to which we put them.

Material well-being and power and prestige, having grown to be the most desirable things in life in the West, all the resources of mind and matter are there directed pitilessly towards inventing means and ways which can secure the realization of these objectives with the utmost ease and speed. Gradually, the means have become an end in themselves. Europeans have developed a childish fancy for machines and have in a thousand ways delegated to them the very functions of living.

Only half a century ago, comfort was regarded by the Europeans as the *sine qua non* of progress. Then, due to various reasons, the emphasis was shifted to speed and now everyone is compulsively seeking it. To quote Joad again:

> Disraeli remarked of his contemporaries that they talked of progress because 'by the aid of a few scientific discoveries, they have succeeded in establishing a society which mistakes comfort for civilization'. To adapt Disraeli's remark to ourselves, we might merely substitute 'speed' for 'comfort'. Indeed, it might in truth be said that the ability to change the position of his body on the surface of the earth with ever-increasing speed is probably the most concrete conception of Utopia that the mind of the contemporary young person is capable of entertaining. Speed, indeed, is his peculiar god, and upon its altar, quiet, comfort, security and consideration for other persons are ruthlessly jettisoned.[193]

Have the contemporary achievements of science brought man nearer to fulfilment of the purposes and ends of his life? Does modern man, with all his power over nature, find himself in a happier position than those who lived, let us say, a couple of centuries ago? For the answers to these questions, we turn once again to Joad, who says:

> We are enabled to travel very fast from place to place, but places to which we travel are diminishingly worth travelling to. Distances are destroyed and nations brought to one another's doorsteps, with the result that international relations were rarely worse, and the strains and stresses engendered by these new facilities for knowing our neighbours bid fair to engulf our world in war. The invention of broadcasting has enabled us to speak to the neighbouring nations, with the result that each nation exhausts the resources of the air in irritating its neighbours, by attempting to convince them of the superiority of its form of government to theirs.[194]

> Look at that aeroplane humming across the summer sky; the knowledge of mathematics, of dynamics and mechanics, the familiarity with electricity and internal combustion, the ingenuity in the application of knowledge, the skill in the working of woods and metals that have gone into its making, are such as to suggest that its inventors were supermen. The intrepidity, resolution, and courage which were shown by the early flying men were the qualities of heroes. Now consider the purposes for which the modern aeroplane has been and seems increasingly again to be used – to drop bombs to shatter and choke, burn and poison and dismember defenceless people...; these, one feels, are the purposes of idiots or devils.

> Let us consider how our treatment of the metal, gold, will strike the future historian. He will describe how we had learnt to signal for gold by wireless telegraphy. He will reproduce photographs showing the ingenious contrivances by which bankers weighed and counted it. He will dwell on the daily miracle by which we defied gravitation as we transported it from capital to capital; and he will then have to record how these semi-savages, skilful and daring as they were in their mechanical triumphs, were so incapable of slight efforts at international co-operation which the control of gold demanded that, having acquired the metal, their sole concern was to bury it again as quickly as possible. Thus, the operations of international finance would appear to him as a process whereby, with infinite cost and labour, men extracted metal from the bowels of the earth in South Africa in order that they might re-bury it in the vaults of London, New York and Paris.[195]

The Destructive Nature of Scientific Inventions

Western people are so preoccupied with the pleasures of the senses that they have lost all regard for mental and spiritual needs. Irresponsible literature and erroneous philosophical concepts have perverted their minds as the most wholesome food turns into poison in an unhealthy stomach; their clever scientific achievements have become in their hands a curse, not only for themselves but for the whole world. It was remarked by Sir Anthony Eden in the course of a speech during the last World War that:

> Unless something can be done the people of this world, in the latter part of this century, are going to live as troglodytes [cave people] and go back to the days of cave-dwelling. It is fantastic that all countries are now spending millions on protecting themselves against a

> weapon of which they are all afraid, but on the control of which they cannot agree. I sometimes wonder how the world to-day would strike a visitor from another planet, who would find us preparing the means for our own destruction and even exchanging information on how we are to do it.[196]

When Eden spoke these words, he could scarcely have imagined that science, freed from the control of religion, would, within the course of that very war, perfect the technique of genocide to a degree that would stagger even its most fanatical enthusiasts.

After years of intense toil and after spending immense amounts of money, the United States, at last, succeeded in manufacturing the dreadful atomic bomb. Its destructive power and range of effect were first tested at 5.30 a.m. on July 16, 1945, on a lifeless steel tower and an unfeeling atmosphere. Then the second experiment was made on the living enemy. On August 6, 1945, the Japanese town of Hiroshima was blasted out of existence. With the thunderous intensity of the explosion and the heat and the heavy pressure of the atmosphere, the whole town was instantaneously reduced to a heap of debris. Within a few minutes the explosion sent a mountain of smoke rising high into the air, beneath which raged a terrific fire.[197]

Of the deadly after-effects of the atomic bomb, Stuart Guilder writes:

> It is now clear that, although they did not know beforehand what the detailed results would be, the atomic scientists did know that they were deliberately using a weapon the secondary effects of which might leave mankind itself without defence against extermination. These are being described by reporters in Hiroshima as 'Atomic Plague'. Victims apparently untouched by blast or heat have died and are continuing to die through disintegration of their blood. First their white and then

> their red corpuscles disappear, their hair falls out and they perish by rotting to pieces as they live. This appears to be due to radioactive substances which are released into the atmosphere when the explosion occurs and are absorbed through the skin or breathed into the lungs.

Guilder goes on to say:

> This news is shocking and horrifying for the whole world which did not know that such a bomb existed and is still ignorant of the properties of radioactive metals. But it was well known to the scientists more than 30 years go that the most fearful feature of this bomb was that there would be no remedy for its fearful effects and that it would be destructive for the whole of humanity.
>
> It has been reported that in an attempt to protect themselves, the Japanese survivors have been wearing home-made masks. Apparently these masks are the same as are worn by the Japanese to protect themselves from the effects of severe cold. They are, of course, as useless as the wet pieces of cloth which some of the Abyssinian soldiers had wrapped round their noses to ward off the effects of poisonous gases sprayed by Mussolini's bombers.

Another report says:

> Air crews of Super-fortresses which made the atomic assaults on Japan reported that after the fall of the bomb dust and smoke rose nine miles into the air. It was propelled by a most tremendous force. Prof. Plesch suggests that there should be careful scientific checks on the condition of the people living as far as 100 miles from the point of the explosion to discover whether they have

absorbed, through inhalation or other means, any of the radio-active gases given off from particles of dust.

It would not be surprising if the world may waken one grim morning to hear the news that people living thousands of miles away from Japan are developing symptoms of atomic plague. If the effects of the atom-bombing of Japan are to deter the world from war, then the world must know all the facts of its effects as quickly and in as much detail as possible. If a small atom bomb propels poisonous dust nine miles into the air, then it is reasonable to suppose that a bigger one will propel it higher and scatter it over a far wider area.[198]

VI

MANKIND'S REAL LOSS UNDER WESTERN DOMINATION

We will not speak now of the grievous material losses the Eastern countries have suffered since the rise of the West. We will speak only of the real – the moral and spiritual – losses of mankind as a whole. In this regrettable development of history the greatest losers have been the followers of Islam. Their philosophy of life was radically opposed to Western ideas and way of life. With the domination of the new barbarism, therefore, it was but natural that they should suffer the greatest loss.

Absence of a Spiritual Sense

The Oriental character has always tended towards the spiritual. Since time began thousands of questions have entered the mind of the Easterner. What is the end of this world? Is there life after death? Where should one look for guidance regarding the After-life? What is the secret of eternal happiness? The Easterner never failed to take note of these questions, not even on occasions of his deepest absorption in secular needs and interests. He gave them an unqualified priority in the manifold occupations of his life. During the whole course of his intellectual and cultural endeavours he kept himself steadily engaged in finding satisfactory solutions to them. His asceticism, his philosophy, his metaphysics, his mysticism were all directed towards it. Sometimes this quest took him along wrong paths. Sometimes he erred and stumbled. But he never shut his ears to the voice of his soul.

Questions relating to spiritual truths arose in Europe before the Renaissance, but as the innate character of its civilization gradually unfolded and the West got lost in the adoration of its material achievements, they were disregarded. If one still hears of them, it is only as problems of metaphysics. They do not occupy any place in practical life. The anxiety, the solicitude, the uneasiness which for thousands of years these questions evoked in the East is not at all felt in the West. And this is so, not because the soul of the West has become illumined with Divine truth or that peace has dawned upon it. The surroundings that the West has succeeded in creating for itself are not related to the Eternal and the Infinite; they have imprisoned man in the world of matter and the West has made him forgetful of his true self.

The fundamental psychological difference, therefore, between an Easterner of earlier times and a modern Westerner is that, while the former possessed a keen and quick spiritual instinct, the latter lost it in the process of his evolution. When a person loses any one of his senses, he loses the consciousness of all things the knowledge of which is dependent on it. One who loses the sense of hearing, for example, becomes insensitive to sound and the whole world of songs and sweet melodies is dead for him. Similarly, one who is devoid of the sense of religion is dead to all feelings and sensations that arise out of religious faith. Things like Futurity, Resurrection, Divine Pleasure and Salvation have no meaning for him.

Religious preachers have, in all ages, encountered the stiffest opposition from people who were devoid of religious feelings. Such people made fun of even the prophets of God. They listened to their soul-warming sermons and said: "*There is nothing except our life on this earth, and never shall we be raised up again*" (Holy Qur'ān, al-Anʿām 6:29).

In the modern age there has appeared a class of people in every community whose material cravings and worldly occupations have ejected religion from the domain of practical calculations. The hearts of such people are adamant and their minds sealed against truths. However hard a religious preacher may try, he does not find an opening through which to reach the inner depths of their souls. Those who have had occasion to preach among them have come to appreciate the real significance of many verses of the Holy Qur'ān, such as: "*God hath set a seal on their hearts and their hearing, and over their eyes is a veil*" (al-Baqarah 2:7), and their difficulties in respect of them would have been removed. The Qur'ānic truth, "*The parable of those who reject faith is as if one were to shout like a goat-herd, to things that listen to nothing except calls and cries; deaf, dumb and blind, they are devoid of wisdom*" (al-Baqarah 2:171), would have presented itself before them in flesh and blood.

Most of the evils of the modern age come from this indifference to religion. The propagation of religion was far easier in the days of open and violent opposition than in the current atmosphere of quiet disinterestedness. One may put one's very heart into one's preaching, but when the inner selves of the listeners have become paralyzed, they cannot be moved to realize the beauties of Divine Revelation.

Lack of a God-Seeking Spirit

We have already seen widespread longing for Truth during the days of Islamic rule. It was customary then to undertake long and arduous journeys in the search for spiritual guides. These guides, who later came to be known as "Mashā'ikh" and "Sufis", kept the spirit of God-seeking alive even after the world of Islam had fallen on evil days. Their abodes functioned as islands of celestial bliss in an ever-growing ocean of materialism. The presence of such men in any society is the standard by which we can judge the strength of religious consciousness in it. Among the Muslims, in particular, the way they turn towards the saints and "sufis" in their midst is a sure indication of the extent of their moral and spiritual awareness.

In former times, in nearly all important towns in the Islamic world, there were men who were actually beacons of spiritual light; Muslims were drawn to them from every corner like moths to a lamp. The subcontinent, situated as it is on the fringe of the Islamic world, has itself been a great centre of religious endeavour. Independent seats of spiritual power existed here side by side with powerful kingdoms throughout the course of Muslim rule. The spiritual settlement of

Niẓāmuddīn Auliyā', Ghayāthpur, offers an admirable illustration of it. Situated in the capital city of Delhi, it maintained its independence through the reigns of eight powerful kings, from Ghayāthuddīn Balban to Ghayāthuddīn Tughlaq (664-725 AH). People of truth from Sanjar[199] to Oudh[200] used to make their way there to seek spiritual guidance.[201]

If we were to give an account of the religious establishments of the saints of all the "sufi" sects in India, and the manner in which people flocked to them from far and near, it would fill a whole volume. We will, therefore, confine our inquiry to the saints of only one sect, the *Naqshbandis*.

Shaikh Aḥmad Sirhindī Mujaddid Alf Thānī (d.1034 AH) had innumerable disciples. They were drawn from all parts of India and Afghanistan. Several influential nobles of the court of Jahāngīr were included among them.

The average number of people staying daily at the *Khanqāh*[202] of his venerable "*Khalīfah*",[203] Sayyid Ādam Bannūrī (d.1053 AH) was about a thousand. They all took their meals at the *Khanqāh*. A great throng followed Sayyid Ādam Bannūrī wherever he went. It is stated in the *Tadhkira-i-Ādamiyah* that ten thousand people accompanied him when he went to Lahore in 1052 AH. Seeing the boundless popularity of the saint, Emperor Shāhjahān became so worried that he devised a plan to send him out of India. He sent him a sum of money and then suggested that since the amount of money made the *Ḥajj* pilgrimage incumbent on a Muslim, he should now proceed to the Ḥijāz to perform the *Ḥajj*. The saint, thereupon, migrated from India.

Mujaddid's eminent son, Khāwājah Maʿṣūm (d.1079 AH) had nine hundred thousand followers, who offered homage of repentance for their sins[204] at his hand. Of them, seven thousand had the honour of being his "*Khalīfahs*".[205]

The Khāwājah's son, Shaikh Saifuddīn Sirhindī, also had an overwhelming following. According to the author of *Dhayl ar-Rashḥāt* about 1,400 persons dined with him daily at his *Khanqāh*, each of whom was served with food of his own choice.

The rich were as enthusiastic in their loyalty to the spiritual leaders as the poor. It is said that noblemen used to cover the path with their scarves and shawls when Khāwājah Muḥammad Zubair Sirhindī went to the mosque to say his prayers so that his feet might not fall on bare ground. When he went out to visit the sick or on any other business, it used to travel in royal style with the carriages and palanquins of the wealthy lords bringing up the rear of the procession.[206]

This ardent devotion to holy men was still very much in evidence among Indian Muslims even during the time of the East India Company, until shortly before the final overthrow of the Mughal Empire in 1857. During the days of Shāh Ghulām ᶜAlī (d.1240 AH), the "*Khalīfah*" of Mirzā Maẓhar Jān-i-Jānān, the Mujaddidiyah *Khanqāh* of Delhi, was a mighty centre of attraction for pious Muslims from all over the Islamic world. Sir Sayyid Aḥmad Khān says in the *Āthār-uṣ-Ṣanādīd*: "I have seen with my own eyes votaries from Turkey, Syria, Baghdad, Egypt, China and Ethiopia coming to the *Khanqāh* and taking the *baiᶜat* at the Shaykh's hand, and considering it a rare good fortune to be of service to the establishment, not to mention the votaries from the adjoining areas of Hindustan, Punjab and Afghanistan who were continually swarming round the saint like bees. No less than five hundred destitute persons used to live in the *Khanqāh*, all of whom were fed and clothed by him."[207]

Shāh Ra'ūf Aḥmad Mujaddidī gave details of the places from which visitors to the *Khanqāh* hailed on a single day – Jumādā I 28, 1231 AH – which includes places like Samarkand, Bukhārā, Ghaznī, Tashkand, Kandhār, Kābul, Kashmir, Peshāwar, Multān, Lahore, Sarhind, Amroha, Sambhal, Rāmpūr, Bareilly, Lucknow, Jāis, Bahrāich, Gorakhpūr, Azīmābād, Dacca, Hyderābad and Poona.[208] All this happened at a time when there were neither railways nor other easily accessible travel facilities.

On the eve of the establishment of British rule, the majestic call of "Run back to Allah" was raised by Sayyid Aḥmad Shahīd (d.1246 AH) and his glorious lieutenants, Shāh Ismāᶜīl Shahīd (d.1246 AH) and Maulānā ᶜAbdul Ḥayy Burhānavī (d.1242 AH). The spectacular manner in which the cream of Muslim society in India rallied round the leader of this group, ultimately to be mingled with the dust at Balākot (May 1831), was proof of the high sense of religious enthusiasm and courage Indian Muslims were still capable of manifesting even at this stage of their decadence.

Unprecedented scenes of religious ardour were witnessed during Sayyid Aḥmad's tour of the Doāb[209] and Oudh when he undertook to pull out the Muslims from the demoralization they had fallen into.[210] In 1032 AH he set out for *Ḥajj*, and a wave of great enthusiasm swept over the whole of Northern India. Muslims came out in their hundreds and thousands to meet him as his caravan travelled from place to place. They invited his party (that finally consisted of 750 persons when they reached Calcutta) to their towns and villages and entertained them for days. It is said that Shaikh Ghulam ᶜAlī, a *ra'is*[211] of Allahābād, spent about twenty thousand rupees in entertaining Sayyid Aḥmad and his companions for a fortnight – about a thousand rupees a day were spent on food alone. In the many towns that fell along Sayyid Aḥmad's route, there were few who did not offer the *baiᶜat* at his hand. His followers in Allahābād, Mirzāpur, Benāres, Ghāzipur, Aẓīmābād (Patna) and Calcutta must have numbered hundreds of thousands. In Benāres patients at Sadar Hospital sent a petition to him saying that since they were unable to come to him, might he take the trouble to grace them with a visit so that they could take the *baiᶜat*. The Sayyid went to the hospital and gave the oath of allegiance to the patients.[212]

About a thousand people became his *murīds* every day during Sayyid Aḥmad's two-month stay in Calcutta. From morning till late at night a stream of men and women poured into the place where he was staying. When it became impossible for the *baiᶜat* to be administered individually, it was arranged for the aspirants to collect in a large house where Sayyid Aḥmad initiated them into his fold. Seven or eight turbans were unrolled on the ground and the aspirants were told to hold them at different places, while one end was held by Sayyid Aḥmad himself. He then taught the fundamental principles of Islam and read out the vow in a loud voice like the *Adhān*[213] which the aspirants repeated and thus completed the ritual. This took place seventeen or eighteen times every day.[214]

For about twenty days at Calcutta, Sayyid Aḥmad delivered the sermons after *Fajr* (morning) prayers. These sermons were attended by over two thousand *ᶜulamā'*, noblemen and countless commoners. On Tuesdays and Fridays, Maulānā ᶜAbdul Ḥayy also addressed the congregation after *Ẓuhr* (midday) prayers, which lasted till the evening with a break for *ᶜAṣr* (afternoon) prayers. Between ten and fifteen non-Muslims accepted Islam daily.[215]

One immediate effect of these religious endeavours was that the liquor business in that great city was suddenly brought to a standstill. The liquor merchants complained to the authorities that though they paid their taxes regularly, they had been forced to close down their business since the arrival in the city of a saint under whose influence more and more Muslims were being reformed daily and were taking the vow to abstain from the use of intoxicants.[216]

On their way back from *Ḥajj*, Sayyid Aḥmad and his companions stopped for a few days at Murshidābād with Diwān Ghulām Murtaḍa. The Diwān had it announced in the market-place that he would pay for any purchases made by his pilgrim guests and services rendered to them by the merchants. Sayyid Aḥmad protested that it was too much, but he replied, "It is a great honour for a Muslim that a 'Ḥājī'[217] should be his guest. I can never be proud enough of my good luck that so many 'Ḥājīs' have graced me with a visit."[218]

Finally, when Sayyid Aḥmad launched the *Jihād*, there was a marvellous response from the rank and file of the Muslim population. The ploughman forsook his plough, the merchant his shop, the servant his master, the nobleman his castle and the theologian his pulpit and they all rose like one man in the defence of God's word.

We have dealt with these facts at some length to bring home to the reader how very susceptible to religious emotion the Muslims were, even at a time when they had entered the gloomiest phase of their existence as a free people, and before the thunderbolt of Western Imperialism had descended to shatter the fabric of their society.

Traces of this earnestness lingered on for some time among Muslims during the early stages of British rule, but they were diminishing fast.

The joy of faith had not yet deserted the hearts of Muslims. Religion was still valued as a vital factor in life. Apart from the educated and the enlightened, the common Muslims, too, had a share in their religious inheritance. There was hardly a Muslim hamlet that was without a moral teacher or a spiritual guide. If one cared to look at the India of thirty or forty years ago, one would find it illumined by a cluster of spiritual lights.[219]

One by one, these lights extinguished. The British Government, of course, never demanded that the *madrasahs* and *khanqāhs* should be closed. Yet the inner urge that used to bring devotees from Samarkand and Bukhārā to Delhi had died down and the higher values of the mind and the spirit had been discarded by the people, and the *madrasahs* and *khanqāhs* were utterly abandoned.

The Epidemic of Worldliness

The new ideal of material advancement has completely gripped the modern mind. In the present age of material progress, there is a great lack of love for learning, nor is love of religion much in evidence. The instinct of hunger has completely dominated human existence. Everywhere people now talk of problems concerning the flesh. Conversations on the problems relating to the spiritual or moral aspects of life are rarely heard in society.

Moral Degradation

When the British arrived in India, moral degradation had already spread a great deal. Many of the ancient ideals of the Eastern and Islamic ways of life had been forgotten. But certain domestic and social virtues were still valued above all things by the people of the subcontinent.

Family and social relations were based on extremely strong foundations. Filial love, parental affection, respect for elders, affection for the young, marital fidelity, loyalty of servants, sincerity of friends – under each of these headings authentic stories have been handed down to us which appear legendary when viewed in the context of the present-day.

The Holy Prophet of Islam ﷺ is reported to have said to a young man: "You and your possessions belong to your father." The dutifulness of children to their parents was modelled on this command. It included respect for the friends and relatives of one's parents as well. The love and regard for one's parents is to be continued even after their death, as stressed by the Holy Prophet ﷺ who is reported to have said, "The best of the good things to do is to do good to the friends of one's deceased father."[220]

Parents were living examples of loving care and self-sacrifice. They never hesitated to subordinate their own desires and interests to those of their children. Yet, when it was necessary to use the rod, they would harden their hearts and do so. It was beneath the dignity of a father to show partiality for his child who was chastised by the teacher. Even illiterate parents would support the teacher on such occasions, though the teacher might have been to blame for being too severe. "The claim of the teacher is greater than that of the father" was a common saying among parents.

Between the old and the young relations were determined by the old Islamic maxim, "He who is not affectionate to those who are younger to him and respectful to the elders of the community is not one of us."[221]

Constancy is a virtue of great merit in the Oriental pattern of morality. Astonishing instances of it were experienced even during the period of decadence. In the daily routine of life, in dress, manners and customs, people were generally consistent and unvarying. If they struck up a friendship, they remained loyal to it.

Wealth was not the sole criterion of respectability in the family or clan, neither was it a dominant factor in friendship. It was inconceivable that at family gatherings there should be discrimination among members of a family on the basis of wealth and, if it chanced to be so, the whole family united against the offender, and sometimes broke off relations with him. A poor young man of noble birth did not feel embarrassed at facing a more prosperous cousin, and the latter took great care to ensure that the former's indigence was not made known to anyone outside the family circle.

A man used to value his conscience above his life. He could not be persuaded to sell his honour at any price. During the official inquiry following the catastrophe of 1857, many a Muslim preferred mounting the gallows to bartering away his honour by feigning innocence while he had actually taken part in the uprising.

Honesty was highly valued both in private life and in cases where communal or national interests were at stake. Communal prejudice was unknown in India and Muslims invariably acted upon Qur'ānic injunctions like the following:

> *O ye who believe, stand out firmly for justice, as witnesses to God, even as against yourselves, or (your) parents or (your) kin...*
>
> al-Nisā' 4:135

> *And let not the hatred of any people make you swerve to wrong and depart from justice, be just; that is next to piety; and fear God...*
>
> al-Mā'idah 5:8

> *And when ye judge between mankind, (God doth command) that ye judge with justice.*
>
> al-Nisā' 4:58

> *Whatever ye say, speak justly, even if a near relative is concerned...*
>
> al-Anʿām 6:152

Once, during the early days of the British administration, there arose in Kandhla, in the Muzaffarnagar District, a dispute between Hindus and Muslims over a plot of land which both claimed as their place of worship. The English Magistrate of the district privately inquired from the Muslims if they could name a Hindu in whose honesty they had full confidence so that the case might be decided on the basis of his evidence. The Muslims said that they knew of no such Hindu. The Magistrate then asked the Hindus whether there was a Muslim upon whose word they would be willing to let the decision of the dispute be made. The Hindus said that, grave as the matter was, there was a Muslim who had never uttered a falsehood and it could be hoped that he would not compromise his integrity over the issue in hand. The man came from the family of Muftī Ilāhī Bakhsh, who was a pupil of Shāh ᶜAbdul ᶜAzīz and a *Khalīfah* of Sayyid Aḥmad Shahīd. The Magistrate, thereupon, summoned him to his court but he declined, saying that he had sworn never to look at the face of an Englishman. The Magistrate said that he need not look at his face if he did not want to, but come he must, because the matter was serious and its settlement depended on him. At last, the Maulānā agreed. He came with his face covered with a mask and stood in the court, his back turned towards the Magistrate so that there could be no possibility of his vow being broken. The case was explained to him and he was asked to state whether he knew anything about the ownership of the plot of land. The Maulānā declared that the plot in dispute belonged to the Hindus; the Muslims had nothing to do with it. The Magistrate decided accordingly. The Muslims lost the case, but Truth scored a magnificent victory. A number of Hindus embraced Islam on that very day at the hand of the Maulānā.

Learning and wisdom were held sacred in those times. Those who occupied a high place in the field of learning were not inclined to sell their intellectual wealth at any price because it was regarded as a precious gift and a sacred trust of God. To allow one's ability or knowledge, directly or indirectly, to serve the cause of injustice and unbelief was in their view tantamount to betrayal.

Compare this intellectual loftiness with the prostitution of the intellect that is practised everywhere today. Some modern men of learning are open to be bought by the highest bidder. They have put themselves up for auction. If they are earning a certain amount in an Islamic institution and a Christian institution offers them more, they will accept the latter. And if a Jewish company offered even more, they would agree to that with equal readiness. And increasingly there is no question of one's mental aptitude or preference. If circumstances allow, a teacher will join the police or the Air Force for a nominal consideration. A Doctor of Philosophy will join a military or a political department where his academic achievements will be of little or no use. A writer sees no difference between writing the biography of a national hero or that of a scoundrel.

In the past, the ties that bound persons to one another were free from the taint of selfishness. These ties were forged in their hearts, with the result that often they acquired an emotional significance that was far beyond the scope of material explanation. The bond of affection that endured, for example, between the teacher and the pupil was so strong that the existing relations between the father and the son or the lover and the beloved pale into insignificance. It will be difficult for a modern person to believe that when the news of the death of Mullā Nizāmuddīn of Lucknow was received (which later turned out to be false), one of his pupils, Sayyid Kamāluddīn Azīmabādī, died of the shock, while another, Sayyid Ẓarīf Azīmābādī, wept so much that his eyes were permanently damaged.[222]

In the West today ethical questions are confined to considerations of practical utility. It is just the opposite in Islam, as its real goal is the inner progress of man. Material utility came to dominate Western thought and morals in the 17th century when its social philosophers propagated the view that all ethical principles that did not have a direct bearing on the material betterment of society were not deserving of serious attention. This view gradually gained strength until it acquired a commanding hold on all fields of human activity. Those virtues that had a purely ethical value were relegated to obscurity and condemned to a mere theoretical existence.

In recent times, Western literature has exhibited a striking fondness for the word "nature". But the context in which it is used and the meanings that are sought to be conveyed show that it implies only animal nature. It stands for the world of flesh and shuts out the soul. Now, as Western society is becoming more and more technological, even animal warmth is vanishing from the nature of man and the individual is turning into so much inanimate matter.

"In the profound transformation the social life of the West is at present undergoing", says Muhammad Asad, "that new, utilitarian morality becomes daily more and more visible. All virtues having a direct bearing upon the material welfare of society, as, for example, technical efficiency, patriotism, nationalist group-sense, are being exalted and sometimes absurdly exaggerated in their value, while virtues which, until now, have been valued from a purely ethical point of view, as, for example, filial love or sexual fidelity, rapidly lose their importance because they do not confer a tangible, material benefit upon society. The age in which the insistence on strong family bonds was decisive for the well-being of the group or the clan is being superseded, in the modern West, by an age of collective organization under far wider headings. And in a society which is essentially technological and is being organized at a rapidly increasing pace, on purely mechanical lines, the behaviour of a son towards his father is of no great social importance, so long as those individuals behave within the limits of general decency imposed by the society on the intercourse of its members. Consequently, the European father daily loses more and more authority over his son, and the son loses respect for his father. Their mutual relations are being slowly over-ruled and – for all practical purposes – annihilated by the postulates of a mechanized society which has a tendency to abolish all privileges of one individual over another, and – in the logical development of this idea – also the privileges caused by family relationship; and the old relation between father and son is becoming obsolete."[223]

The Muslim Rulers of India

In the Islamic Orient the conception of human progress and perfection was so high that in order to meet its demands one had to cultivate such diverse qualities and merits as would seem opposed and contradictory to the lethargy and short-sightedness of the modern age. To take from the world of Islam only the Muslim rulers of India and their ministers and courtiers, there are such rare examples of human perfection as can scarcely be dreamt of today.

Shamsuddīn Iltutmish

The vastness of the Empire of Sultān Shamsuddīn Iltutmish is known to all students of Indian history. What, however, is not so generally known is that, despite the great responsibility of ruling over such a vast Empire and waging numerous wars, the Sultān was highly scrupulous in his religious duties. When it was made known at the death of the saint, Khawājah Quṭbuddīn Bakhtiyār Kāʿkī, that the saint had asked that his funeral prayers be led by him, who had never in his life missed the "*sunnahs*"[224] of the ʿ*Aṣr* (afternoon) prayers and the first "*takbīr*" of any congregational prayer, the Sultān reluctantly conducted the service. Likewise, Sultāns Ghayathuddīn Balban, Naṣīruddīn Mahmūd and Fīroz Tughlaq were all known for their piety.

The Sultāns of Gujrāt

The Sultāns of Gujrāt were particularly celebrated for the way they epitomized the splendid Islamic ideal of integrated material and spiritual progress. Maulvi Sayyid ʿAbdul Ḥayy throws light on the life and character of one of them, Sultān Muẓaffar Shāh Ḥalīm, in the following words: "After the death of Maḥmūd Shāh, his son, Muẓaffar Shāh Halīm, who was a worthy son of a worthy father, became the king. He had been a pupil of ʿAllāma Muḥammad ibn Muḥammad al-Ijī. The Science of Ḥadīth he had studied with ʿAllāma Jamāluddīn ibn Muḥammad ʿUmar Bahraq. He had learnt the Qur'ān by heart in his youth, an age about which Shaikh Saʿdī has rightly said, 'You know what happens in youth.'

"Side by side with these intellectual attainments, God had endowed him with great piety and strength of purpose. Throughout his life he strictly followed the *Sunnah*[225] of the Prophet, remained always with *Wudu* and offered his prayers in congregation. He did not touch wine, was not unnecessarily hard on anyone, and never sullied his tongue with a foul word. Moreover, in this picture of piety there were gathered the highest qualities of a soldier and a statesman. When Maḥmūd Shāh II of Mālwā was deposed by his minister, Mandlī Rāe, and the rites of Islam began to be wantonly outraged there, his religious pride was stirred. Setting out with a powerful army, he covered the distance to Mālwā with the utmost speed and besieged its fort. Mandlī Rāe, realizing that he was no match for the besieging force, begged Rānā Sāngā to come to his aid. But before Rānā Sāngā could advance as far as Sarangpur, Muẓaffar Shāh sent a detachment of his valiant army to deal with him. Soon the fort of Mālwā fell.

"The sum and substance of the story is that when Muẓaffar Shāh entered the fort and the chiefs of his escort beheld the great treasure the rulers of Mālwā had amassed and heard accounts of the richness of the land, they ventured to suggest in his presence that since 2,000 of their horsemen had been killed in the fighting, it would not be wise to restore the kingdom to a ruler who, owing to his incompetence, had lost it to his minister. As soon as Muẓaffar Shāh heard it, he cut short the round of inspection and came out of the fort, instructing Mahmūd Shāh not to allow any member of his party into the fort. The latter entreated him to rest in the fort for a few days more, but he firmly declined. On a later occasion, explaining the implications of his action Muẓaffar Shāh said, 'I had waged that war simply to earn Divine approbation. When I heard the talk of the chiefs, I became apprehensive lest some unwholesome desire should crop up in my heart to ruin the sincerity of my act. I have not done any favour to Maḥmūd Shāh. On the contrary, I am indebted to him, for it was through him that I got the opportunity of performing a noble deed'."[226]

When the hour of his death drew near, Muẓaffar Shāh, by way of public acknowledgement of the benefits conferred upon him by God, related to the courtiers and the pious who were assembled around his bed, "By the grace of God, in addition to knowing the Qur'ān by heart, I have a full command over the points of law and precepts arising out of every verse of it, the occasion of its revelation and the method of its recitation. I remember by heart all the Traditions of the Prophet – their texts, references, the antecedents of their narrators and everything – about which I have received the certificate from my teacher, ʿAllāma Jamāluddīn Muḥammad ibn ʿUmar Bahraq. I possess such knowledge of Fiqh (Islamic Jurisprudence) that I hope to bear testimony to the veracity of the Prophet's words that 'Those for whom God makes a decision of virtue, are made by Him the jurists of His faith'. I have been engaged for some time in the purification of the soul after the system of the Sūfis and aspire for their blessings on the strength of the principle that 'whoso makes himself resemble a people becomes one of them'. I have read the *Tafsīr Maʿālim-ut-Tanzīl*[227] once. I am now revising it and have gone through it half-way. I hope to finish it in heaven."[228]

His condition deteriorated at the time of *Jumuʿah* (Friday) prayers. He sent away his attendants to attend the prayers, while he himself offered the *Ẓuhr*[229] prayers. After the prayers, he observed, "I have offered the *Ẓuhr* prayers in your midst; I hope to offer the *ʿAsr* prayers in heaven." Then, reciting the following prayer of the Prophet Yūsuf عليه السلام, which was truly in keeping with his own condition, this saintly king passed away.[230] "*O my Lord, Thou hast given me (something) of sovereignty and hath taught me (something) of the interpretation of events – Creator of the heavens and the earth, Thou art my Protecting Friend in the world and the Hereafter. Make me die submissive (unto Thee), and join me to the righteous*" (Holy Qur'ān, Yūsuf 12:101).

Sher Shāh Sūrī

Likewise, the following account of the daily routine of Sher Shāh Sūrī, an emperor who set himself to complete the task of a century in five years, reveals a diligence for religion which the average man could hardly manage today:

"Sher Shāh got up when two-thirds of the night had passed, had his bath and offered the *Nafl*[231] prayers. He used to finish the supererogatory devotions before the *Fajr* prayers. Then he would look into the accounts of the various administrative departments and issue the necessary instructions so that he might not be disturbed by them during the day. After that, he would perform the *Wuḍū* for the *Fajr* prayers which he offered in congregation and remained at his devotions till the high functionaries of the Empire came to pay their respects to him. After the *Ishrāq*[232] prayers, the Emperor attended to the applications of the people and made to them grants of land, money and horses according to their needs. Then he heard the petitions and redressed grievances. Afterwards, he went out to inspect the troops and the arsenal and sanctioned the appointment of new recruits to the army after testing their ability. Then he inspected the Treasury. On returning from there, he met the grandees of the Empire and foreign emissaries. Then the reports of the provincial governors were presented to him. He listened to them and dictated orders. The he sat down to the mid-day meal at which a number of *ʿulamā'* would be present. After the meal, he retired for two hours till the *Ẓuhr* prayers, which he always offered in congregation. Then he recited the Qur'ān. After it, he again occupied himself with the affairs of the Empire.

"The emperor adhered strictly to his routine, whether he was in the capital or out on a journey. He used to say that a great man was he who spent his time wisely."[233]

Aurangzeb

The Empire of Aurangzeb stretched from Kābul and Kandhār to the Deccan and he used to look into everything connected with it personally. Yet, he was able to find time to offer the daily prayers at the earliest hour and in congregation, and the Friday prayers in the *Jāmiʿ* Masjid and observed the *sunnahs* and the *nawāfil* with scrupulous attention. He kept the fasts of Ramaḍān even in the hottest weather, and participated in the nightly *Tarāwīḥ*[234] prayers and did the *Iʿtikāf*[235] during the last ten days of the month. As well as Ramaḍān fasts, he fasted regularly on Mondays, Thursdays, Fridays and Saturdays. He took care never to be without *wuḍū'* and recited the Holy Qur'ān and the other traditional prayers every morning. Notwithstanding the vexations and worries with which he was surrounded throughout his reign, he paid full attention to the spiritual lessons he received from Khawājah Saifuddin (the grandson of Mujaddid Alf Thānī), and with such success that the latter used to remark upon the progress made by him in his letters to his father, Khawājah Maᶜṣūm. He listened, from day to day, to the *Fatāwā ᶜĀlamgīrī*, a Code of Laws, which religious scholars were compiling under his guidance and offered his own suggestions. He knew the Qur'ān by heart and wrote the commentary of his own book, *Arbaᶜīn*, in which he had collected forty Traditions of the Holy Prophet ﷺ.

ᶜAbdur Raḥīm Khān-i-Khānān

Among the ministers and courtiers of the Mughal Court, there were such versatile men as ᶜAbdur Raḥīm Bairam Khān-i-Khānān, Saᶜdullāh Khān 'Allāmī, Majduddīn Muḥammad ibn Muḥammad al-Ijī, Ikhtiyār Khān, Afzal Khān and ᶜAbdul ᶜAzīz Āsaf Khān. Here we give brief summaries of the lives of two of them.

ᶜAbdur Raḥīm Khān read religious textbooks with Maulānā Muḥammad Amīn Andjānī and Qāzī Nizāmuddīn Badakhshānī and advanced books from ᶜAllāma Fatḥullāh Shīrāzī. Later, when he resided in Gujrāt, he took instruction from ᶜAllāma Wajīhuddīn ibn Nasrullāh Gujrāti. He also regularly held academic discussions with scholars he maintained in his retinue. Consequently, he became perfect in learning and on some subjects he was recognized as an authority. He was an accomplished linguist. ᶜAbdur Razzāq Khawānī says in the *Ma'āthir-ul-Umarā'* that he enjoyed complete mastery over Arabic, Persian, Turkish and Hindi and could compose excellent poems in all four languages.

ᶜAbdur Raḥīm Khān's passion for learning was so strong that he was often seen reading a book while on horseback on the battlefield. He would also read while in the bathroom. At the same time he was second to none as a soldier. The conquests of Gujrāt, Sind and the Deccan speak volumes for his military prowess.

His manners were sublime. He was benevolent, forbearing and generous. Āzād Bilgrāmī observed that if one were to put the riches given away by ᶜAbdur Raḥīm Khān in one side of a balance and those by all the Safavid rulers (of Iran) in the other, the former would turn out to be the heavier.[236]

So far as the religious and spiritual side of his life was concerned, it is enough to know that he was one of the few favoured ones who enjoyed the confidence of Mujaddid Alf Thānī, and with whom the latter kept up a regular correspondence. The *Letters* of the great Mujaddid reveal how highly he regarded ᶜAbdur Rahīm Khān.

Āṣaf Khān

The story of Āṣaf Khān is another example of composite excellence and versatility. His real name was ᶜAbdul ᶜAzīz. He received elementary education from his father, Ḥamīd-ul-Mulk, and studied *Ḥadīth* and *Fiqh* with Qāzī Burhānuddīn and ethics and philosophy with ᶜAbul Faḍl Ghādhrūni and ᶜAbul Faḍl Astrābādī. When his education was complete, he gained admission to the Imperial Court, rising to be a minister in the reign of Bahādur Shāh. When Maḥmūd Shāh succeeded to the throne, he appointed Āṣaf Khān as prime minister of the Empire. But neither position nor wealth made any difference to his thirst for knowledge. He remained a scholar up to the moment of his death.

Āṣaf Khān was once compelled, for political reasons, to migrate to Arabia where he lived for a number of years. The religious circles of Arabia were overwhelmed by his intellectual and spiritual attributes. Ibn Ḥajar Makkī, the most distinguished Arab scholar of that time, wrote a book about him in which he paid a glowing tribute to Āṣaf Khān's great learning and spiritual merit.

Āṣaf Khān's life in Arabia was that of an ascetic in spite of the pomp and splendour by which he was surrounded. He recited ten *Juz'*[237] of the Qur'ān every day in the *Tahajjud* prayers.[238] We know from Ibn Ḥajar that, "There was not a single occasion during the ten years he lived in Makkah in which he failed to offer his prayers in congregation at the Holy Mosque. His lodgings being by the side of the *Maṭāf*,[239] his activities were constantly under full view of the people. One almost never saw him except when he was engaged in prayer or meditation or study or religious discussion. Books of the highest standard were discussed at all hours in his presence in which the *ᶜUlamā'* of the *Ḥaram* participated eagerly." Ibn Ḥajar goes on to say:

> A peculiar glow had come over Makkah during Āṣaf Khān's stay. The learned and the wise considered it a privilege to converse with him. There was a great fostering of learning...Students hurried to Makkah from all sides...They took great trouble to think out literary problems so as to make them the vehicles for getting nearer to him. This was because the liberality with which he patronized learning and bestowed favours upon students had not been witnessed in Makkah for a long time. His name was blessed in the streets of Makkah in the same way in which the cries of *Labbaik*[240] are raised during the *Ḥajj* days.

Āṣaf Khān was invited to Constantinople by the Sultān of Turkey. It was narrated by a friend who accompanied him that during this journey he always preferred to practise *ᶜazīmah*, the best and more rewarding way of worship, instead of opting for *rukhṣah*. While in Egypt, the governor, Khusrau Pāshā, sent him a robe of honour by a special envoy. The envoy begged him to put on the robe if only for a minute, so that he could tell the governor that Āṣaf Khān had worn it. The governor would be very happy to hear this. But Āṣaf Khān politely refused. The garment was made of silk and he could not wear it on any account.

It is not implied that in former times every monarch was a Muẓaffar Shāh or an Aurangzeb, or that every minister or saint of the realm was an ᶜAbdur Raḥīm Khān or an Āṣaf Khān. What we want to convey is the fact that generally the quality of human material was much better in the past than it is now. Many of the things that were then considered essential for bringing the human personality to maturity have now been ruled out of existence under the devastating spell of Western ideals and inclinations.

Moral, Religious and Spiritual Decline

Since religion used to be pursued as a programme of life, worldly success could not thwart spiritual progress. However, with the levelling to the ground of the ethical ideals of Islam by Western convictions and aspirations, humanity in general has degenerated rapidly, mentally and morally, in the Muslim East. A few noteworthy exceptions such as Muftī Sadruddīn Khān, Nawāb Quṭbuddīn Khān, Nawāb Wazīruddaulah of Tonk, Nawāb Kalbe ʿAlī Khān of Rāmpūr, Munshi Jamāluddin Khān, the Wazīr of Bhopal, and Nawāb Sayyid Siddīq Ḥasan Khān did, however, grace the scene occasionally during the period of transition, in whom the severe self-discipline of an ascetic, the love for learning of a scholar and the alertness of a soldier were combined with princely power and wealth. But the process of social disintegration, having once started, proved irresistible. Dazzled by the power and progress of Western nations, Muslims began to imitate Western social and economic institutions regardless of the consequences, although they were much inferior to their own and consisted of little more than the ardent pursuit of material success. The prestige of religion was diminished. The teachings of the Prophet ﷺ were forgotten. All those ideals of life, which truthfully displayed within themselves both the spiritual and the temporal aspects of life and did not subordinate the former to the latter, ceased to impress the minds of the great mass of Muslim society. Their place was taken by ideals far inferior to them. Life was filled with frivolous desires and occupations to a degree that it had to eschew religious and spiritual cravings and activities. If one were to compare the daily occupations of present-day Muslims with those of the aforementioned specimens of the old Islamic civilization, one would find it hard to believe that both professed the same ideology or that only a few generations separated one from the other.

VII

THE REVIVAL OF THE MUSLIM WORLD

In the 6th century, when the world was hovering between life and death and there was no one to whom man could look for help, the advent of Prophet Muḥammad ﷺ gave humanity a fresh lease of life. He placed human welfare under the care of a community that was in possession of the Revealed Word and the Divine Law and in the light of these did everything that was the symbol of purity and justice. This community was blessed with the most harmoniously blended disposition and temperate outlook and had risen to the position of the trusteeship of mankind after going through rigorous moral training and attaining complete spiritual adjustment.

The emergence of this community marked a turning point in human history. It immediately arrested the progress of mankind towards its doom and made it safe, for centuries to come, from the moral and material hazards that were threatening to engulf it. Under its guidance humanity made a well-balanced advance towards its true goal, the various capabilities of man were called splendidly into play and an environment was created in which it was made possible for him to advance to the highest goal of progress in the shortest and the surest way.

Under the influence of this new community the lives of men, their minds and their morals were revolutionized. Unbelief and depravity of character were replaced by faith and virtuousness; false ethical values and wrong ideals gave way to high moral patterns. Politics was placed under the control of ethics. In the system of Islamic civilization there was unremitting care for spiritual as well as material prosperity. Economic development was matched with moral advancement; political expansion corresponded with spiritual development. A deep, inner unity of faith, an unswerving oneness of purpose, and peace and fellow-feeling had demolished all barriers between man and man in the world of Islam and made it into a society which, in spite of it being composed of diverse racial elements, was blissfully free from all social inhibitions, tensions and prejudice. The path of virtue that had been deserted for so long and had become so difficult to tread was now a smooth, even road on which people could walk in perfect freedom and security. Man's right to worship and obey God was restored. The call of religion developed great vigour that lifted millions of men from the depth of degradation to the greatest heights of glory. The spirit of man was aroused, and his genius was set to a noble purpose. In short, the caravan of humanity was brought nearer to its destination and its vanguard did, indeed, arrive.

But before the rest of the travellers could arrive at the journey's end, the caravan suddenly stopped and its leadership underwent change. The old leader had to relinquish charge because he had not made adequate arrangements for the safety of the travellers. An unknown fellow-traveller assumed the reins of leadership at the point of the dagger and proceeded to take the caravan along a path that was tortuous and uneven and over which nocturnal darkness prevailed even at high noon. He is engaged still in the same mad pursuit. The travellers stumble and fall headlong and groan, but the leader, in his arrogance and haste, presses heedlessly on.

Western Nations

This, surely, is no figment of the imagination, for the Western nations, which succeeded the Muslims to the stewardship of the world, had, from the very beginning, been labouring under a serious disadvantage. They were never in possession of an unpolluted source of Revealed Knowledge or an uncorrupted fund of Divine Wisdom. The insignificant part of the teachings of Jesus Christ that had reached them had become lost owing to distortions and interpolations. Western nations tried to make up for the light of heavenly guidance with the learning of the Greeks and the Romans, and the entire pagan legacy of Ancient Greece and Rome had fallen to their lot. They had received the worship of the perceptible, devotion to pleasure, local patriotism and libertinism from the Greeks and the bankruptcy of religious belief, racial pride, power-worship and imperialism from the Romans.

We have seen how what was left of the religious teachings of Jesus Christ was devoured by Roman paganism. What remained was lost in the dogmatic quarrels of the clergy. This was followed by the epidemic of monasticism and then, in reaction, the Christian world became immersed in sensual enjoyment. The depravity and luxury of the clergy produced, in the European mind, a pronounced revulsion towards Christianity which was replaced in unthinking minds by religion in general. In the Middle Ages there occurred a bitter conflict between the Church and the State, which was succeeded by an even more violent clash between Christianity and Science. The ghastly atrocities committed by the Church officials during the course of its struggle sealed the fate of Christianity in the West, and succeeded in creating a distrust of religion in general. Western intellectuals did the rest. They broke the remaining link with transcendental ethics. As a result, the West turned to materialism, and power and wealth became the sole objects of its worship.

A further outcome of the peculiar development of the West was the growth of aggressive nationalism. For the preservation of national existence it became necessary to bear ill-will towards the rest of humanity. Europe, on the one hand, decided that the whole of the East was an opposite camp, and on the other, it divided itself into a number of water-tight compartments on the illusory basis of national self-determination. The world was converted into a huge market-place for the sale and purchase of the weaker nations.

The coupling of moral and religious depravity with phenomenal progress in the scientific and industrial fields led to the creation of a striking disparity between power and ethics. Men learnt to fly in the air like birds and to swim in the water like fish; but they forgot how to walk straight on the earth. Undisciplined knowledge and unenlightened wisdom furnished every highwayman with a sword. Deadly weapons were placed in untrained hands which repeatedly plunged the world into horrible blood-baths. And now science has given the atomic and hydrogen bombs to humanity as weapons for suicide.

Under the influence of these godless nations the sciences relating to inanimate matter made great progress while human material was brought low in every respect. Religion was ostracized and secularized; moral enthusiasm was crushed under the weight of material cravings. The religious instinct of Eastern peoples, too, which was the pivot of their lives, was seriously impaired.

The Universal Sway of Materialism

It is a tragic fact of modern life that there exists no community worth naming in Europe, Asia, Africa, or America which is genuinely opposed to the pagan philosophy of materialism. Nations like the Germans in Europe, the emerging independent states of the former Soviet Union, and the Japanese or Indians in Asia, are all becoming increasingly convinced of the merits of materialism. The ideological differences that one encounters in the modern world are merely the off-shoots of an all-out struggle for political supremacy. They have no relation to moral or spiritual convictions. It is simply too much for the pride of a powerful nation that another should be in command of the international scene. No nation feels inclined to address itself to the moral regeneration of humanity should the opportunity ever arise.

Eastern Nations

Eastern nations are by no means rejecting materialism and secularization. The same urges and ambitions that rule over the West are enshrined in their hearts, too. Their leaders have only one quarrel with the West: they do not want their nations to be exploited by Western nations. They now aspire to be their own masters. Apart from this, there is no fundamental difference in the mental attitudes of Eastern and Western nations. What the people of the East are opposed to is that the Western ideas and ideals should be brought to their lands by Westerners; they want to be left free to do it themselves. They do not wish to give up the ideals of Western civilization. They only desire that they themselves should be the torchbearers of that civilization. Further, many Eastern communities have their own traditions of paganism, together with which they are becoming imbued with the pagan attitudes of the West.

The New Allies of Paganism

What is so regrettable is that the traditional enemy of paganism, the Muslim, has become its ally in many parts of the world. What better proof of the universal triumph of paganism can there be than that Muslims should regard those countries as their friends and well-wishers who are the leaders of the pagan movement in the present age? The modern Muslim has totally given up the idea of leadership; he has lost faith in himself. His whole mental attitude is being moulded by the undercurrents of paganism. Muslim states are exhibiting the same materialistic tendencies which are the hall-mark of the Western social system. The same enslavement to earthly longings is fast becoming the creed of the community, the cornerstone of whose religious faith is the idea that the real life is the life to come. These nations' love for the After-life is declining day by day. They are subordinating ethical principles to material expediency with astonishingly cheerful readiness. In some respects Muslims are actually outdoing some Western nations in the glorification of material wealth.

A Ray of Hope

With the solitary exception of the followers of Islam, in which alone one sees a ray of hope, all the communities in the world have lost touch with their heritage of Divine guidance. The light of the Prophetic teachings has departed from their hearts. The passage of time has severed their connections with the real origins of their spiritual inspiration. Past experience of religious reform movements among the various nations precludes the possibility of a fundamental change being brought about in their outlook by bringing religion into their lives. Their primary ideals are rigidly opposed to a religious conception of life.

Against this backdrop the entire spiritual inheritance of the Muslims is preserved in its pristine purity. A full record of the life and Traditions of the Holy Prophet ﷺ and of the lives of his Companions, which holds the key to the understanding of the memorable rise of Islam, is still available in its original form. Moreover, a chain of religious reformers has been continually operating among Muslims, sustaining their spirits, nourishing their souls and guarding them against a relapse into Ignorance.

The Muslim mind, by the very nature of its ordering, is such that it can never be made to imbibe pagan materialism unless, of course, its very structure is destroyed and recast in a new form.

The Standard-Bearers of Faith

In an earlier chapter it was pointed out that the Holy Prophet ﷺ said of Muslims in the Battle of Badr: "O God, if these (Believers) are destroyed, no one will be left on the earth to worship Thee." This is equally true today because, if anyone can challenge paganism and offer to the world an alternative plan of life, it is the Muslims. The plan of Islam is an eternal plan. It will remain valid for all time to come. By virtue of their religion, Muslims are the moral guardians of mankind and they will return to their duty when they wake up. That day will be a day of reckoning for the nations of the world. Muslims possess a spark which, if and when it is ignited, will burn down the whole structure of Ignorance.

ʿAllāmā Iqbāl used the medium of the presiding genius of the Order of Ignorance, the Devil himself, to express this in his poem *The Advisory Council of the Devil, 1936*. The evil spirits of the world are shown in the poem to have gathered together to ponder over the new challenges that are threatening their nefarious system. One adviser mentions democracy as "the latest evil of the new world". Another mentions communism. Says the great poet:

Such an awe this budding menace has struck,
That the brooks, the hills and the yonder mountains shake.
The world, my Lord! is about to crumble.
The world that depends upon Thy guidance alone.

The Devil allays their fears and explains the plans he has devised for meeting those threats. Then he speaks of what, in his opinion, is the real menace and says that though he has thought out the most appropriate campaign against it, too, its potentialities are so terrifying that he is constantly brooding over it. He goes on to say:

If any fear attends me, it is from the people whose ashes
yet the spark of Desire contain.
Occasionally still, I see among them men who,
with tears, perform the *wuḍū* in the early morn.
He who knows the secrets of History knows
That Communism is not morrow's menace, but Islam.
That they from the Qur'ān have departed, I know.
And Capitalism is now the faith of the Believer;
In the pitch-dark night that upon the East has fallen,
The wise men of the 'Ḥaram'[241] are without the light
of faith.
But from the exigencies of this age I fear the Law of the
Prophet may re-appear.

Beware of the Law of the Prophet, a hundred
times beware!
The safeguarder of women's honour, the tester of men,
the Maker of men,
The voice of death for all forms of slavery.
There is no distinction of the Ruler and the ruled
in its domain.

It purges wealth of foulness,
And the rich the trustees of their goods it makes.
Can a more radical thing than this there be –
That the earth belongs to God, not to the kings?
The more this Law from the world's view is hidden the better.
Luckily, the Muslim himself is devoid of faith.
Let him in meticulous interpretations of the Book his energies waste.
And a helpless groper in the gloom of Theology be.

Satan then gives the following advice to his council:

Whose mighty '*takbīrs*' the spell of time and space can break,
May his night of decay no day-break see.
You keep him a stranger to the world of deed, I say,
That all his movements on the life's chess-board be frustrated.
For him such poetry and mysticism are, indeed, the best,
Which from his eyes life's broad spectacle conceal.
Every moment do I at the thought of their awakening tremble,
The real purpose of whose faith is the supervision of the Universe.

The Message of Faith

The World of Islam can still give the message of faith and life to disillusioned humanity. It is the message the Holy Prophet ﷺ imparted to humanity 1400 years ago. It is a simple, dynamic, radiant message, a grander and more majestic message than anything the world could hope to receive.

It is the same message which prompted the Muslims of Madīnah to leave their homes and spread throughout the world; it is the same message which was so exquisitely summed up by a spokesman of the Muslims before the Emperor of Iran who had asked the followers of Islam as to what had brought them to his land: "We have been sent by Allah to deliver whom He pleaseth from the overlordship of His slaves to His overlordship; and from the narrowness of this world to the boundlessness of the Hereafter; and from the oppression of other religions to the equity and fairness of Islam."

Not one word of this message can be altered even today, more so many years after it was first delivered. It is just as capable of moving the minds and filling the hearts of men in the 20th century as it was in the 6th.

Today, too, humanity prostrates before false deities, sculptured and unsculptured; the worship of One Transcendent God is becoming rare, the animal in man has been let loose and the priests, the rulers, the capitalists and the political leaders have lifted themselves to the dizzy heights of godhood.

The world with all its vastness has become more constricted, murky and suffocating today than ever before. Being the devotee of material power the man of today refuses to admit the existence of any other power. He has been captivated by his own material achievements. He finds himself deceived, and frustrated and is growing increasingly petty, exclusive, selfish and sceptical. Everyone believes that he alone has the right to live, regardless of other people. Politicians and national leaders have made life still more narrow and difficult by erecting artificial barriers in society. They have laid hold of the wells of life, and bound up the structures of economic and political forms with the wishes and necessities of the privileged classes. Lands which, in the past, were renowned for their richness and fertility have been rendered barren. Entire populations have been placed, like helpless children, under the trusteeship of aliens. The modern way of life is constantly forging new fetters for the spirit of man, the levies and imposts are growing heavier day by day, peace is assailed from all sides, and mental stress, dissension, riots and strikes have become the inevitable constituents of daily existence.

Today, again, it is necessary to "deliver men from the oppression of other religions to the equity and fairness of Islam". Even in the 20th century there are religions abounding in superstitious beliefs and fantastic teachings that tyrannize their followers and drive them like deaf and dumb animals. Then there are the new – political and economic – religions such as collectivism, nationalism and socialism that are a step ahead of the ancient pagan faiths in fanatical intolerance and coercion. The last two World Wars were the "gifts" of these very dogmas to humanity, besides which the bloodthirsty religious strife of ancient Rome and the bitter conflicts between the Church and the intelligentsia of Europe in the Middle Ages recede into insignificance.

Today, too, the message of Islam is an open invitation to the worship of, and surrender to, One God and belief in the Mission of the prophets, particularly that of Prophet Muḥammad ﷺ and in the Resurrection and Final Judgement. In return for submitting to this call the world will emerge from the darkness of Ignorance and the spirit of man will be set free. Man will rediscover his equilibrium and from the narrow confines of the world of matter he will come out into a world which, although enclosed within himself, stretches beyond time and space.

There has never been a clearer appreciation of the need and the utility of this Message as there is now. The civilization of Ignorance has been publicly disgraced. Its shame is being flagrantly exposed. People are disgusted with life; they despair of their intellectual and cultural leaders. Modern civilization is seriously ill. From all indications the psychological moment has arrived when a radical change in the leadership of human affairs is necessary. So far changes in leadership have only been in the nature of a change of personnel. There has been no major shift in thought.

The only thing that can cure the world of its present ills is that its leadership should pass from the hands of those who worship materialism to the hands of those who worship the One God.

Renaissance of Faith

To attain this objective the world of Islam will have to rediscover its spiritual roots. It will have to re-dedicate itself to Islam. There is absolutely no need for a new religion, a new Canonical Law or a new set of moral teachings. Like the sun, Islam was, is, and will be timeless. The Mission of Prophet Muḥammad ﷺ is endowed with the quality of timelessness. No other Messenger of God is to be raised now. His religion is everlasting, his teachings are immortal. But the Muslims do require a renaissance of faith. One cannot face new hazards and meet new challenges with a weak faith and unauthorized practice. A decaying building cannot withstand a flood. One must have a living, glowing and firm faith in the cause one seeks to uphold. If the Islamic world aspires to inject new life into humanity, to give it the courage to resist and reverse the torrents of materialism and religious disbelief, it will first have to produce that enthusiasm and life in itself.

The Muslims will have to regenerate themselves internally. They cannot brave the onslaught of the ungodly West by imitating its empty cultural forms, customs and social concepts, for these have no place in the growth and rise of nations. All cultural imitations are bound to make a people small. The Muslims can exert themselves only by means of that inner force, regarding which the West is becoming increasingly worried.

The secret of a Muslim's strength lies in his faith in the Divine recompense and reward in the After-life. If the Muslim world, too, establishes the same worldly ideals and gets caught in the same web of material desires as the West, the latter, with its larger fund of material knowledge and power, has a prior claim to superiority.

History speaks of times when Muslims grew indifferent to the value of the inner force and the wells of spiritual vigour within them dried up owing to disuse. Then occasions arose calling for great feats of faith and the Muslims tried to draw upon that force, but to their dismay they learnt that it had deserted them long ago. It then dawned upon them that they had done themselves a great injury by neglecting it, and they made frantic efforts to induce it artificially but this proved futile.

During such times there also occurred events in the course of which the honour of Islam seemed to be at stake, and it was hoped that the entire Muslim world would be set ablaze with fury and Muslims would rush forth from every quarter to defend their sacred rights, but nothing happened beyond a ripple here and a wave there. Under the surface everything remained motionless and dead.

The major task before the Muslim leaders and thinkers today is to rekindle the flame of faith in the hearts of Muslims. They should do all that the early preachers of Islam did, and at the same time avail themselves fully of all the opportunities the modern age has put into their hands.

The Qur'ān and the *Sunnah* can still revitalize the withered arteries of the Islamic world. Their study and influence still fire one with the desire to smash the citadel of Ignorance. They have a rousing quality about them that can spur a slumbering people into new life. Under their inspiration mighty struggles can once again ensue between belief and unbelief, faith and treachery, heart and intellect. The world can once again be made to rouse itself to the battle between the tranquillity of the mind and ease of the body – a battle which all the prophets had to wage, and without which no vital change in the moral make-up of men can be brought about. There will then be born in every Muslim home good men who will fully correspond to the description contained in the following verses of the Holy Qur'ān:

> *They were youths who believed in their Lord, and We advanced them in guidance. We gave strength to their hearts; behold, they stood up and said: 'Our Lord is the Lord of the heavens and of the earth; never shall we call upon any god other than Him; if we did, we should indeed have uttered an enormity.*
>
> al-Kahf 18:13-14

The world will then again see living specimens of the religious earnestness and sacrificial spirit of Bilāl and ʿAmmār, Khabbāb and Khubaib, Ṣuhaib and Musʿab ibn ʿUmair and ʿUthmān ibn Maẓʿūn and

Anas ibn an-Naḍr; the gentle breeze of faith will once again kiss the face of the earth and a new world quite different from the one we know will come into existence.

Today, Muslim society is a victim of complacency and compromise with prevailing circumstances. The perils which are so relentlessly closing in from all sides leave it unmoved. It is drifting and it does not know to what end. Its heart is without the warmth of desire.

There is a dire need to disturb the complacency of this Community of the Faithful; it must be persuaded to care for human welfare more than its own interests.

Maturity of Outlook

No matter how well-provided with material resources a nation may be, it cannot hope to go far in the world without maturity of thought. In such a predicament it will always be playing into the hands of adventurers and exploiters.

Unfortunately, the followers of Islam cannot distinguish between good and bad and will just as happily place their trust in a foe as in a friend. Often, indeed, it turns out to be easier for their enemies to win their confidence than for their well-wishers to do so. The Holy Prophet ﷺ once said, "A Muslim is not bitten twice from the same hole".[242] Now it is just the reverse. The political awakening among Muslims is almost nil. They are constantly acting so as to invite foreigners and their own selfish leaders to exploit them.

Conversely, Western nations are characterized by a keen political awareness. No one can easily misguide them and they choose their leaders with care. However glorious a leader's record might be, if they feel that he has done all he can a new man is called for, and he will be replaced without hesitation. This is why these nations are, on the whole, safe from the machinations of manipulative politicians and dishonest leaders – their rulers know that an enlightened public is difficult to deceive.

The Muslim world cannot afford to lose time in catching up with the West in inculcating proper consciousness among its masses and educating them in the responsibilities of good citizenship. It goes without saying that mere education is no proof of consciousness in a community, though it is a necessary condition thereof. Deliberate and systematic steps will have to be taken in this direction. It is for a Muslim leadership to realize that people who cannot do their own thinking cannot constitute a reliable people, however much enthusiasm they may show for a cause. There is no stability in their thoughts and emotions. They have a weakness for clever words; they are prone to think with their heart rather than with their head. Any slogan can lure them away, any charmer can fool them.

In spite of being a revealed religion, having its roots in Divine Revelation and the Holy Prophet's Mission, Islam worked out a typical consciousness among its people – a consciousness that was deeper, stronger and wider than what we mean by it today. It developed a frame of mind that was anti-pagan and an understanding which, with all its breadth and flexibility, could not for a moment accommodate beliefs and notions which were inconsistent with its own basic pattern.

Take, for example, the following incident. Owing to the teachings of the Prophet ﷺ, it was fixed firmly in the minds of the Companions that injustice was an evil which was not to be permitted in any circumstance. They had given up their ancient family and tribal predilections, believing that there was no place for such things in Islam. Then one day they heard the Prophet ﷺ say: "Stand by your brother, be he the aggressor or the aggrieved."[243] Had there been the slightest weakness in the development of their new understanding, they would have readily accepted the command in its apparent meaning; firstly, because of the background of their native traditions and, secondly, because they believed as a matter of faith that what the Holy Prophet ﷺ said was not from his own umderstanding but from Divine inspiration. Their loyalty to the Prophet ﷺ was unmatched. Yet, they could not resist speaking out, "Helping the aggrieved is all right, O Prophet of God, but how can one help the aggressor?" The Prophet ﷺ explained that the way to help the aggressor was to restrain him from committing aggression. This gave them a new understanding. But until they had heard it, they were not disposed to accept even the advice of the Prophet ﷺ in spite of their implicit faith in him. This was because Islam had taught them to exercise their judgement and they learned how to use it.

Similarly, the Prophet ﷺ once despatched an army under the command of a Companion and enjoined on it to remain obedient to its commander. On the way the commander became upset with his men and had kindled a large fire. He ordered the soldiers to march into the fire. The soldiers refused. They said that they had embraced Islam to save themselves from fire and not to march into it.[244] When the incident was reported to the Prophet ﷺ he commended the action of the soldiers and said that had they stepped into the fire, they would never have come out of it (meaning that they would have gone straight to hell).

The Companions did not hesitate to challenge even the Caliph publicly if they suspected him to be guilty of a wrong act. Once, as the mighty Caliph ʿUmar, may Allah be pleased with him, arose to address a gathering, he was cut short by Salmān al-Fārisī, may Allah be pleased with him, who said that he would "neither listen to, nor obey" the Caliph unless he explained how he happened to be wearing a garment made of two pieces of cloth while to others he had allotted only one piece each. ʿUmar, may Allah be pleased with him, advised him to be patient, and then he called upon his son, ʿAbdullāh. At first there was no response. ʿUmar called again, "O ʿAbdullāh, the son of ʿUmar!" This time ʿAbdullāh got up. ʿUmar said to him, "Tell them whether the *ḥullah*[245] I am wearing is my own or one borrowed from you." ʿAbdullāh affirmed that it was his (ʿAbdullāh's) and that he had only lent it to his father for use. On hearing this, Salmān said, "Proceed Amīr'-ul-Mu'minīn, we will now listen to you."[246]

This powerful awakening proved to be the strongest obstacle against the imperialistic ambitions of the Umayyads. It was not until the entire generation that had been brought up under the influence of the Prophet ﷺ had passed away that the Umayyads could breathe a sigh of relief.

Intellectual Core

Every movement has an intellectual background. No revolution can succeed unless the minds of the people have been prepared. A study of the French Revolution will show how irresistible the masses can become once their minds are aroused. The French Revolution was not the outcome of a sudden impulse. Its leaders had patiently prepared the minds of Frenchmen much in advance. There was an army of intellectuals who had given meaningful content to the popular urges that ultimately found expression in the three-word slogan of "Liberty, Equality and Fraternity". Though its leaders were not able to make the revolution beneficial for humanity, it proved to be a mighty force in human history because it sprang from the minds of the people.

That the West is still alive and powerful, is due to the keen political consciousness and the civic sense of its people. One hears rarely of anyone in the West violating his allegiance to his country or subordinating national interests to personal considerations.

Leaders in Muslim countries, on the other hand, though they mortgage the destiny of their people, yet people will still swell their ranks and dance to their tunes. In a number of Muslim countries conditions are extremely deplorable – the common man leads a sub-human existence, the authority of God is brazenly violated and all sorts of shameful acts are committed – and yet this arouses neither pain nor indignation among Muslims. This is so because the process of thinking among Muslims is stagnant and their social consciousness almost dead.

It is essential for the revival of Islam that conscious efforts are made for the development of an enlightened and responsible public opinion in Muslim countries. Without it all manifestations of religious enthusiasm or political fervour will be merely superficial and of no significance.

No Place for Selfishness

The Arabian Nights tells the story of an age when the State or the Empire was the lengthened shadow of one man – the King or the Caliph – who held sway over society like a huge tree that sends out enormous branches in all directions and robs the tiny plants growing under it of sunshine and air. The wheels of the nation's life moved for him alone; for him alone did the farmers till the soil, the traders ply their trade and the workmen use their tools; for him alone did the authors write, the poets sing, the soldiers march, the mothers give birth, the earth open up its bowels and the seas give up their treasures.

This book exerted enormous influence on Muslim social organization from Baghdad to Cairo and Damascus. The stories of *The Arabian Nights* and the literary masterpieces of *The Book of Aghānī* are living proof of the strength of this influence. But, for all that, the spirit of this age was diametrically opposed to the spirit of Islamic civilization. Islam brought the structure of such a civilization down to earth. The Holy Prophet ﷺ dubbed it the "Age of Ignorance" and foretold the end of the reign of all imperial rulers.

This age has now forfeited its right to continue. The very idea of such an age is revolting to our minds. Who in the current context of things would like a state or society to exist in which a few individuals were permanently sick with indigestion due to over-eating, while the rest were permanently in the throes of death due to starvation? Such a situation is unnatural and unjust. It should not have been tolerated even for a day. If it flourished in the past, it was because Islam had not yet acquired enough strength to expose its hypocrisy. As the Islamic movement spread and people learnt to distinguish clearly between right and wrong, they progressively emerged. The age of *The Arabian Nights* has quit the stage of history for ever.

Islam can have nothing to do with egotism or self-conceit, individual or collective. Whether these sentiments take the form of family or sectarian pride, as in Eastern and Islamic countries, or American capitalism, they are patently un-Islamic. These systems may succeed in putting off their doom for some time, but they are bound ultimately to go. The conscience of humanity cannot be cheated indefinitely. The future of the world is inseparably linked with the social justice of Islam.

Industrial and Military Self-Sufficiency

If the Muslim world really wants to rise up and make Islam once again the instrument of realizing human destiny, it can no longer afford to ignore its educational, scientific and industrial development and the organization of its military strength. It must quickly make itself independent of the West and attain a position wherein it can use its natural resources, manufacture its weapons and feed and clothe its people without having to look to others for assistance. It must build up its economic and military strength so that it does not have to rely on another power for security and protection.

As long as Muslim countries depend on the West for economic and military aid, the West will continue to keep them weak and disorganized. In the past, Muslims were neglectful of their duty to themselves and to the rest of the world, and they were condemned to a long period of servitude and misery. The rule of the West was imposed upon them, which proved to be the starting point of the degeneracy of man in modern times. If Muslims do not pay immediate attention to their intellectual and economic re-birth, the period of their suffering will be extended and the world will be damned indefinitely.

Educational Reorganization

The educational set-up of the Islamic world will have to be thoroughly overhauled in the light of Islamic ideals and precepts. To learn from Western countries which are scientifically and technologically advanced is one thing, but the moment Muslims forget that their roots are in Islam, and become the intellectual followers of others, their creative energies will be dampened. In former times, the intellectual leadership of the Muslims was accepted all over the world. Their culture and learning could be observed in every sphere of human life all over the globe. For a long time the world continued to think in the Islamic way and draw inspiration from Islamic life. Arabic was the vehicle of learning in the Western world and every writer of note used this language to express himself. Sometimes an original book was brought out in Arabic and a summary of it was produced in another language, such as Imām al-Ghazālī's *Kīmiyā-i-Saʿādat.* Though the educational system introduced by the ʿAbbāsids was more Greek and Iranian in its essence than Islamic, and had a number of defects from the academic point of view, it gained currency almost everywhere.

But times changed, and Western rule began. This brought with it a new attitude towards learning, which was the product of Europe's own cultural experiences and needs. The world began to follow the new structure blindly. Muslim countries, too, on account of their intellectual sluggishness, succumbed to the illusion that their salvation lay only in slavish submission to the West and to its educational system.

The ground was thus prepared for not merely intellectual adoration but also for imitation of Western civilization by the Muslim intelligentsia. Religious scepticism, conceit, discontent and other characteristics of the modern Western mode of living began steadily to replace the cultural ideals of the rising generations of Muslims. The spiritual civilization of Islam began systematically to be replaced by the material culture of Europe.

For the regaining of world leadership for Islam it is vital that Muslims should re-establish their intellectual superiority over the West. For this the Islamic culture will have to re-assert itself. Crusading endeavours will have to be made in all branches of learning. This, obviously, cannot be achieved by a few individuals or associations; Muslim states should take the task of intellectual regeneration seriously in hand. High-powered committees and institutions should immediately be set up for the purpose of evolving an educational structure that fully conforms to the spirit of the Qur'ān and the *Sunnah* without overlooking the requirements of modern learning and scientific research. Muslim educationists and scientists should apply their own speculative reasoning to the empirical sciences so that they can save the coming generations of Muslims from developing a feeling of contempt for their own past and a despair for their future.

This is how an Islamic revival can be brought about. This is the way in which Muslims can spread the light of Islam to far-away lands and save mankind from the stark ruin that is staring it in the face. Such leadership will not be easy – it will call for tremendous faith, labour and sacrifice.

VIII

LEADERSHIP OF THE ARAB WORLD*

The Arab world occupies a very significant place on the world map. It has been the birth-place of people who have played an important and determining role in history. In it lie treasures of unlimited wealth and power. It has oil which is the life-stream of industrial and military power. It is a link between Europe and the Far East and is the pulsating heart of the entire Muslim world, to which this world turns, with everlasting affection and devotion, for its religious and spiritual needs. Its significance is also heightened by the possibility of it becoming the stage for a third World War. It has hands that are strong and minds that are sharp and bodies that can endure the hardships of war. It has big markets and land of great fertility. It has Egypt, through which runs the Nile, and which, with its fertile soil and its long tradition of civilization and culture, occupies a special position in the world. In the Arab world lies Palestine which, with its neighbouring lands is distinguished for its natural beauty, delightful weather and its strategic importance. It contains Iraq which is famous for its boldness, valour, courage and for its great reservoirs of oil.

The Arabian peninsula is unique in that it is the religious and spiritual nerve-centre of the Muslim world, where the annual assembly of people from around the globe for *Ḥajj* has no parallel anywhere. It has wells that produce huge amounts of oil.

---

* Translated into English by Asadullah Kazmi.

These are some of the factors that have made the Arab world the focus of attention of the Western powers, the centre of their aspirations for supremacy, and the battleground of their struggle for leadership. All this, in turn, has created a strong sentiment of Arab nationalism.

The Prophet Muḥammad ﷺ

There is a world of difference between the way in which a European and a Muslim look at the Arab world. Even the way a nationalist Arab regards it is quite different from that of a Muslim from another part of the world. To Muslims in general, the Arab world is the cradle of Islam, a refuge for humanity, a tower of light and the very source of Muslim leadership. A Muslim believes that Muḥammad, the Prophet of Islam ﷺ, is the soul of the Arab world, the cornerstone of its prestige and the title to its glory. Without Muḥammad ﷺ this land, in spite of its riches and wealth of resources, will be no more than a picture without colour or a body without spirit. It is Muḥammad ﷺ alone who brought the Arab world into being. This world, before he came, was a world of divided people and warring tribes over which hovered clouds of ignorance and darkness. Its potentialities lay untapped and its real virtues undiscovered.

The Arabs at that time could not, even in their wildest dreams, think of waging a successful war against such imperial powers of the day as Rome and Persia. The very thought was impossible for them to conceive. Syria, which subsequently became an important part of the Arab world, was still a Roman colony and was at the mercy of a ruthless and cruel dictatorship. It did not understand the concept of justice or know the meaning of freedom. Iraq was the victim of the greed and plundering of the Sāssānid rulers of Persia. New levies and ever-increasing taxation had almost broken the back of the people. The Romans held Egypt and treated it like a domestic animal from which is to be squeezed out the last drop of milk but which is badly looked after and poorly fed. Along with political domination, it was also subjected to religious persecution.

Then came a breath of fresh air. Muḥammad ﷺ appeared. He

arrived at a time when the Arab world was on the verge of destruction and the pulse of its life at a very low ebb. He gave it a new life, a new sense of direction, knowledge, wisdom and enlightenment and taught it discipline and self-reliance. Through him, the Arab world was completely transformed. It was now the ambassador of Islam, a messenger of peace and security, a source of comfort and grace to the people and the torchbearer of culture and civilization.

Today we speak of Syria, Iraq and Egypt with pride. Had there been no Prophet of Islam ﷺ with his message, there would be no Syria, no Iraq, no Egypt; in fact, no Arab world. Not only that, the world could not have reached the high level of culture and refinement it did, nor could knowledge, arts and science have achieved such high standards.

If today any one of the countries wishes to turn its face from Islam to the West, cast nostalgic eyes at its pre-Islamic state or emulate the West in its ordering of life, its laws, its forms and systems of government and does not accept the Holy Prophet ﷺ as its teacher, guide and leader, it should give up the blessings he brought and revert to its previous state. It will then go back to an age in which Roman and Persian imperialism held absolute sway, persecution and tyranny reigned supreme and in which people were steeped in ignorance and darkness and the Arabs stagnated in a life of obscurity.

The Arab world, with its glorious history and its great achievements in refinement and culture, in knowledge and scholarship, in arts and science is the product of the advent of Muḥammad ﷺ and the message he brought.

Faith is the Real Strength of the Arabs

Faith in Islam is the only unifying force of the Arab world and the Holy Prophet ﷺ its only leader and guide. It was this faith that enabled the Arabs to successfully face all opposition and conquer all difficulties in their march forward to secure a fair deal for humanity. It is still the real source of all its strength and is available even today. It still remains the most effective weapon with which the Arab world can hold its own against its foes, preserve its existence and forge ahead and recover the prestige and power it once had. If the Arab world has to fight any of its foes, it cannot do so with the support it receives from England or the arms it accepts from America or even the money it earns by selling its oil to the West. It can only fight with the help of that faith, spiritual strength and fervour with which it fought Rome and Persia simultaneously and inflicted on both of them a crushing defeat. It cannot fight with a heart that is in love with life and fears death, a hand that has been enfeebled by a life of ease and luxury and a mind that has been riddled by doubt and scepticism and in which high ideals and mean urges, noble thoughts and base instincts keep up a constant struggle. It has to be remembered that no one can fight the battles of life on borrowed arms, with a faith that is weak and a mind that is torn with doubt.

The most important duty of Arab leadership is to inspire the hearts of its soldier, farmer and its common man with faith, rekindle in them the zeal for righteous strife and struggle in the path of God, breed in them contempt for material wealth, its pomp and ceremony and train them to face death with ease. They should be taught to give once again their best in life so that it is blessed as it was blessed by the sweat and toil and sacrifice of their forefathers.

The Supreme Importance of Keeping up the Martial and Manly Spirit of the Arabs

It is unfortunate that the Arabs today seem to be neglecting habits and practices that kept their martial characteristics alive and active. Take, for instance, horsemanship for which the Arabs were famous throughout the world. Horsemanship is now almost a forgotten art and is fast disappearing from the daily life of the Arabs. If horsemanship is allowed to disappear completely from Arab life, it will be a national loss and will greatly impair their manly spirit which used to be the most distinguishing trait in the Arab character. The horse is now superseded by the car and there is a real danger of the Arab horse, the pride of the world, becoming extinct. The Arabs have practically given up all those manly activities – such as horsemanship, archery, wrestling – that keep up the martial spirit and have instead adopted games and sports which have but little value. It is incumbent on Arab educators to revive the martial spirit in their people, rekindle in them a love for the hard life and train them to face difficulties and hardships with courage and fortitude. ʿUmar, the Leader of the Faithful, wrote thus to the Arab governors appointed to non-Arab countries:

> Keep aloof from a life of ease and avoid expensive and ornate styles of dress; keep up your habit of working in the sun for sunshine is the bath of the Arabs. Remain accustomed to simple dress, hardship and labour and be steadfast and patient; retain the habit of leaping on horseback with alacrity and keep up the practice of archery and marksmanship.[247]

The Holy Prophet ﷺ has said: "O Ye Arabs, keep up practising archery because your great ancestor (Ismāʿīl) was a great marksman";[248] and again: "Remember (the power which the Qur'ān emphasizes) is marksmanship."[249]

It is an essential part of the duties of Arab educators to fight against everything that saps the spirit of manliness and breeds effeminacy or incompetence, ban all indecent journalism and obscene literature that corrupts youth by propagating hypocrisy, shamelessness, and the pursuit of sensuous pleasures. They should not let those who propagate such things enter the camp of the Holy Prophet ﷺ as they corrupt the morals of Muslim youth and who, for a handful of silver, paint in glowing colours sin and libertinism, indecency and immorality.

History bears witness to the fact that whenever a people begins to lose its manliness, sense of honour and discipline, and its women fight against their very nature, give way to license in the name of freedom, and ape man in the name of equality, become indifferent to domestic virtues and seek to avoid the responsibilities of motherhood, then such a people is doomed. Hardly any trace is ever left of its greatness. Such was the fate of the Greeks, the Romans and the Persians and towards such a fate seems to be heading Europe and the world at large today.

A Curb on Extravagance and Liquidation of the Growing Difference among People

Owing to various influences the Arabs have, unfortunately, acquired habits of spending extravagantly on the non-essentials of life. And alongside this extravagance there exist poverty and wretchedness, want and hunger. When a person visits the cities of the Arab world he is filled with shame and distress as he witnesses the appalling difference between rich and poor. He sees, on the one hand, a man who spends lavishly on the luxuries of life and, on the other, a destitute who cannot afford even one meal a day or a good piece of cloth to cover his naked body. When Arab men of wealth cruise by in their powerful limousines, a host of hungry children clad in rags runs by, begging for coppers.

As long as lofty mansions stand beside hovels and hunger and want exist alongside opulence, the doors on forces of disruption can never be closed. No propaganda, however loud and persuasive, and no power, however strong and pervasive, can do it. Unless the Islamic system with all its virtues is established in those lands, the unchangeable retributive laws of God will come in and, as a reaction, a system that will be ruthless and cruel.

Self-Sufficiency in Finance, Commerce and Industry

It is imperative for the Arab states, as it is for the rest of the Muslim world, to acquire self-sufficiency in all their financial, commercial, industrial and educational needs. These countries possess all the necessary prerequisites for self-sufficiency. The people of these lands should, to begin with, use only what they produce with their own efforts out of their own resources.[250] These states should learn to exist without Europe in all spheres of life. They should not look to Europe for food, clothes, arms and machines.

The situation today is that, if for some unforeseen reason, the Arab world is obliged to take up arms against a European power, it cannot fight because it is indebted to that power and depends a great deal on its help. This dependence has reached such lengths that even the fountain pen with which an Arab state signs an agreement with a

European power is made in Europe. If and when the Arab world has to fight, it fights with arms and ammunition manufactured in Europe. The great tragedy of the Arab world today is that it cannot utilize, without outside help, its great reservoirs of wealth, energy and power. Instead of flowing in its own veins, its life-blood is transfused into the veins of others. It is the army officers of European powers that train its armies and European experts and agents that look after the other departments of its life.

If the Arab world has to stand on its own feet, as it must, then it should be the master in its own house. It should be able to look after its own needs and requirements, have complete control over its economy and over the training of its soldiers and technicians. It should certainly train its own people to shoulder responsibilities and discharge them efficiently with integrity and loyalty.

The Personal Sacrifice made by the Arabs in the Past for the Welfare and Happiness of Mankind

As said earlier, the Prophet of Islam ﷺ came with his message at a time when mankind had reached almost the last stage of misery and wretchedness.

To relieve humanity of its misery was beyond those who were, at that time, the overlords of life. They had neither the vision, courage, nor desire to undertake such a task. Luxurious living had sapped their energies and greed and avarice undermined their courage. They had become incapable of giving up even a fraction of their comforts for any noble cause. They could not face hardships and had no stamina left for the trials and tribulations inherent in such a struggle. They could not look beyond their immediate interests, they could have no thought for others and were not willing to give up anything for the collective good of mankind.

Mankind was in dire need of those who were cast in a different mould. It needed men who held life cheap and who could risk their wealth and prosperity, even their lives for its sake. Mankind cried out for those who cared neither for loss nor gain and who would not hesitate to sacrifice the high hopes and aspirations entertained of them by their own people and about whom these people would say what the people of Ṣāliḥ said about him: "*O Ṣāliḥ, thou hast been of us! – a centre of our hopes*" (Holy Qur'ān, Hūd 11:62).

The salvation of humanity is not achieved by force. It depends on the moral courage and the spirit of self-sacrifice of a handful of people who, by worldly standards, are often considered to be lacking in good fortune. It is they who, courting dangers and trials, release millions of people from their miseries and lead them from despair to hope and from wretchedness to grace. They are the people who consider it a cheap bargain if, by the sacrifice of a few, many are able to achieve dignity and prosperity and if, by some loss of prosperity and wealth, the doors of material and spiritual well-being are opened for many.

At the time of the Prophet of Islam ﷺ, the Romans and the Persians, who shared power in the world, had become weak and had neither the moral courage to risk the comforts of life nor the stamina to face the trials and hardships of the struggle for humanity at large. They would not give up even a small portion of the luxuries with which they had surrounded themselves. Such people were scarce among them who, by controlling their physical appetites and instincts, greed and avarice, liberate themselves from the bondage of luxurious living and lead a more purposeful life, dedicated to high and noble ideals. For such a cause a different people were chosen by divine providence. The Arabs were chosen to be the companions and followers of the Holy Prophet of Islam ﷺ, and his great mission to ennoble life. The people were filled with a spirit of dedication and sacrifice and prepared themselves to sacrifice all that they possessed in meeting the great trials that faced them in fulfilling the mission. The falseness of sophisticated culture and luxurious living could not lure, nor worldly pomp and show charm them. They were rich because they knew contentment; they were wise because they understood the higher values of life. The Prophet of Islam ﷺ himself faced, in full measure, trials and hardships, privations and dangers in carrying out completely his great mission. He set his face against all worldly desires and ambitions, and everything that stood in the way of his mission. Worldly success with all its allurements could cast no spell on him, nor could any power on earth make him deviate from his path. The choicest gifts of life, like political power and supremacy, wealth and luxury which could ensnare the heart of any man, were readily rejected by him when offered, while he was still a young man, by the Quraysh. Again when, on the insistence of the Quraysh, his own uncle tried to dissuade him from his mission, he said: "O My uncle, I swear by God that if the Quraysh put the sun in my right hand and the moon in my left, I will not give up my mission until it prevails or I perish in my efforts."[251]

This striving for truth at all costs, this supreme indifference towards worldly ease and comfort and this deliberate choice of a life of dedication, hardship and trial set an inspiring example to his followers and to those who had a noble mission to discharge and a high destiny to fulfil. In the discharge of his mission, the Holy Prophet of Islam ﷺ denied ease and comfort and good living not only to himself but to all those who were near to him like his wives, children, relatives and friends. Those who were closest to him received less and much was taken from them. They were the first in the struggle and the last to reap its benefits. Whenever he prohibited anything, he prohibited it first for his own people. Whenever there was any opportunity for material gain, others were considered first and his own last. They were often deprived of the good things of life when and if they came the way of the Muslims in general. When he prohibited usury, he began with his own uncle ʿAbbās ibn ʿAbdul Muṭṭalib, whose money-lending business was the first to be closed and the interest that had gathered annulled. He acted in the same manner when he stood up to mitigate the evils of blood feuds and forgave those who had killed his own kinsman, Rabīʿah ibn al-Ḥārith ibn ʿAbdul Muṭṭalib. When *zakāh* was distributed, he forbade for ever his own family and his descendants from accepting any portion, however poor they might be.

When, after the conquest of Makkah, his cousin ʿAlī ibn Abī Ṭālib, may Allah be pleased with him, claimed, on behalf of Banū Hāshim, the custody of the key of the Kaʿbah, he was met with a stern refusal. The

Holy Prophet ﷺ sent for ʿUthmān ibn Ṭalḥah and putting the key before him said: "ʿUthmān! This key is yours, take it. This is the day of recompense for obligations and pledges fulfilled. This key will remain with you for ever. Nobody can take it from you unless he takes it unjustly with a cruel hand."[252] He preached austerity and simplicity of life to his wives and told them, in clear terms, that if they were willing to share with him a life of hardships they could stay with him. If, on the other hand, they preferred a life of ease and comfort, they were free to leave him. He told them of what God has said:

> *O Prophet, say to your wives: 'If you desire the comforts of life then come, I will give you some worldly goods and send you away with good grace. If, however, you prefer God, his Prophet, and the life Hereafter, then for those of you who do good deeds, God has prepared a great reward.*
>
> Holy Qur'ān, al-Aḥzāb 33:28-9

The world knows what their choice was. When his own daughter, Fāṭimah, approached the Holy Prophet ﷺ, with her hands blistered by constant grinding of corn and asked for a servant from the common pool so that she might receive a little help with this burdensome work, she was told that her request could be considered only after the claims of other people had been met. Instead of a servant she was given a special form of prayer for the glorification and praise of God. This was how all the Prophet's relatives were treated. The nearer the relation, the greater his responsibility.

Such examples of selflessness inspired and sustained those who, by embracing Islam, had lost a great deal of their worldly possessions. Many of them were used to a life of ease and comfort and were known for their rich and luxurious way of living. Many had lost even the very means of earning a livelihood. Events that were to shape the destiny of mankind seemed to wait for these people to decide whether they were willing or not to sacrifice themselves for the ultimate good of man. The decision was given in no uncertain terms. The Arabs decided to face the struggle and triumphed. They withstood trials and faced hardships with a fortitude that is rare in the history of man. And more was demanded of them. When the *Ansārs* in Madīnah, who, in serving Islam, had severely neglected their farms and orchards, their main source of subsistence, asked for a little time to look after them, they were told abruptly, in the words of the Holy Qur'ān: "*Spend in the path of God and do not destroy yourself with your own hands*" (al-Baqarah 2:195).

Such were the lessons of self-restraint and discipline which the Prophet ﷺ taught, not merely by word of mouth but also by example to those who were to carry the message and discharge its great responsibilities. Such was also the training of those Arabs and others who subsequently accepted the mission and who had their full share of the difficulties and hardships in the struggle for its development. They are admonished by God thus: "*If you hold your parents and children, your brothers and sisters, your wives and families, the wealth you have acquired and the trade you fear to lose dearer than God and His Apostle, then wait till God sends His judgement. God never leads to victory those who obey not (His judgement)*" (Holy Qur'ān, al-Tawbah 9:24). At another place it is said: "*It is not for the people of Medina and the Arabs of the neighbourhood to refuse to follow God's Apostle or to prefer their own lives to him*" (al-Tawbah 9:120).

Such were the people on whose resolve and courage, renunciation and sacrifice were to be built the prosperity and happiness of mankind. And they were tested again and again. They are told: "*But surely we will test you with something of fear and hunger, some loss of goods, or lives, of the fruit (of your toil)*" (al-Baqarah 2:155). Again they were told: "*Will they be left alone by merely saying we believe and not be tested*" (al-ʿAnkabūt 29:2). If the Arabs had hesitated to accept this leadership and feared to shoulder its great responsibilities, the darkness and ignorance of contemporary life could not have diminished, nor the period of its misery and wretchedness shortened: "*If you do not do this, there would be tumult and aggression on earth and great mischief thereof*" (al-Anfāl 8:73).

The world stood at a crossroads in the 6th century CE. Two alternatives were available. One was for a group of dedicated and divinely-inspired people to go forward, risk prosperity and wealth, kith and kin and all that is dear to man's heart, deny all pleasures of life and offer even their lives for the collective good of mankind. The other was to remain unchanged and continue a life of narrow self-interest, of self-indulgence, of preferring personal gain to the general well-being of human beings. In that event the world lulled by ignorance and apathy would have remained immersed in the bog of misery and darkness.

God, however, gave the Arabs the strength and courage to take up the first alternative. The fate of humanity was decided and man began to march forward under the leadership of the Arabs. The Prophet ﷺ breathed into the Arabs the spirit of faith and sacrifice, and taught them to believe wholeheartedly in the life to come, and the great rewards it offered to those who believe and do righteous deeds. Uplifted by hopes of this reward and inspired by the spirit of service, these Arabs turned their eyes away from the comforts of life, gave up all that man's heart covets and sacrificed themselves in order to help humanity achieve happiness and dignity. They toiled with faith and sincerity and did not hesitate even to give up their lives. God, therefore, blessed them with the best of rewards: "*Verily God loves those who do righteous deeds*" (Holy Qur'ān, al-Mā'idah 5:93).

The world today has reached a state very similar to that in which it found itself in the 6th century CE. The time has surely come when the Arabs should come forward and offer once again their lives in order to change the fate of humanity. To release it from its present miseries and save it from impending disasters, they should risk once again their ease and comfort, wealth and possessions, even their future prospects. Then the course of humanity would be transformed once again and man would walk in dignity towards the goal of his destiny. The other alternative is that the Arabs remain engrossed in petty aims of personal gain, of preference for offices, salaries and securing better and still better means of personal comfort. In that case the world will remain in the swamp in which it has been floundering for some time.

If the Arab youth, enslaved by thoughts of selfish ends, remains tied down to the comforts and distractions of big cities, if the pivot around which its life revolves is but the stomach and material comfort, if all its efforts and energies are directed towards its personal well-being and worldly success, then the resurgence of humanity will remain a mere dream never to be realized. The youth of the pre-Islamic period had equally big stakes in life and the same high intelligence but, in pursuing the path of its choice, it sacrificed its physical comforts and even its future for the sake of Islam. The poet Imra'ul Qays said: "Were I trying for an ordinary life, a little would be enough. But I aspire for a greatness that lasts and is worthy of a man like me."

Once again the courage of the Muslim youth is needed. With its sacrifice, it could build a bridge so that life could cross over to its essential nobility and happiness. Life, like soil, needs fertilizers. That, which can fertilize life so that it gives of its best, is the sacrifice of the Muslim youth of its personal ambitions in order to bring Islam to its full fruition and fill God's earth with peace and plenty. Today a forsaken humanity demands the courage and determination of those who can, for its sake, give up ease and comfort, opportunities of worldly gain and concern for individual success and prosperity.

If the Muslims in general and the Arabs in particular decide to take up the challenge and if, by the sacrifice of a few, humanity is brought back from the path of ruin to the path that leads to salvation, then it will be an excellent bargain indeed, the gains of which will far outweigh the sacrifices. An Urdu poem says:

> O heart, it is all gain in the bargain of love.
> Its only loss of life, and it is not such a loss after all.

What the Islamic World Expects from the Arab World

Because of its characteristics, its situation, and its political importance the Arab world has the right and the necessary competence to shoulder the responsibilities of the mission of Islam. It can easily take up the leadership of the entire Muslim world, strengthen itself to look Europe in the face and, by the grace of God and the strength of its faith, acquire supremacy and lead the world once again from darkness into light, from wretchedness to grace, from destruction and ruin to peace and prosperity. In the words of the Muslim messenger to the court of Xerxes it could once again: "lead men from the worship of Man to the worship of God, from the narrowing trivialities of life to the expanse of faith, from the injustices of creeds to the justice and equality of Islam."

The whole world is looking towards the Muslims as its saviour and the Muslim world is looking to the Arabs for guidance and leadership. Can the Muslim world fulfil the expectations of the world? Can the Arab world rise to the challenge? For a long time a bruised and maimed humanity has been crying out, in the words of Iqbal, for help, still believing that the hands that built the Kaʿbah can rebuild humanity:

> Thou art the custodian, the trustee of the Eternal Order.
> Thou art the right and the left flank of the Lord
> of the Universe;
> O! thou creature of dust, thou art the Time and thou
> art the Earth.
> Drink the wine of conviction and get away from the
> tavern of uncertainty.
> Wake up! wake up! from thy deep slumber.
> From thy deep slumber, awake, from thy deep slumber,
> awake, awake.
> From thy deep slumber, from thy deep slumber awake.
> I cry mercy from the wantonness of Europe.
> I cry mercy from the Sheerins and Purvazes of Europe.
> The world has become dissolute by the dispoilation
> of Europe.
> O! thou builder of the Kaʿbah, arise and build a new
> world again.

NOTES

CHAPTER I

1 Sale, *Translation* (1896), p.62.

2 A.J. Butler, *Arabs' Conquest of Egypt and the Last Thirty Years of the Roman Dominion*, pp.29-30.

3 Ibid., pp.183-9.

4 *Encyclopaedia Britannica*, art. 'Justin'.

5 Sale, *Translation*, p.72.

6 *The Decline and Fall of the Roman Empire*, Vol.V, p.31.

7 Ibid., Vol.VII, p.175.

8 *A Short History of the World*, p.170.

9 Robert Briffault, *The Making of Humanity*, p.164.

10 Butler, Ibid., pp.133-4.

11 *Historians' History of the World*, Vol.VIII, p.84.

12 *Tārīkh Ṭabarī*, Vol.III, p.138.

13 A.I. Christensen, *L'Iran Sous Les Sassanides* (Urdu translation by Muhammad Iqbal), p.430.

14 Ibid.

15 Shahrastānī, *Al-Milal wa'l-Niḥal*, p.86.

16 *Tārīkh Ṭabarī*, Vol.II, p.88.

17 *Tārīkh Ṭabarī*, Vol.II and *Tārīkh-i-Iran* by Makarios Irani.

18 Christensen, *L'Iran Sous Les Sassanides*, pp.421-2.

19 At the museum of Taxila, the visitor is amazed at the number of idols and images that have been excavated from ancient Buddhist sites. They reveal how idolatrous the Buddhist religion and civilization had become. Dr. Gustave le Bon writes: "In order to understand what Buddhism really is one should study its relics, not books. These relics tell us a completely different story from the theoretical principles taught by the Western writers. They show that the religion the Western scholars are so fond of presenting to the world as monotheistic is, in fact, at the head of all idolatrous and polytheistic faiths" – *Les Civilisations de l'Inde* (Urdu translation by Sayyid Ali Bilgrami), p.265.

20 Ishwar Topa, *Hindostani Tamaddun*.

21 P.J. Nehru, *The Discovery of India*, pp.201-3.

22 *Tamaddun-i-Hind*, pp.440-1.

23 *Safarnama-i-Hiuen Tsang* (*Maghribi Saltanat*).

24 Ibid.

25 Ibid., p.447.

26 Dayanand Saraswati, *Satyarath Prakash*, p.344.

27 Ibid., p.211

28 Ibid., p.236.

29 Ibid., p.238.

30 Al-Kalbī, *Kitāb-ul-Aṣnām*, p.33.

31 Bukhārī, *Kitāb-ul-Maghāzī*.

32 *Kitāb-ul-Aṣnām*.

33 Ibid., p.44.

34 Ibid., p.34.

35 Ṣāʿid Andalusī, *Ṭabaqāt-ul-Umam*, p.430.

36 The term *Tābiʿī* is applied *par excellence* to those Muslim doctors who followed immediately the '*Aṣḥāb*' or the Companions of the Prophet ﷺ (Translator).

37 *Tafsīr Ṭabarī*.

38 *Al-Maidānī'*.

39 *Kitāb-ul-Aghānī*.

40 *Sunan Dārimī*, Vol.I.

41 Name of a place, some twelve miles from Makkah, where pilgrims have to make a brief halt during the *Ḥajj*.

42 See Qur'ān 2:199.

43 *Dīwān al-Ḥamāsah*.

44 Ibid.

45 *Ayyām-ul-ʿArab*.

46 *Tārīkh Ṭabarī*, Vol.II, p.133.

47 R.V.C. Bodley, *The Messenger, The Life of Muhammad*, pp.18-19.

48 James Carkern, *History of China*.

49 Robert Briffault, *The Making of Humanity*, p. 159.

50 A.J. Butler, *Arabs' Conquest of Egypt*, p.42.

51 Muhammad Kurd Ali, *Khiṭāṭ-ush-Shām*, Vol.I, p.101.

52 Ibid., p.103.

53 Christensen, *L'Iran Sous Les Sassanides*, p.161.

54 A *mithqal* is equal to 4 '*mashas*' 3.1/2 '*rattis*' [4.325 grams] (Translator).

55 The "crown was made of gold and silver and was studded with rubies, emeralds and pearls. It was hung from the roof with a gold chain which was so thin that it could not be seen until one stood very close to the throne. To a viewer from a distance it appeared that the crown was resting on the Emperor's head. But, in truth, it was so heavy that no human being could support it. It weighed 91 kilograms (Christensen, p.531).

56 Ibid., pp.30-7.

57 Briffault, *The Making of Humanity*, p.160.

58 Christensen, *L'Iran Sous Les Sassanides*, p.424.

59 Shahin Makarios, *Tārīkh-i-Iran*, pp.90-211.

60 *Tārīkh Ṭabarī*.

61 Ibid., Vol.IV, p.178.

62 A fragrant gum (Translator).

63 *Aghānī*, Vol.XIV, p.2.

64 A silver coin. Originally it was an unstamped piece of silver, shaped like a date stone. About fifty years after the death of the Prophet ﷺ, it was altered into a round form and stamped. Its value in these days is uncertain (Translator) [a *dirham* is 3.98 grams].

65 *Tārīkh Ṭabarī*, Vol.IV, p.134.

66 Christensen, *L'Iran Sous Les Sassanides*, p.681.

67 *Tārīkh Ṭabarī*, Vol.IV, p.161.

68 Christensen, *L'Iran Sous Les Sassanides*, p.161.

69 Muhammad Kurd Ali, *Khiṭāṭ-ush-Shām*, Vol.V, p.47.

70 Shāh Waliyyullāh was born in 1703 and died in 1762. He wrote on Sociology, Economics, Politics,

Ethics, Mysticism and World History and particularly on Islamic History. His views on Cosmology compare very favourably with those of modern Physicists. The *Ḥujjatullāh-i'l-Bālighah*, the *Budūr Bāzighah*, the *Tafhīmāt-i-Ilāhiyah* and the *Izālat-ul-Khifā'* are his masterpieces. He was mainly instrumental in the defeat of the Maharattas in the third battle of Panipat, 1761 (Editor).

71 The allusion is to the Mughal Emperors of India.

72 *Ḥujjatullāh-i'l-Bālighah*, Vol.I, p.105.

73 The famous Companion of the Holy Prophet Muḥammad ﷺ (Translator).

74 An authentic account of the experiences of Salmān is given in the *Musnad* of Imām Aḥmad Ibn Ḥanbal and in the *Mustadrak* of Ḥākim.

CHAPTER II

75 The reference is to the dispute over the fixing of '*Ḥajar Aswad*' (the Black Stone) when the Kaʿbah was being rebuilt (Translator).

76 The case of Mr. Gandhi provides a striking example. He set himself two moral objects at the beginning of his public career, in the service of which he used all his vast energies and resources, resources such as have been available to few men in modern times. One of these was non-violence. He developed it as a creed and a philosophy of life, and made it the very breath of his existence. But as his approach was different from that of the prophets, he could not produce that fundamental change in the minds of his people which is essential to the success of a moral movement. The principle of non-violence was torn to pieces in his own lifetime (during the holocaust of 1947), and, in the end, Gandhi himself fell a victim to violence. His other objective was the removal of untouchability. In this, too, he did not register any remarkable success. We can, thus, say that the methodology of the prophets is the only sure and successful way of bringing about a radical change for the better in the religious and social affairs of humanity at large.

77 Ibn Hishām, *Sīrah Nabawiyyah*, Vol.I, p.266.

78 Al-Nasā'ī, *Kitāb al-Jihād*.

79 The Madinite Muslims were called '*Ansār*' (meaning 'helpers'), while the Muslims who had migrated from Makkah were called '*Muhajirs*' (meaning 'emigrants') – (Translator).

80 *Jihād* literally means any effort made in a righteous cause, the highest form of which is a war waged for the defence of the Faith.

81 Muslim, *Kitāb-ul-Ḥudūd*.

82 Meaning the tax-collectors of the pre-Islamic days who were extremely cruel in the discharge of their duties.

83 Muslim, *Kitāb-ul-Ḥudūd* (Translator).

84 *Tārīkh Ṭabarī*, Vol.IV, p.16.

85 Ibn Kathīr, *al-Bidāyah wan-*

Nihāyah, Vol.III.

86 Ibid.

87 Bukhārī and Muslim.

88 Muslim.

89 Muslim.

90 *Zād-ul-Maʿād*, Vol.III, p.135.

91 Ibid., p.190.

92 The ceremony of walking round the Kaʿbah at Makkah (Translator)

93 *Zād-ul-Maʿād*, Vol.II, p.332.

94 Ibn Abī Ḥātim.

95 Aḥmad ibn Ḥanbal, *Musnad*, VI, 5, 15.

96 Abū Dāwūd.

97 Ibid.

98 Bukhārī.

99 Ibn Kathīr, *Tafsīr*.

100 Bukhārī and Muslim.

101 Ibn Kathīr, *al-Bidāyah wan-Nihāyah*, Vol.II, p.30.

102 Ibn Isḥāq.

103 Ibn Kathīr, Vol.IV, p.63.

104 *Zād-ul-Maʿād*, Vol.II, p.134.

105 Ibid., p.130.

106 Ibid., p.136.

107 *Ibn Hishām Sīrah*.

108 Ablution performed before prayers (Translator).

109 *Zād-ul-Maʿād*, Vol.III, p.125.

110 Ibid., p.130.

111 Bukhārī and Muslim.

112 *Tafsīr Ibn Jarīr Ṭabrī*, Vol.VII.

113 *Tafsīr Ṭabarī*, Vol.28.

114 Meaning Persia (Translator).

CHAPTER III

115 Bukhārī and Muslim.

116 Ibn al-Jawzī, *Sīrah ʿUmar ibn al-Khaṭṭāb*.

117 It is related by Abū Mūsā Ashʿarī that the Holy Prophet ﷺ once said, "The message with which God has sent me into the world can be compared to a heavy shower of rain that fell over a vast stretch of land. Part of this land was soft and smooth and it absorbed the rain and was turned into a meadow; part of it was uneven and hard and it retained the water which proved to be of great benefit to mankind; people drank it themselves and gave it to others to drink; part of it was altogether flat and barren, which could neither retain the water nor grow anything. The first two instances apply to those who drank in the Divine message to their own advantage and to the advantage of their fellow-beings, while the last one refers to those who paid no heed to what God had revealed to me" – Bukhārī, *Kitāb-ul-ʿIlm*.

118 The Traditions of the Prophet Muḥammad ﷺ (Translator).

119 Islamic Jurisprudence (Translator).

120 Ibn Khaldūn, *Muqaddimah*, p.499.

121 Aḥmad ibn Marwān Mālikī, *Kitāb-ul-Mujālasah*.

122 Ibn Kathīr, *al-Bidāyah wan-Nihāyah*, Vol.VII, p.53

123 Ibid., p.18.

124 Ibn al-Jawzī, *Sīrah ʿUmar ibn al-Khaṭṭāb*.

125 Muhammad Asad (Leopold Weiss), *Islam at the Crossroads* (Lahore, 1955), pp.26-9.

126 Aḥmad Amīn, *Duḥa'l Islām*.

127 *The Making of Humanity*, p.190.
128 Ibid., p.202.
129 Ibn Jubair, p.302.
130 Ibn al-Jawzī, *Ṣaydul-Khāṭir.*
131 *Taḍhkiratul-ʿUlamā'.*

CHAPTER IV

132 Maidānī, *Al-Amthāl.*
133 Stanley Lane-Poole, *Saladin*, p.25.
134 *Encyclopaedia Britannica* (9th Edition), Vol.VI, art. 'Crusades'.
135 During the Caliphate of Abū Bakr, may Allah be pleased with him (Translator).
136 *Al-Kāmil*, Vol. XI, p.164.
137 *Saladin*, p.214.
138 *Tārīkh* of Abul Fidā' Ḥamawī.
139 *Saladin*, p.234.
140 Ibid., p.358.
141 Ibid., p.359.
142 *Al-Kāmil*, Vol. XIII, pp.202-3.
143 Ibn Kathīr.
144 Tax levied by a Muslim State on its non-Muslim subjects in lieu of exemption from military duty (Translator).
145 Ibn Kathīr, Vol.XIII, p.304.
146 M. Jamil Beyham, *Falsafat-ut-Tarikhil-Usmani*, p.274.
147 Ibid., pp.280-1.
148 Jurji Zaydān, *Tārīkh-u-Misr.*
149 Halide Edib, *Conflict of East and West in Turkey*, pp.480-2.
150 Expounding the thesis that modern England has been made great by wealth plundered from India, Brooks Adams says: "Very soon after Plassey the Bengal plunder began to arrive in London, and the effect appears to have been instantaneous, for all authorities agree that the 'Industrial Revolution, the event that has divided the 19th century from all antecedent time began with the year 1760...Plassey was fought in 1757, and probably nothing has ever equalled the rapidity of the change which followed...In themselves inventions are passive, many of the most important having lain dormant for centuries, waiting for a sufficient store of force to have accumulated to have set them working. That store must always take the shape of money, and money not hoarded, but in motion...Before the influx of the Indian treasure, and the expansion of credit which followed, no force sufficient for this purpose existed...The factory system was the child of the 'Industrial Revolution', and until capital had accumulated in masses, capable of giving solidity to large bodies of labour, manufactures were necessarily carried on by scattered individuals...Possibly since the world began, no investment has ever yielded the profit reaped from the Indian plunder, because for nearly fifty years Great Britain stood without a competitor" (*The Law of Civilization and Decay*, London, 1898, pp.313-17).

Writing in the same vain, Sir William Digby says: "England's industrial supremacy owes its origin to the vast hoards of Bengal and the Karnatik being made available for her use...Before Plassey was fought and won, and before the stream of treasure began to flow to England, the industries of our country were at a very low ebb" (*Prosperous India: A Revelation*, p.30).

151 Dr. Ahmad Amīn, *Zu^c^amā'-ul-Iṣlāḥ fil ^c^Aṣr-il-Ḥadīth*, p.6.

CHAPTER V

152 Halide Edib, *The Conflict of East and West in Turkey*, pp.226-7.

153 W.E.H. Lecky, *History of European Morals* (London, 1869), Vol.I, pp.344-5.

154 *Republic*, Book VII.

155 Lecky, *History of European Morals*, Vol.I, p.243.

156 Ibid., p.178.

157 Ibid., p.179.

158 Ibid., p.178.

159 Ibid., p.177.

160 Muhammad Asad, *Islam at the Crossroads*, pp.38-9.

161 J.W. Draper, *History of the Conflict Between Religion and Science* (London, 1927) pp.31-2.

162 Ibid., pp.34-5.

163 Ibid., p.40.

164 Ibid., pp.40-1.

165 *Iqtiḍā'-uṣ-Ṣirāṭ-il-Mustaqīm*, p.143.

166 *Kitāb-un-Nubuwwāt.*

167 Abū Dāwūd.

168 Bukhārī.

169 Lecky, *History of European Morals*, Vol.II, pp.162-6.

170 Draper, *Religion and Science*, p.230.

171 Ibid., pp.234-5.

172 *Islam at the Crossroads*, pp.55-6.

173 C.E.M. Joad, *Guide to Modern Wickedness*, pp.114-5.

174 *Philosophy for Our Times*, pp.338-40.

175 Agha Muhammad Ashraf Dehlavi, *Hawa'i Hamla.*

176* Ibn Hishām, *Sīrah Nabawiyyah.*

177 *Ṭabā'i^c^-ul-Istibdād.*

178 *Guide to Modern Wickedness*, pp.235-6.

179 Convocation Address, Aligarh Muslim University, January 1938.

180 *Guide to Modern Wickedness*, pp.150-1.

181 Abū Dāwūd.

182 Bukhārī.

183 Muslim, Nasā'i.

184 Muslim.

185 *Guide to Modern Wickedness*, pp.152-3.

186 Ibid., p.261.

187 Ibid., pp.262-3.

188 Alexis Carrel, *Man, the Unknown*, p.30.

189 Ibid., p.33.

190 Ibid., p.38.

191 Ibid., pp.38-9.

192 Ibid., pp.50-1.

193 *Guide to Modern Wickedness*, p.241.

194 Ibid, p.247.

195 *Man, The Unknown*, pp.261-2.

196 Ibid., pp.234-5.

197 On 20 August, 1949, the Mayor of Hiroshima disclosed that the number of those killed by the atomic bomb was between 220,000 and 240,000 – P.T.I.

198 *The Statesman*, 16 September, 1945.

CHAPTER VI

199 E.g. Shaikh Hasan ^c^Alā' Sanjarī.

200 E.g. Shaikh Naṣiruddīn Chirāgh-e-dehlī.

201 Khawājah Nizāmuddīn came to Delhi in the reign of Ghayāthuddin Balban and settled down at Ghayāthpur. All the kings who sat on the throne of Delhi during his lifetime keenly desired to meet him and they did their utmost to make him agree to it, but the saint would have nothing to do with them. For fully sixty years he and his disciple remained superbly indifferent to the Imperial Court.

202 Religious establishment (Translator).

203 Deputy. In *Sūfī* terminology, a *khalīfah* is the one to whom permission is given to take *bayʿah*. (Translator).

204 See Chapter IV.

205 *Nuzhat-ul-Khawāṭir*, Vol.V.

206 *Durr-ul-Maʿārif*, *Irshād-e-Raḥmānī*, and *Nuzhat-tul-Khawāṭīr*.

207 *Āthār-uṣ-Ṣanādīd*, Chapter IV.

208 *Durr-ul-Maʿārif*, p.106.

209 The flat region between the Ganges and Jamna rivers (Translator).

210 A full account of the tour is given in *Sīrat Sayyid Aḥmad Shahīd* by the same author.

211 I.e. the chief landlord (Translator).

212 Maulavi Muhammad ʿAlī, *Makhzan-e-Aḥmadī*.

213 I.e. Muslim call to prayer (Translator).

214 *Waqa'iʿ-i-Aḥmadī*.

215 Ibid.

216 Ibid.

217 One who has performed the *Ḥajj* pilgrimage (Translator).

218 Sayyid Jaʿfar Ali Naqvi, *Manzūrat-us-Suʿadā'*.

219 Meaning Muslims of exceptional holiness (Translator).

220 Muslim.

221 Imām Bukhārī, *al-Adab al-Mufrad*.

222 *Nuzhat-ul-Khawāṭir*, Vol. 6.

223 *Islam at the Crossroads*, pp.51-2.

224 Non-obligatory prayers (Translator).

225 The system of action, customs, orders and prohibitions derived from the life-example of the Prophet ﷺ (Translator).

226 Sayyid Abdul Ḥayy, *Yād-i-Ayyām*.

227 A commentary of the Holy Qur'ān by ʿAllāma Baghavi, running into thousands of pages.

228 *Yād-i-Ayyām*.

229 The midday prayers on Fridays are called *Jumuʿah* prayers if offered congregationally. Otherwise these are known by the usual name of *Ẓuhr* prayers (Translator).

230 *Yād-i-Ayyām*.

231 Voluntary prayers (Translator).

232 *Nafl* Prayer, offered after the rising of the sun (Translator).

233 *Yād-i-Ayyām*.

234 Extra prayers offered during Ramaḍān nights after the *Ishā* prayers (Translator).

235 Living in the mosque for constant devotion and prayers (Translator).

236 *Khizāna-i-ʿĀmirah*.

237 The Holy Qur'ān is divided

into 30 parts of about equal length (Translator).

238 Offered during the last one-third of the night (Translator).

239 The path on which the *Ṭawāf* (the ceremony of walking round the Kaᶜbah) is performed.

240 Meaning "Here I am" or "I am ready" (Translator).

CHAPTER VII

241 The Kaᶜbāh at Makkah (Translator).

242 Bukhārī, *Kitāb al-Adab.*

243 Bukhārī, *Kitāb al-Maghāzī.*

244 An-Nasā'ī, *Kitāb al-Bayᶜah.*

245 A garment worn by Arabs (Translator).

246 Ibn al-Jawzī, *Sīrah ᶜUmar ibn al-Khaṭṭāb.*

CHAPTER VIII

247 Baghawī.

248 Bukhārī.

249 Muslim.

250 That this method can work in modern times has been amply demonstrated by Japan.

251 Ibn Hishām, *Sīrah Nabawiyyah.*

252 Ibn Saᶜd, *Ṭabaqāt*, Vol.12.

INDEX